ELIZABETH BISHOP

Elizabeth Bishop

HER ARTISTIC DEVELOPMENT

by

THOMAS J. TRAVISANO

University Press of Virginia

Charlottesville

THE UNIVERSITY PRESS OF VIRGINIA
Copyright © 1988 by the Rector and Visitors
of the University of Virginia

First published 1988

Design by Janet Anderson

Library of Congress Cataloging-in-Publication Data

Travisano, Thomas J., 1951-
    Elizabeth Bishop : her artistic development.

    Bibliography: p.
    Includes index.
    1. Bishop, Elizabeth, 1911-1979—Criticism and
interpretation. I. Title.
PS3503.I785Z88   1988   811'.54   87-23096
ISBN 0-8139-1159-1

Printed in the United States of America

FOR ELSA

CONTENTS

ACKNOWLEDGMENTS

My fascination with Elizabeth Bishop's poetry began at the University of Virginia in the classrooms of two stimulating poet-teachers, Alan Williamson and Mark Strand. Formal study of Bishop's work followed, under the direction of J. C. Levenson, for whose continuing advice and encouragement I remain grateful. Discussions with David Rosenwasser helped me, at an early stage, to see Bishop's work in the context of other literary studies of enclosure. Candace MacMahon very kindly arranged for me to read her bibliography of Elizabeth Bishop while it awaited the printers at the University Press of Virginia, and she steered me toward important unpublished and uncollected material.

Portions of the manuscript were read by John Willis and Scott Donaldson, colleagues at William and Mary, and by David Baldwin, Thomas Beattie, Robert Bensen, Terrance Fitz-Henry, and Carol Frost, colleagues at Hartwick College. Each offered suggestions and criticism that have made this a better book.

Profs. M. L. Rosenthal, Ashley Brown, and Paul Breslin have read the entire manuscript, and each has made numerous suggestions for which I am grateful. Walker Cowen, late director of the University Press of Virginia, was ever gracious, and unflagging in his encouragement at difficult moments.

My wife Elsa has seen this book through many drafts, and it owes to her whatever claims it can make to clarity or stylistic grace.

Quotation from Elizabeth Bishop's *Complete Poems: 1927–1979* and *Collected Prose* is by permission of Farrar, Straus and Giroux. Quotation from Bishop's letters to Marianne Moore is by permission of Alice Methfessel and the Rosenbach Museum & Library, Philadelphia. Quotation from Bishop's letters to Robert Lowell is by permission of Alice Methfessel and the Houghton Library. Quotation from Lowell's letters to Bishop is by permission of Frank Bidart and the Vassar College Library.

1911   Born February 8, Worcester, Massachusetts, of Canadian-American parents; father dies when she is eight months old.

1916   Mother, after several breakdowns, becomes permanently insane and Bishop never sees her again; is raised by maternal grandparents in Nova Scotia and an aunt in Boston.

1927   After being kept from school by various illnesses, enters Walnut Hill School.

1930   Enters Vassar.

1934   Meets Marianne Moore who becomes a lifelong friend; mother dies; graduates Vassar.

1935   First poems published in *Trial Balances* with introduction by Moore.

1935–38 Lives in New York and travels to France, England, North Africa, Spain, and Italy, using an inheritance.

1939   Moves to Key West.

1946   Receives Houghton Mifflin Poetry Award for first book, *North & South*.

1947   Guggenheim Fellowship; friendship with Robert Lowell and Randall Jarrell.

1949–50 Consultant in Poetry at the Library of Congress.

1951   Settles in Brazil with Lota de Macedo Soares.

1955   Second book, *Poems*, published; it receives the Pulitzer Prize.

1965   *Questions of Travel* published.

1967   Lota de Macedo Soares dies.

1969   *The Complete Poems* published; it receives the National Book Award.

1970–73 Alternates fall terms at Harvard with seasons in Ouro Prêto, Brazil.

1974   Moves permanently to Boston waterfront; begins teaching both terms at Harvard.

1976   *Geography III* published; *Books Abroad* / Neustadt International Prize.

1979   Dies of a stroke at her Boston home.

INTRODUCTION

Introduction

Elizabeth Bishop's reputation has grown steadily since she published her first poems in the mid-1930s. She is now recognized as one of the best poets of her time. This is the first comprehensive study of her career. Bishop's work has received much close analysis of its local effects but comparatively little evaluation in terms of its larger patterns, which reveal a powerful intelligence and sensibility at work. It is these patterns that give her poems their major significance. Her art went through important stylistic and expressive changes. One must assess these changes if one is to appreciate not just her delicacy, craft, and precision, which have long been valued, but the coherent and consistent approach she took to fundamental human problems. To analyze the stages of her development is to bring into bolder relief concerns that underlay her life's work and give it artistic unity.

I have divided Bishop's career into three phases, which I will briefly outline. The early phase, "Prison," was devoted to the exploration of sealed imaginary worlds. It includes such dreamlike, introspective fables as "The Man-Moth" and "The Weed" and is limited to the first half of her first book, *North & South*. The middle phase, "Travel," breaks through early enclosures and engages imaginatively with actual places and people. Reflecting her many years in Florida (especially Key West) and Mexico, it includes such marvels of fresh observation as "The Fish" and "Over 2,000 Illustrations and a Complete Concordance," works found in the remainder of *North & South* and in the whole of *A Cold Spring*, her second book (published with a reprint of her first book as *Poems*). The last phase, "History," goes further still. It takes on the challenges of public and private history. It includes her last two books, *Questions of Travel* and *Geography III*, which explore her many years' sojourn in Brazil and her ultimate return to Boston and the scenes of her youth. The cautious, even defensive, stance of the early Bishop, which apparently prefers the abstractly colored landscapes of a map to the world itself, a preference that implies a bias toward art rather than history, gives way to the recognition that "our knowledge is historical, flowing, and flown." This phrase, from a middle-period poem, "At The Fishhouses" (*CP*, 66), helps to explain her early reluctance to engage with historical knowledge. To explore history is to face loss in that transient world that every moment is flowing and flown. As a child who lost both parents by the time she was five, one through death and one through madness, who experienced a youth marked by periods of sickness and isolation, and who never afterwards knew a permanent home, transience was a well-learned and intimidating fact and solitude an old acquaintance. One's own deepest feelings were dangerous terrain, terrain that could only be traversed after careful preparation. She was a shy woman; she told her good friend Robert Lowell in the late 1940s that she was canceling a reading engagement because she was "scared—it is idiotic."[1] Facing up to fear is a buried but powerful theme throughout her work. She would later sufficently control this fear to give readings fairly extensively. In the context of the anxieties that dominated her early life and writing, the rich, calm, melancholy, and quietly humorous poems of personal experience that emerged from her last years stand out as a courageous achievement. They are all the better for the restraint with which they are uttered. As a poet, she kept getting richer and stronger as she came more directly to terms with inner necessity and as the concerns of her work moved closer to the surface.

Bishop has been highly valued by critics and fellow poets but is too often overlooked by literary historians. Her style is understated, and as a result, historians have tended to overlook her not inconsiderable contribution to the development of contemporary poetic idiom. Bishop's work is not only large and complex but coherent and powerful. She responds with imagination, wit, emotional honesty, and keen intelligence to problems that have haunted the contemporary imagination: isolation, emotional loss, rootlessness, and the limits and possibilities of fiction. Self-pity, arguably the most pernicious of contemporary spiritual diseases, is her central subject. In poem after poem, self-pity is entertained but given no quarter. She vanquishes it to such a degree that one acute reader, the poet Mark Strand, was moved to say, in only partial error, "There is no self-pity in Elizabeth Bishop's writing."[2] She is so subtle that some of her closest students can feel the major effect of her work (the purgation of self-pity) without quite recognizing its cause.

Bishop was not a world-historical figure, like Yeats, Eliot, or Lowell. Instead, she was one of those startlingly individual lyric voices who vex the historian, a voice as fresh and unique as Gerard Manley Hopkins, Emily Dickinson, or her own beloved George Herbert. As with them, complete recognition has taken time. Her historical importance rests, not on her immediate impact on her day, although that was greater than has been measured—she contributed importantly to the idiom of Robert Lowell and many of her younger contemporaries—but on the uniqueness and lasting value of her poetic creation.

Although she has always had devoted readers, and although she won more than her share of prizes and fellowships, only with the publication of her most recent books, *Geography III* in 1976 and the posthumous *Complete Poems: 1927–1979* (1983) and *Collected Prose* (1984), have the dimensions of her achievement begun to be generally appreciated.[3] The reasons for the delay are complex. For one thing, she published sparingly—four small volumes of original work that appeared, a decade apart, over a span of forty years. Bishop was thirty-five before her first book appeared, and many of the poems in this book were reticent and enigmatic fables of the isolated soul, very different in character from her later poetry. It took time for a substantial body of writing to accumulate and for the major directions of her work to emerge. Even so, this first book, *North & South* (1946), contained poems of such concentration and distinction that many praised it, and a few readers, including Randall Jarrell and Robert Lowell, hailed it as a classic.[4]

Her second book, *A Cold Spring*, which appeared together with the reissued *North & South* as *Poems* in 1955, was not published until she was forty-four. It received the Pulitzer Prize. Still, at an age when many poets have their best work behind them, she had only some fifty short poems in print. These included much varied and masterly work, for poems like "The Fish," "The Weed," "A Miracle for Breakfast," "Roosters," "Over 2,000 Illustrations and a Complete Concordance," "The Bight," and "At the Fishhouses" have long been rated highly, but it was possible to lament that she had produced too little. Bishop's last two volumes, *Questions of Travel* (1965) and *Geography III*, were vital in two ways: they made it obvious that she had written a great number of superb poems, and they extended and confirmed directions in her career that until then had been only subliminally present. Not least, they placed a newfound access to direct emotion alongside the intense but submerged emotion found in earlier work. The recently published *Complete Poems: 1927–1979* and *Collected Prose* round out the picture, bringing nearly all of Bishop's poetry, stories, and memoirs together in two volumes, and adding significant writings she either did not publish or did not live to collect. The *Complete Poems* includes, as well, some significant juvenilia, and two dozen translations, the most important of which are her splendid versions of modern Brazilian poems.

As David Kalstone said, Bishop "to her credit, has always been hard to 'place.'" She is, for him, "probably the most honored yet most elusive of poets."[5] In an age when many contemporaries were mining poetry directly out of private tragedy, she held to principles of personal reticence and artistic restraint. Not identified with any particular school, she did none of the extras that attract attention; remote, in Key West, Mexico, or Brazil, she remained aloof from literary politics, issuing no manifestos, writing little criticism— not even explaining or defending her own practice. She did not cleave to the New Critics. She did not kneel at the Confessional. She was neither a Beat nor an Academic. She offered no private myth. She attracted no cult of personality. She offered no target to the popular press. She simply wrote poems.

Looked at in mid career, Bishop's work did not clearly reflect what Anne Stevenson, her first biographer, called "a sense of growth, of what might be called a development in understanding." Stevenson's 1966 book was based on the premise that "Bishop's work, elegant and eloquent as it often is, does not achieve this kind of organic unity." Stevenson saw Bishop's as a series of "meticulous observations" made "in passing." This assessment was echoed by many others, including Jerome Mazzaro, who, commenting on the separateness of individual poems, concluded in a 1969 review: "This sense of boundaries, which makes her an ideal poet for anthologies, militates against any cumulative effect and keeps her work discrete."[6] More recently, Kalstone made a contrary observation. Noting that "she has become known as the author of single, stunning poems," Kalstone rightly suggests the inadequacy of Stevenson's and Mazzaro's view: "Wonderful as the anthologized poems may be, they give, even for anthologies, an unusually stunted version of Bishop's variety, of the way her writing has emerged, of her developing concerns."[7] Unfortunately, Kalstone does not survey Bishop's development himself. This suggests the need for a chronological study of her artistic evolution, a study that outlines and explores the "developing concerns" of Bishop's career, defining the nature of its "organic unity."

The three major phases of Bishop's career imply an evolving response to the important poetic movements of her time. Her early phase shows her as a reluctant master of the symbolist's private world, a world that renounces history for the ambiguous pleasures of enclosure. Her middle phase reflected years of travel and observation, through which isolation might be at least temporarily bridged. It "extends the Imagist instant,"[8] combining the precision and conciseness of imagism with a liberating dimension of temporal development. Her last phase reverses the earliest, engaging with personal and private history. The yearning for enclosure is still powerful, but it is controlled by a calm and expansive vision. Bishop dealt with more widely shared concerns than many have recognized, and she may be seen, not as an isolated—though brilliant—observer, but as a figure who has helped to define the subject matter of contemporary poetry and who has tried to identify the technical and spiritual resources it can offer in response to inevitable human limitation. Bishop's technique, governed by roots in symbolist and surrealist poetry and thought, grounds her work in actuality and allows her philosophically to confront the necessities of life, surrendering neither to despair nor to a longed-for affirmation. The claim for her importance begins with her formal elegance, but it rests on the continuity and courage of her writing, its philosophical freshness, its moral complexity and soundness.

Although Bishop quietly maintained her privacy and individuality, she was never really isolated. Among the older generation, she was most closely associated with Marianne Moore, her patron, encouraging reader, correspondent, and intimate friend. But she was influenced at least equally by a wide range of modern poets, including Wallace Stevens, W. H. Auden, the French symbolists (especially Jules Laforgue, whose work she knew well), and the

French and Spanish surrealists. Among earlier poets, she was particularly drawn to Herbert and Hopkins. At different times, she created original work in response to a *frottage* (or charcoal rubbing) by Max Ernst, a poem by Pablo Neruda, and a poem by Herbert. However, her responsiveness to the work of other writers never diluted what Donald Sheehan called "the strange *isolated* quality of [her] poems, that air they seem to wear that no other poems really exist."[9] There is a curious aura to even her earliest published writings.

Among poets of her own age, her closest friends and advocates include Lowell, Jarrell, and in later years, Octavio Paz. Younger poets who have acknowledged her importance include James Merrill, John Ashbery, Mark Strand, Richard Howard, Frank Bidart, Sandra McPherson, and Robert Pinsky. For these, her work was not a rallying point but a touchstone. To Lowell, who called her "one of the best craftsmen alive," she offered an escape from the "ponderous armor" of his early style. Her "Armadillo" led directly to Lowell's "Skunk Hour" and its companion poems in *Life Studies,* as he often gratefully acknowledged. Bishop's example encouraged Lowell and others to let the image speak for itself in what might be called a semiopen structure, involving the presentation of a succession of images without direct authorial comment, and to write in a voice sophisticated yet natural: prosaic and conversational, yet capable of rising to moments of lyric exaltation. On the other hand, Bishop was not greatly interested in, nor, one surmises, of great interest to, those contemporaries such as Charles Olson, Robert Creeley, and Allen Ginsberg, who abandoned any drive toward closure in favor of the possibilities of open forms. Her influence, then, while not universal, was significant. It continues to be felt in the clear, colloquial intensity of some of the best poets now writing.

Although she has been the subject of numerous essays and reviews, many of them by fellow poets, there has been comparatively little critical work on Bishop when measured against the libraries rapidly assembling around Lowell, Olson, Theodore Roethke, and even some younger poets. Surprisingly, this is only the second critical book on Bishop, and the first, Stevenson's, was written twenty years ago. Perhaps her charming but deceptive surfaces have kept critics at a certain distance. Her poems refuse generalization, and in that way they resist explication. Bishop said she liked to present a complex problem in the simplest way possible. But this simplicity can be devious. As Robert Mazzacco has said, "You'd have to go back to Frost to find another poet as slyly unaccommodating."[10] The success with which her art conceals art has caused many readers to enjoy her poems deeply without quite knowing why. The critic's first job is to uncover the sources of their sometimes mysterious authority. So far, this delicate job has been only partially done.

Which means we are still in an early stage of Bishop studies. Until the mid-seventies, most of the comment on Bishop took the form of brief reviews. Only in the past decade has she become the frequent subject of considered essays. Two schools of Bishop criticism have emerged. The earliest to establish itself, and the one with the most obvious limitations, might be called the objective school. Emphasizing the visual accuracy and formal control of her work, this school sees her as an objective observer whose main value lies in the exactitude of her descriptions. Because her poems have an air of cool detachment, the adherents of this school see little or no subjectivity in her writing. For example, James G. Southworth wrote that "The poetry of Elizabeth Bishop, except for some ten poems, is as objective as poetry can well be," and he points to "carefully and skillfully selected objective details," as the essential feature of her style, while Peggy Rizza states that "She possesses what might be called an 'objective imagination.'" Rizza goes on to suggest that her poems "are absent of the pathetic fallacy."[11] The failure of this approach is that it cannot account for the imaginative play and passionate undertones that color Bishop's precise observations. The objective school has particular difficulty explaining Bishop's dreamlike early work, which is overtly fantastic and subjective. Although Southworth does not name them, the ten exceptions to Bishop's objectivity that he alludes to must include such enigmatic early fables as "The Man-Moth," "The Unbeliever," "The Imaginary Iceberg," and "A Miracle for Breakfast." These important fantasies are not isolated exceptions to be brushed aside but a closely related series; they provide the foundation for any serious reading of her work. Nor does the objective approach explore the underlying emotional and moral concerns that give life to her observations. It cannot account for the more straightforward emotion of Bishop's last book, which is not so much a departure as a more direct treatment of questions she had handled indirectly before. Mazzaro laments that "her poems offer a method for observing the world which must remain discrete from the observer as well as from any attempts by him to free experience by making it subjective."[12] But a descriptive passage like the one that follows, from Bishop's most famous poem, "The Fish," not only offers accurate observation but is permeated with nostalgia and compassion. Studying a very large and very old fish she has just caught, the observer notes:

> Here and there
> his brown skin hung in strips
> like ancient wallpaper,
> and its pattern of darker brown
> was like wallpaper:
> shapes like full-blown roses
> stained and lost through age.[13]

This writing is free of the constraints of photographic objectivity; it invites one to explore not only the fish itself but the experience of an observer crowded with conflicting feelings and associations. These lines do not call attention to their subjectivity by stating feelings outright, but these feelings are palpable even so. Adherents of the objective approach tend to find Bishop's work, for all its precision, rather narrow and artificial. Their view provides a convenient formula for dismissing the poet as a "mere" observer, emotionally and imaginatively inhibited, or for erecting a small monument to her as a "perfect" but perfectly minor poet.[14]

Over the past decade and a half, a second school of Bishop criticism has established itself. This rightly finds Bishop's work permeated by controlled subjectivity and recognizes that she consistently explores the border ground conjoining imagination and fact. One advocate of this second school, Willard Spiegelman, states, "Bishop's best poems show her to be an epistemological poet in the tradition of William Wordsworth and Samuel Taylor Coleridge." He might have added Wallace Stevens, to whose playful, high spirited way of "twanging [the] wiry string" of imagination Bishop is really closer.[15] The presence of Stevens may be felt throughout Bishop's work. Although she eventually rebelled against what she felt to be Stevens's excessive subjectivity—she was more in love with what Pound called "the thing itself" than he—Bishop learned a great deal from him about how imagination shapes perception. While this second group of critics has recognized the thought, emotion, and mystery that animate Bishop's work, they have not applied this recognition to a thorough exploration of her achievement. Nor have her chief artistic sources been adequately defined.

Her technique is hard to pin down because it successfully reconciles apparently contradictory qualities. The surface of Bishop's poetry, with its wit, control, and incisive vigor, seems to display the standard classical virtues. Her highly polished surfaces, her elegant fancies, her formal control, her cool, hard, linear qualities, her self-conscious artistry, are classical or, more properly, neoclassical features that adherents of the objective school like to point out. By contrast, Spiegelman and Harold Bloom find Bishop's work a response to the romantic tradition because of her attachment to nature and her experiments with the powers and limits of imagination.[16] In her poems, conscious control is persistently undermined by the lure of dreamlike visions and by the seductions of empathy. If it is to apply at all, the term *romantic* must be understood in its broadest sense, to include not only the English romantic poets but also the French symbolists (especially Laforgue and Baudelaire) and the French surrealists: in short, the broad tradition defined by Octavio Paz in *Children of the Mire*—a book by one of Bishop's admirers and colleagues that I will have occasion to refer to again.[17] But neither term, *classic* or *romantic*, adequately defines her. Her mature work is really postneoclassical, postromantic, postsymbolist, and even postsurrealist in that she derives much from each of these movements—a devotion to craft, a concern for nature, a superiority to rhetoric, an alertness to the promptings of the unconscious—but she is really *of* none of them. Her poems imply what her interviews and letters sometimes state, that she sees the limitations of each approach with cool detachment, and that she has deliberately chosen her own path. If there is one artistic movement to which she felt closest, it is an older one—the baroque. She identified her two favorite poets, Herbert and Hopkins, as baroque masters. By this she meant that they attended to the twists and turns of perception, that they displayed those qualities that, as M. W. Croll stated in a famous essay that Bishop studied at Vassar and referred to on more than one occasion, are the characteristics of the great baroque writers. "Their purpose," said Croll in lines quoted by Bishop in reference to Hopkins, "was to portray, not a thought, but the mind thinking." They attempt to capture "the moment in which the truth is still *imagined.*"[18] As a result, they achieve freshness and surprise. The element of surprise, of unlooked for discovery, was the quality Bishop most prized in baroque art. She found that surprise in the rhythms of Scarlatti (a Scarlatti recording by Ralph Kirkpatrick helped her to complete the stalled "Roosters") and in the Jesuit baroque architecture and folk art of Brazil. She also found it, for example, in a bad picture by a great-uncle and in a newspaper misprint for "Mammoth," and these surprises led to splendid poems. Surprise, that access to delight, is the favorite antidote to self-pity in her writing.[19]

Aside from Anne Stevenson's study, which, as I have indicated, appeared too early to consider *Questions of Travel* and *Geography III* and thus could not take Bishop's most decisive work into account, this is the first book-length analysis, but it is not the first book of which she is the subject. The bibliography of Bishop's work has been well done. Candace MacMahon's superbly detailed *Elizabeth Bishop: A Bibliography* made the breadth of the Bishop canon available and established the chronology of her work. Diana E. Wyllie's *Elizabeth Bishop and Howard Nemerov: A Reference Guide* is particularly strong as a source of critical essays. Schwartz and Estess' recent *Elizabeth Bishop and Her Art* is a valuable collection offering ready access to much of the best writing on Bishop to date (including good new essays), in addition to selections from Bishop's few, but suggestive, critical writings (sometimes, unfortunately, abridged). David Kalstone's long essay on Bishop in *Five Temperaments* (also included in the Schwartz and Estess collection), along with John Unterecker's essay in the *American Writers* series, provide the best discussions to date of Bishop's imagination.[20] None of these works, valuable as they are, attempts to provide a thorough critical evaluation of the major patterns of Bishop's work, of her governing emotional and intellectual concerns, or of her growth as an artist. Such an overview is plainly needed.

This book attempts to evaluate Bishop's artistic development. Because each of her four separate books (*North & South, A Cold Spring, Questions of Travel,* and *Geography III*) was the product of a decade's labor and has unique things to say, each will be closely examined in turn. Her first book rates two chapters because it reflects two distinct stages of development. Representative poems from each book will be discussed in terms of that book's place in her artistic evolution. I will be turning often to Bishop's interviews and critical writings and to unpublished letters.

The critic of twentieth-century poetry who means the most to me is Bishop's friend and admirer Randall Jarrell, a reader of just taste within broad limits and a penetrating critic. While I cannot hope to match Jarrell's compressed insight, nor the colloquial vigor of his style, I have tried to emulate his clarity and his freedom from jargon. In method, this study might be called eclectically traditional. It adopts the well-tested approach of close reading informed by knowledge of historical and cultural contexts and by analysis of manuscripts—following this as the best route toward understanding the complex and evolving art of a poetic genius. I have intended to write a book that will be useful to anyone, general reader or specialist, who is curious about Elizabeth Bishop, and I have considered it important to make my work clear even to those with little background in critical theory. Bishop herself loathed writing that was pretentious, needlessly obscure, or condescending. I have left to others the exploration of Bishop's work in the light of poststructuralist aesthetics, an approach that sometimes threatens to make criticism more esoteric and obscure than the work itself. Jarrell had little time for theory, but he was a master of the practice of criticism who had plenty of news to bring us about Whitman and Frost and Stevens and Auden. I have tried to say a few new things about Elizabeth Bishop.

One way of coming to terms with a poet is to define what makes the poet difficult. The difficulty of Bishop's poetry appears when one tries to probe beneath the engaging surface in search of a poem's elusive meaning. One *feels* this meaning to be present, but it seems to reside apart somewhere, deep in the image-making process itself. Although her poems invariably explore deep-seated emotional, moral, and intellectual concerns, Bishop felt that leaving the thesis of her poems unstated was a strategy of the greatest importance—because the reader must share the process of observation and discovery. For her, there are no shortcuts to the emblematic significance of things. An emblem arises naturally, sometimes painfully, out of the act of perception itself. Since, at the same time, the greatest simplicity and economy have been maintained, we are confronted by poems like fathomless mountain lakes: crystal clear, yet so deep one can hardly see the bottom.

Most often, the way Bishop creates and joins a poem's images offers the best route to its significance. Patient attention, watching as the act of observation unfolds, is what Bishop demanded of herself, and it will reward her readers. She does not attempt to hide her meaning, but she does insist that the reader seek it through careful, imaginative observation. Bishop's images, often presented in the form of simple enumeration, cohere at last in surprising moments of recognition. In the same way, the body of her work, which might seem to lack unity, to amount to little more than mere observations made in passing, coheres at last into a rich and significant pattern.

Bishop's work began as a conversation with herself and evolved into a conversation with the world at large. Her first instinct was for the inward life. For all her talent as an observer, her command of the outer world was a deliberate acquisition. The path she traces is difficult and strewn with obstacles, but it leads toward fresh engagement with an ominous but captivating world.

EARLY PHASE: PRISON

1934 – 38

Fables of Enclosure

NORTH & SOUTH I

Early Life and Work
« Islands of the Imagination »

Elizabeth Bishop's first book, *North & South,* can be divided into two chronological phases reflecting two stages of artistic development. These phases can only be identified, however, through study of the dating of the poems in this book, which was eleven years in the making. The hermetic early phase is set in the North. The early poems received their first magazine publication between 1935 and 1938. Among these are many probing, enigmatic fables of the curious rewards and penalties of the inward life. Revealing an affinity to the rising New Critical aesthetic, these poems demonstrate her to be a keen ironist, a master of intricate verse forms, and a deft handler of understatement and ambiguity. She was devoted to the critically fashionable Metaphysical poets, which might seem to confirm her orthodoxy. And yet her work implies that, from the start, she found the latent artistic conservatism of the New Critics confining.

Bishop was fortunate to launch her career at a time when she could choose among a wide range of viable poetic idioms. She seems never to have felt that oppression in the face of the achievement of her modernist predecessors that James Breslin argues was an essential characteristic of her generation. Some twenty years earlier, pioneers like Pound, Williams, Stevens, and Marianne Moore had had to grope and experiment, freeing themselves from outdated models while producing, some of them, a considerable body of problematic or derivative verse before they could originate a suitable style and voice. According to James Laughlin, Basil Bunting said that "when Pound came to London in 1908 'he was

forty years behind' and that 'his father—and his mother—were
Rosetti.'"[1] Bishop's first collection bears her own stamp from the
very start, and some of its earliest poems—one thinks of "The
Map" (1935), "The Man-Moth" (1936), "The Weed" (1937), "A
Miracle for Breakfast" (1937), and "The Unbeliever" (1938)—
continue to be widely anthologized and to rank with her best.[2] It
would be hard to come up with a similar list for, say, Roethke or
Berryman, whose earliest poetry seems emotionally and intellectually constricted by a too-pious formalism. Of course, Bishop
wrote several early poems that aren't nearly so successful, such as
"The Colder the Air," "Wading at Wellfleet," and "From the Country to the City," poems in which interesting ideas are not quite
fully realized. But even these have a certain individuality and
freshness of attack. Bishop's early verse alludes to traditional
forms—the blank-verse line, the quatrain, the sestina—but it
treats them with considerable freedom. One is impressed by the
sense this early work gives of its range of stylistic options. Still, it
does express anxiety about the power of poetry to address spiritual
poverty, an anxiety that compelled her to write a series of parables
exploring imaginative (or imaginary) enclosures.

I have called this first phase "Prison" because the theme of
deliberate or unwilling imprisonment, within walls that are
ultimately psychological rather than physical, reappears so persistently. The later poems in the volume, mostly set in the South,
were first published between 1939 and 1946. I have assigned them
to her middle phase, "Travel," because like the poems of her second
book, A Cold Spring (1955), they are devoted to external facts observed in transit. The early phase provided training for the later
one; Bishop discovered early her sensitivity to the surprising levels
of inwardness latent in even the most ordinary objects. The later
phase is also an answer to the first. The freedom and immediacy
of her observed South redresses the loneliness and vulnerability of
her imagined North. This is not to say the early work lacks
power—in fact, the emotional current runs high. The early poems
and stories contain surprises at every turn, and though narrow,
they dig deep. They are marked by a keen, though sometimes groping, intelligence. The austere tone does not dampen their strange,
telling flights of imagination, nor does it rule out humor. Alto-
gether, while they show affinities to elements of symbolist, surrealist, and New Critical thought, the atmosphere of these early

pieces is hard to find elsewhere in literature. While they reveal a general debt to Anglo-American modernism, perhaps the closest relatives are Kafka (for his hermeticism, his somber ironies, and the cool concreteness of his fantasy) and Laforgue (for his delicate wit and odd sense of play, for what Bishop herself called his "new sub-acid flavor"[3]).

Elizabeth Bishop was famous for the precision with which she saw. What Randall Jarrell said of *North & South*, "all her poems have written underneath, *I have seen it*," applies equally to everything that followed.[4] At first, though, that famous eye was directed neither at the people she knew nor at the landscapes and seascapes she observed, but at what she once called "islands of the Imagination"—dreamlike alternative worlds.[5] The people (and animals) found there come from strange, neurotic reaches of the land of fable. Bishop's enclosures are psychologically and morally complex objectifications of tense emotional and intellectual states.

The chief biographical sources for "those horrible 'fable' ideas that seem to obsess me"[6] were traumas from a difficult childhood that taught her painful lessons in the reality of loss, isolation, and homelessness, as well as in the necessity of seeking imaginative compensations. The chief literary sources include the tales of Andersen, which Bishop devoured as a child, as well as English metaphysical poetry (especially Herbert's), French and Anglo-American symbolist poetry (especially that of Laforgue, Stevens, and Auden), and the poetry and visual art of Parisian surrealism, which she explored on lengthy trips to France in the mid-thirties.[7] Although the title of the first book suggests a dialogue between South and North, one critics have ever since considered basic to her work, that dialogue only began after the hermetic early work had been written. A catalytic event, the move from New York City to Florida in 1937, opened a new and sympathetic field of observation that precipitated the discovery of the middle-period style. Before this, introspection dominated. Yet the early poems themselves reveal discomfort with the constraints of introspection and find imaginative compensations alone not wholly adequate. They betray an awareness that to look resolutely inward is to find a vast and fascinating arena but one that ignores or blocks out essential realities.

Many readers have found these early poems difficult. Robert Lowell's review of *North & South* points to poems about "some fantastic object. . . . One is reminded of Kafka and certain abstract paintings, and is left rather at sea about the actual subjects of the poems." Anne Stevenson calls early fables like "The Imaginary Iceberg" and "The Map" "tantalizing and exasperating."[8] These poems camouflage their true concerns while creating fantastic subjects or, more often, ordinary subjects made fantastic by a shift in point of view. They reveal their unstated significance only when one recognizes what they have in common—that each depicts a struggle for peace and fulfillment within the confines of a wholly imagined world. Rather than follow the poems in their published sequence, I will order my discussion around different aspects of this struggle.

Bishop arranged North & South on geographical, and to some degree on chronological, lines. The poems of the North appear on pages 3–31 of the Complete Poems: 1927–1979, the poems of the South on pages 32–52. Almost all the Northern poems should be classified as early. This means, as I have already suggested, that they were published by 1938, that they experiment with enclosure, and that their landscapes are formulated by the mind. That these poems are set in the North is not surprising. Bishop was born in Massachusetts and resided there or in Nova Scotia as a child. She was living in New York City when she wrote most of the poems, and had not yet ventured to Florida. Bishop's arrangement admits two Northern poems that were written later: "Large Bad Picture" and "Chemin de Fer." Both were published in 1946; both are Northern in subject matter; but each belongs chronologically and spiritually to the less dream-bound middle period. The Southern poems that complete the volume appeared later, between 1939 and 1946. They relate in style, spirit, and subject matter to the poems of A Cold Spring. An artistic breakthrough, leading to this new kind of poetry, was achieved in the 1939 poem "Florida" and in "The Fish" and "Roosters," which quickly followed it. Attitudes about art, nature, imagination, and love expressed in early poems like "The Map" and "The Imaginary Iceberg" underwent transformation in later work.

To isolate and explore her early work is to recognize that, far from Bishop being an impersonal or "objective" poet, her vision begins with a world that is almost wholly subjective, indeed, suffocatingly so. She emerges as a master of one of the central problems of contemporary poetry—introspection—a problem that she treats with insight and imagination and with a detachment unique among her contemporaries. None of these poems are explicitly autobiographical, although the theme of introspection seems to lend itself to autobiography. Instead, Bishop creates personae who embody the introspective urge. Having externalized the impulse, she can then study it freely and without self-pity. She can show the imaginative richness introspection offers, but she can equally show how dangerously constricting it can be. While most of the great contemporary masters of introspection—one thinks of Lowell, Berryman, Plath, and Roethke—sometimes appear to revel in the pungent misery of self-contemplation, Bishop never does. For her, the problem of introspection is universal before it is personal. She moved away from an exclusively introspective poetry as quickly as she could find a way, but even her coolest and crispest later landscapes retain an introspective flavor. And this is an aspect of their strength. In the early work, enclosure dominates, and nature and society seem remote or hostile. In the later poetry the tense but rewarding balance Bishop achieved between introspection and observation allowed her to blossom forth as an imaginative and precise observer of nature and society. However, Bishop's concern with dreams, with the peace that comes from isolation, with the danger of love, with the rewards and distortions of imagination, continued to inform the later work, giving her most precise details an air of mystery.

Bishop is often considered impersonal, even antiautobiographical, but her early experience provides a necessary context for the discussion of her early writing and of her continuing development. The decisive events of Bishop's early life are well-known.[9] She was born in 1911 in Worcester, Massachusetts. Her father was of a prominent Boston family. His father was a wealthy builder. Her mother, of Nova Scotian Baptist stock, was a sensitive woman of fragile spirit. These parents, William Thomas and Gertrude Bulmer Bishop, were not able to care for their only daughter very long. The poet's father died when she was eight months old. His young wife never really accepted his death; her grief and shock led to insanity. After periods in and out of sanitariums, including a final, brief stay with her child and parents in Great Village, Nova Scotia, Gertrude Bishop was placed permanently in a mental institution. Her child was five years old. Bishop never saw her mother again. Events from this last, disastrous visit are heartbreakingly recalled in the story "In the Village" (*CProse,* 251–74). Gertrude Bishop died in 1934, the same year her daughter was graduating from Vassar and launching a career as a writer. As many critics have already suggested, these tragic experiences forced bitter early knowledge upon the child—knowledge that profoundly shaped her writing. Aware of the potential for madness and loss, her work seeks out tenuous islands of sanity and permanence. The lure of a fatal lassitude, of dreamy isolation, which has the look of safety, forms an undercurrent that may be felt throughout her work. The longing for

> freedom at last, a lifelong
> dream of time and silence,
> dream of protection and rest   (*CP,* 72–74)

explored in "Faustina, or Rock Roses" reappears, less explicitly stated, in many poems. The dream is of the calm found lastingly only in death; but even in death one may be met instead with the hellish mockery of

> the very worst
> the unimaginable nightmare
> that never before dared last
>   more than a second   (*CP,* 74)

For her, lucid observation was the alternative to this self-imposed isolation, which is both seductive and frightening.

Bishop's early years were often solitary, and she never knew a permanent home. As an only child and, in effect, an orphan, she shuttled between relatives, spending winters with a paternal aunt in Boston and summers with her maternal grandparents in Nova Scotia.[10] From the beginning, she was an (often unwilling) traveler. When she was six and still living with her modestly placed but affectionate maternal grandparents in Great Village, her rich paternal grandparents, whom she "scarcely knew," appeared one day to "rescue" her from comparative poverty and took her away to their large house in Worcester, Massachusetts. As Bishop related in the autobiographical story "The Country Mouse" (unpublished until after her death), "I felt as if I were being kidnapped, even if I wasn't" (*CProse,* 14). Her grandfather, a successful building contractor, is pictured in Bishop's story as stern, cold, and humorless. The house "was gloomy, there was no denying it" (*CProse,* 17).

Even Beppo, the family dog, seemed susceptible to the Puritanical atmosphere. On one occasion, having vomited unobserved, the dog seated himself "gloomily . . . in the closet facing the wall. He was punishing *himself*. No one had ever punished him for his gastritis, naturally; it was all his own idea, his peculiar Bostonian sense of guilt" (*CProse,* 21). The dislocation the child experienced, following as it did on a pair of catastrophic losses, contributed to a series of illnesses that might have killed her. After nine months in her Bishop grandparents' house, she was rescued yet again, this time by her mother's elder sister, Maude. The child shared her aunt's small apartment in Boston and was nursed back to a degree of health, although she continued throughout her childhood to suffer from nagging ailments, and severe asthma followed her into adulthood. During the summers, she returned to her beloved Bulmer grandparents in Nova Scotia. The sensuous richness of detail found in the many poems and stories set in Great Village and the paucity of writing about the rest of her childhood attest to the importance of those summers.

Because of her many childhood illnesses, Bishop received little formal schooling until she entered secondary school at Walnut Academy in Natick, Massachusetts, at sixteen. She finished college at twenty-three. To compensate for sickness and isolation, she became intensely engaged by visual beauty and by the life of the mind. Bishop's interest in reading, writing, nature, and the arts was largely self-developed, and she continued, throughout her life, to follow an independent course. She determined to become a poet at fourteen. She told an interviewer, "I was very isolated as a child and perhaps poetry was my way of making familiar what I saw around me."[11] Her later poems and stories consistently demonstrate a remarkable visual memory, full of sharp fragments of village experience that she could not understand as a child. A voracious reader, Bishop came early to Shelley, Whitman, and especially Hopkins. For her, books (and pictures) always remained alternative worlds with real depth and dimension, with a distinct, indwelling life of their own. She traveled vicariously, combing books and staring at maps, a habit that accounts for her later preoccupation with imaginary travel. At Walnut Academy, she contributed strange, amusing fancies to her high-school literary magazine, *The Blue Pencil*. At Vassar, she helped to found an alternative literary magazine, *Con Spirito,* when the established one would not accept her work and the work of her friends. Later these rebels were invited to accept positions on the original magazine. In these school outlets and others, she published essays and stories as well as poems at a brisk rate. Some of these offer revealing glimpses of her nascent artistic personality.

The best and most characteristic of Bishop's juvenilia is "To a Tree," written when she was sixteen. It anticipates the fascination with observation-through-a-frame that provides the occasion for so many of her mature poems.

> Oh, tree outside my window, we are kin,
> > For you ask nothing of a friend but this:
> To lean against the window and peer in
> > And watch me move about! Sufficient bliss
>
> For me, who stand behind its framework stout,
> > Full of my tiny tragedies and grotesque grieves,
> To lean against the window and peer out,
> > Admiring infinites'mal leaves.   (CP, 212)

Although the diction flirts with archaism, it is simple and direct. The final line, with its flowing assonance, gives evidence of a sensitive ear. But the aspect most characteristic of Bishop's future work is the keen appreciation of the security of enclosure, which actually encourages observation of the tempting world outside. For the moment, the comfort of security appears to be winning the implicit contest between enclosure and travel, a contest that would be reconsidered in poem after poem throughout her life. When the young writer asserts kinship with the tree, it is because the tree implicitly recognizes her shyness and permits their friendship to remain on a purely aesthetic basis. She can "admire" the tree because she is protected by a "framework stout." This loneliness is pleasing, its melancholy tempered by an awareness of correspondences. The tree seems all the more humanized because it is distanced and framed, yet it retains the miracle and mystery of "infinites'mal leaves."

After college she received encouragement from Marianne Moore, whom she met in 1934, during her last term at Vassar. Bishop, excited by Moore's *Observations,* was introduced to Moore through a Vassar librarian. She described the meeting they arranged as the most important thing to happen in her senior year.

Moore was her first serious reader. She encouraged her protégée to continue writing during a period of doubt, when Bishop considered a medical career. Bishop's letters to Moore, housed at the Rosenbach Museum in Philadelphia, are of great interest.[12] In them Bishop confided her evolving ideas about poetry and art. Bishop's published comments on this relationship in the poem "Invitation to Miss Marianne Moore" and the essay "Efforts of Affection: A Memoir of Marianne Moore" reveal a keen, amused appreciation of Moore's talent, kindness, eccentricity, and devotion to her art. Moore's influence on Bishop has excited frequent comment, but significantly, Bishop's early poetry resembled Moore's poetry less than her later, more mature, poetry does. Bishop had not yet broken through to the tangible world that Moore details so precisely. It is clear from the early correspondence that she wants to, and Moore's importance may be that she offered a way.

During her post-Vassar years, Bishop began to travel. Freed by a small inheritance from her wealthy Bishop grandfather, Bishop visited France, Italy, Spain, and Morocco, keeping New York City as a home base. For a poet later noted as a traveler, the early locations she traveled to appear infrequently, except for a few poems set in Paris. Instead, this early poetry travels inward. The enigmas of these early poems are not impenetrable. An early short story, "In Prison" (1937), offers a key. This story outlines, more explicitly than the poems, what is at stake: the safety of enclosure opposes the ambiguous freedom and danger of life at large. "In Prison" experiments with self-imposed isolation. It offers a sharply drawn portrait of the artist as a consciously alienated, self-intent loner, content to seek out a private den of pure thought. He is a spokesman for many less articulate but similarly driven Bishop characters. David Lehman has rightly contended that "for the way it prefigures attitudes and motifs . . . throughout the poet's career, 'In Prison' commends itself to critical inspection over and beyond its intrinsic merits, considerable though these are."[13] Lehman correctly interprets the story's implication that voluntary imprisonment can be a source of imaginative liberation, and he aptly places Bishop's narrator in a tradition of connoisseurs of the paradoxical liberations of imprisonment that includes Shakespeare's Hamlet, the poets Lovelace and Donne, J. K. Huysmans, and such disciples of Bishop herself as Merrill and Ashbery. But Lehman evidently fails to share my sense of horror at this willing inmate's choice.

Lehman points to the paradox that imprisonment can lead to liberation, but the story conveys the further paradox that voluntary imprisonment is a form of retreat from the challenges of life. The narrator's cool, self-congratulatory tone, so well designed to allay the reader's doubts, is really a veneer to cover the potential cowardice of his action, and one gleans that his artistic vision will be self-contained and never communicated. This man suggests the ultimate sterility of the Huysmans tradition, against which the story may be read as a satiric thrust. Introspection, emblematized by willing imprisonment, is a necessary but not sufficient condition for imaginative creation, as the body of Bishop's work would bear out.

The narrator begins his story thus: "I can scarcely wait for the first day of my imprisonment. It is then that my life, my real life, will begin" (*CProse*, 181). The narrator continues in a vein of modest urbanity. For him, to seek imprisonment is the most natural thing in the world. He yearns for a life of virtually unalloyed idea, untroubled by the tumult and confusion that the world of accidents thrusts upon one.

He details, calmly, articulately, lovingly, the study he had made of prison life. Quoting Hawthorne and Valéry, he expatiates on the forceful figure he will cut in jail, but the real motive for his imprisonment is that it will open the springs of artistic expression. He wishes for "one very dull book to read, the duller the better. A book, moreover, on a subject completely foreign to me; perhaps the second volume, if the first would familiarize me too well with the terms and purpose of the work" (*CProse*, 187). The very barrenness of this hypothetical book appears to open up vast possibilities. "From my detached rock-like book I shall be able to draw vast generalizations, abstractions of the grandest, most illuminating sort, like allegories or poems, and by posing fragments of it against the surroundings and conversation of my prison, I shall be able to form my own examples of surrealist art!—something I should never know how to do outside, where the sources are so bewildering" (*CProse*, 180). Is Bishop speaking for herself here? Her own early work shuns the bewildering complexity of life outside, while mental confines incite her imagination to strange flights. But that work also suggests the inherent emotional and imaginative frustrations of symbolic prison.

Within narrow limits, the narrator seeks a new freedom. Imprisonment apparently means no loss because "I already live, in relation to society, very much as if I were in prison" (*CProse*, 181). Fear of the jostling and confusion of life is never stated but is clearly present. Near the end he admits, "Never, never could I succeed 'at large'" (*CProse*, 190). Instead, the narrator embraces chosen limits. He concludes: "'Freedom is knowledge of necessity;' I believe nothing as ardently as I do that. And I assure you that to act in this way is the only logical step for me to take. I mean, of course, to be acted *upon* in this way is the only logical step for me to take" (*CProse*, 191). The narrator speaks confidently of his future life, as if all the gains he anticipates are guaranteed, but he's too cocksure. He admits that any slight divergence from his plans, "if, for example, I should become ill and have to go the prison infirmary, or if shortly after my arrival I should be moved to a different cell—either of these accidents would seriously upset me, and I should have to begin my work all over again" (*CProse*, 190–91). If his prison career does not go according to plan, his artistic ends might be frustrated. If they were, it would be consistent with the implication of Bishop's remaining early work that the flight to symbolic prison merely heightens the frustration one fled. This implication is supported by a dream the narrator recounts near the end of the story:

> Once I dreamed that I was in Hell. It was a low, Netherlands-like country, all the marsh grass a crude, artificial green, lit by brilliant but almost horizontal sunlight. I was dressed in an unbecoming costume of gray cotton: trousers of an awkward length and a shirt hanging outside them, and my hair cut close. I suffered constantly from extreme dizziness because the horizon (and this is how I knew I was in Hell) was at an angle of forty-five degrees. Although this useless tale may not seem to have much connection with my theme, I include it simply to illustrate the manner in which I expect my vision of the outside world to be miraculously changed when I first hear my cell door locked behind me, and I step to the window to take my first look out.
>
> (*CProse*, 189)

The narrator apparently fails to recognize that this "useless" dream *is* connected to his theme because its vision of Hell is a vision of his future; the "unbecoming costume of gray cotton" must surely be his prison uniform; the hair of prisoners is always "cut close." Far from experiencing the expected liberation when he first looks out of his cell window, he is likely to experience the painful disorientation of perspective prefigured there. Bishop has chosen to depict this willing prisoner *before* his incarceration in order to leave open the tale's sad ironies. Without consciously realizing it, this dreamer may be entering a nightmare.

Bishop's theory of imagination is not, after all, a "theory of absence," as Lehman would have it. Lehman correctly stresses that Bishop's imagery often turns to "room, cell, cage, and box, and usually within the context of aesthetic inquiry,"[14] but in her early work, characters so enclosed are living an imaginatively charged but sterile life (I'm thinging of the empty heroism of her Man-Moth, the useless beauty of her imaginary iceberg) while in her later work the room or box generally opens out into a tangible reality of physical fact and emotional risk, which the framing element encourages her to experience freshly. Lehman points out the "quite explicit echo" of this story in "The End of March," a poem written some forty years later, which contemplates "my proto-dream-house, / my crypto-dream-house," a small, odd shack where one would like to retire "and do *nothing*, / or nothing much, forever, in two bare rooms" (CP, 179), but he fails to note that this place is described as "—perfect! But—impossible." The distant object of a Cape Cod seaside walk in early spring, the house is never reached because tangible facts won't allow it:

> that day the wind was much too cold
> even to get that far,
> and of course the house was boarded up.   (CP, 180)

The dream house offers an impossible ideal, no doubt fortunately impossible, but it does serve as one incitement to the poem's brilliant concluding vision of the "lion sun" that transforms the bleak natural world and allows one to see it in a newly vigorous light. In Bishop's work, early or late, Lehman's theory of absence is always implicitly or explicitly challenged by present realities, and absence by itself, though tempting, is never an adequate value.

In a high school essay for *The Blue Pencil*, the eighteen-year-old poet had already begun her contemplation of deliberate isolation:

There is a peculiar quality about being alone, an atmosphere that no sounds or persons can ever give. It is as if being with people were the Earth of the Mind, the land with its hills and valleys, scent and music;

but in being alone, the mind finds its Sea, the wide, quiet plane with different lights in the sky and different, more secret sounds. But it appears we are frightened by the first breaking of its waves at our feet, and never go on voyages of discovery, never feel the free winds that have blown over the water, and never find the islands of the Imagination, where live who knows what curious beasts and strange peoples? . . . Perhaps we shall never know the companion in ourselves who is with us all our lives, the nearness of our minds at all times to the rare person whose heart quickens when a bird climbs high and alone in the clear air.[15]

Although the language of this charming passage is more naively romantic than the cool, conversational tone she would later employ (she was then under the spell of Shelley), the appeal of being alone persisted. The narrator of "In Prison" has the courage to set sail for "the islands of the Imagination." He seeks the "companion in himself." Despite his relaxed tone, his choice is frightening, because it asks no return.

Most of Bishop's early poems explore related fantasies of self-enclosure. In these poems, small heroes are driven by deep psychological compulsions that betray egotism, fear, and even self-pity. The poet explores these emotions with cool but compassionate irony. The hero of "The Gentleman of Shalott" (1936), a literally split personality, assumes that, because of his physical symmetry, he is half mirror image. The Gentleman is descended on one side from Tennyson, on the other from Laforgue. He has mastered the art of evading experience by inventing an absorbing game; his delusion gives him an excuse to watch himself. Tennyson's high rhetoric has given way to Bishop's relaxed, colloquial idiom and playful way with versification. The short, jerky lines of varied lengths, with their witty, slant rhymes, evoke the precarious balance of the Gentleman's existence. They are typical of the sly, expressive use Bishop made of the "traditional" verse forms she favored in her early poems.

> If the glass slips
> he's in a fix—
> only one leg, etc. But
> while it stays put
> he can walk and run

and his hands can clasp one
another. The uncertainty
he says he
finds exhilarating. He loves
that sense of constant re-adjustment.   (CP, 9–10)

His life is out of kilter, yet he seems quite at home in it. He would not want to be shown that he is whole. Like the narrator of "In Prison," the Gentleman is both genial and hermetic. It is the curiously unembarrassed, even cheerful, way these characters cling to their conditions that makes us wonder whether to laugh or weep over them. When we take leave of the Gentleman, he is enjoying his celebrity and freely dispensing advice, as if to the newspaper: "He wishes to be quoted as saying at present: / 'Half is enough.'" His gesture of renunciation resembles the choice made by the hero of "In Prison"—it seems like sacrifice but is really self-indulgence.

Further exploring the theme of self-incarceration is "The Man-Moth" (1936—CP, 14–15). Written at the age of twenty-five, while Bishop was living alone in New York the year after she left Vassar, this is her first great poem. In six unusual stanzas of controlled free verse, it creates a bizarre yet familiar world. In this fable the central figure is not genial, but the cyclical anxiety of his life forms a pattern so regular he cannot renounce it. Although her Man-Moth suggests the alienated artist, his plight cuts deeper. Through him Bishop explores the thwarted emotional life of urban man, with whom he is compared. The Man-Moth feels more intensely than, and thus suffers as representative of, the more blasé Man. This creature alternates with dogged fixity of purpose between the two halves of a moth's career: the light-seeking moth and the larva in the cocoon. Aboveground, the moth's fluttering and his instinctive pursuit of light at great personal cost symbolize human anxiety and compulsion. His recurrent effort to climb to the moon would seem heroic if it weren't comically doomed from the start. He responds to moonlight imaginatively, but his imagination only distorts the world and troubles his nights. His descent belowground into the subway / cocoon seems a desperate flight from the exposed life above into a fearful isolation that combines enclosure with meaningless travel at breakneck speed, facing backwards on the subway train, paralyzed by fear of the third rail. Here is the symbolist city, where nightmare and reality blend. Remarkably, the poem is able to balance its intense evocation of urban alienation, and of mythic patterns gone awry, with a sly sense of the ridiculous that leads to deliciously humorous moments. For the Man-Moth is also Pierrot.

Robert Lowell stated a decisive opposition in Bishop's poetry when he pointed out two recurring elements, *motion:* "weary but persisting . . . stoically maintained" and *terminus:* "rest, sleep, fulfillment or death. This is the imaginary iceberg."[16] While Lowell's terms have their advantages, I prefer to refer to these poles by two more precise names, *travel* and *enclosure.* The narrator of "In Prison" ignored half of the equation. He chose enclosure or terminus. On the other hand, when the Man-Moth rides backwards on the subway, he combines enclosure with aimless travel. There will be no terminus. His situation also suggests Bishop's recognition that enclosure and anxiety go together, even when one flees to enclosure to *escape* anxiety. Enclosure is not, in Bishop's work, a restful state, but one troubled, as here, by recurring dreams or other reminders of the anxieties one fled.

Bishop had a talent for making offbeat loners seem real and representative. The Man-Moth's naïveté, his humble persistence, his vulnerability, give him a sad and funny appeal. He resembles the narrator of "In Prison" in his loneliness and isolation and in his commitment to psychic voyaging, but he does not share that character's intellectual dimension, his self-consciousness. The Man-Moth instinctively surrenders to necessity without knowledge. Indeed, he seems to emblematize the surrender to the unconscious. Although the Man-Moth is imprisoned, at times he musters the courage to strive, heroically but blindly: "what the Man-Moth fears most he must do." What the poet fears mose *she* must do. Bishop's early work constantly presses against the limitations imposed by neurotic fears.

The Man-Moth is a heroic quester, an artist, a coward, and a clown. The poem combines these features through the myth of regeneration. The moral of "The Man-Moth" appears in the counsel the final stanza offers if one catches him. Impersonating the detached precision of a naturalist, the speaker suggests that one must "hold up a flashlight to his eye": it will reveal the darkness inside the "haired horizon" of his eyelid. Intrusion on this vast inner world will force out "one tear, his only possession, like the bee's sting," a private token of self.

Slyly he palms it, and if you're not paying attention
he'll swallow it. However, if you watch, he'll hand it over,
cool as from underground springs and pure enough to
    drink.

The Man-Moth has a clown's movements, a clown's sadness. His
strangely cool salt-free tear bespeaks his inner purity, an underground part of himself he is loath to reveal. Handing it over suggests the possibility of regeneration through sacrifice and
communion. For all the Man-Moth's fears, only his tear, his token
of hidden loneliness, can really betray (and thus save) him, because it will reveal his vulnerability. A strange miser possessing
nothing but hidden regret, the Man-Moth must part with that
regret to pay the wages of love.

Love as Risk

The Man-Moth's ultimate motive for choosing imprisonment is his reluctance to expose himself. For Bishop, love
means exposure, but isolation from love means empty safety. The
danger of loving someone is that one might be rejected; worse, one
can lose the loved one, as Bishop knew from the early death of one
parent and the lifelong madness of the other. The search for
love—and the fear of love—are absorbing and might lead either to
freedom or to deeper hermeticism. The cost of love is defined in
"Casabianca" (1936). The poem begins with a historical boy who
refused to leave a disabled ship when his father, the French admi-
ral Casabianca, disdaining surrender, went below to blow it up.
The poem's insistent repetitions present the boy's stubborn determination (and his uncertainty) with compassionate irony.

Love's the boy stood on the burning deck
trying to recite "The boy stood on
the burning deck." Love's the son
    stood stammering elocution
    while the poor ship in flames went down.

(CP, 5)

The boy attempts to live up to a cast-iron concept of heroism em-
bodied in the schoolroom verse, applying it to his own perilous
situation. His ship lost, encircled by water and flame, the boy pre-

sents an emblem of frustrated travel. Here love is synonymous with pain and seems to exist in a realm of high rhetoric, where it exacts pointless, self-destructive gestures of devotion.

> Love's the obstinate boy, the ship,
> even the swimming sailors, who
> would like a schoolroom platform, too,
>   or an excuse to stay
>   on deck. And love's the burning boy.

To prove oneself remains painfully desirable, as even the safely swimming sailors know. At last the language doubles back on itself a final time, the "burning deck" enfolds "the burning boy," and love has won dominion.

Bishop consistently ties one's fear of love to the Christian myth of regeneration through suffering. To love is to burn, which makes love fearful. "The Weed" (1937), a rich and a strange poem, is "modelled somewhat," Bishop told interviewer Ashley Brown, on George Herbert's "Love Unknown,"[17] which contains an image of the hard heart made tender and purified by fire. Bishop's lifelong affinity with Herbert was a natural one. She shared with him a sense of the emblematic significance of common things; for either poet, a crumb, a flower, or a church window had a message that would yield itself only to humble observation and disciplined meditation. Meditation must be disciplined to sort out nature's inherently paradoxical implications. Despite their devotion to paradox, each favored a clear, direct style—the sense of the poet speaking. Each was, in this way, a democrat of literature. When asked what she most liked about Herbert, she replied, "To begin with, I like the absolute naturalness of tone."[18] More fundamentally, each combined an unusually unsentimental and intellectually rigorous approach to moral questions with remarkable gentleness and generosity, a spirit that demands much of oneself while wishing clemency for others. Although Bishop was no churchgoer, Christian motifs appear throughout her poetry. She had a religious nature and education, and the foundations of her work are recognizably Christian. Her writing stresses the virtues of humility, patience, and renunciation (and it exposes false pretenses to those virtues). After the breakthrough that led to the work of her middle phase, Bishop celebrates, with Herbert, the miraculous gift of sight. One senses that the commitment of her poems to report what they see without cant or cheating is moral as well as artistic.[19] Her early poems suggest that when you fool yourself about the essentials of what you perceive, you are a moral coward. And this conviction is at the center of "The Weed."

As in Herbert's "Love Unknown," Bishop's "The Weed" takes inspiration from the emblem of the tortured heart. Both poems are about the anguish love costs. Herbert's emblem fits into a well-established tradition illustrating a painful yet ultimately reassuring moral: the value, in Christian terms, of purging the heart's sin through the refining fires of divine love. By contrast, the enigma the heart presents in "The Weed" is consistent with the bitter mystery of *human* love. Bishop converts sacred thought to profane ends. The solemn, dreamlike setting is presented calmly and with utter conviction through a precisely realized series of unlooked for, self-consistent details.

The poem begins with a startling image—a body dead but capable of thought; a heart frozen on an inert idea; time a meaningless measure.

> I dreamed that dead, and meditating,
> I lay upon a grave, or bed,
> (at least, some cold and close-built bower).
> In the cold heart, its final thought
> stood frozen, drawn immense and clear,
> stiff and idle as I was there;
> and we remained unchanged together
> for a year, a minute, an hour.   (*CP*, 20)

The language is of the utmost simplicity—sombre, austere, and weighty—yet the scene is charged with ambiguity. How did the speaker come to dream this? What is the meaning of the cold heart's "final thought"? How is it the "stiff and idle" companion of the speaker? The speaker's voice seems unperturbed, yet here is another restless enclosure. There is the appearance of terminus, but, in fact, motion will dominate.

The key to the fable is "love unknown." The heart's calm is shattered by a

>   motion,
> as startling, there, to every sense
> as an explosion.

The sterile safety of death's "desperate sleep" is disturbed because:

> A slight young weed
> had pushed up through the heart and its
> green head was nodding on the breast.
> (All this was in the dark.)

Frozen thought is shattered by the rude green enigma of life: this personified, emblematic weed is free even of the requirements of photosynthesis. As G. S. Fraser notes, "The precision, there, paradoxically serves to make clear the *impreciseness*—the gappishness, the incommensurability with waking experience—of experience in dreams."[20] The weed signals something ("two leaves moved like a semaphore"); we are not instructed in the code.

> The rooted heart began to change
> (not beat) and then it split apart
> and from it broke a flood of water.

The speaker's bodily parts are not "my" breast, "my" heart, but "the" breast, "the" heart, suggesting mental alienation from these dead features. However, when a few drops from the flood fall "upon *my* face / and in *my* eyes" (my italics), these drops revive emotions. Now she perceives:

> that each drop contained a light,
> a small, illuminated scene;
> the weed-deflected stream was made
> itself of racing images.
> (As if a river should carry all
> the scenes that it had once reflected
> shut in its waters, and not floating
> on momentary surfaces.)   (CP, 21)

The tendency to correct or clarify a statement parenthetically in mid thought, evident throughout this poem, is one of Bishop's favorite devices. It creates the effect of seeking precision while thinking aloud, before an experience or thought has been quite completed. The stream is a repository of the past, of those tearful episodes when her heart was first lost. But the scenes form no readable narrative; they fly past, bright enigmas!

The weed seems triumphant. First cautiously, then with abandon, it has aroused questioning attention.

The weed stood in the severed heart.
"What are you doing there?" I asked.
It lifted its head all dripping wet
(with my own thoughts?)
and answered then: "I grow," it said,
"but to divide your heart again."

The weed dominates the dream ominously and speaks confidently of its ongoing dominion. What can this green, unkillable weed be but the ineradicable vitality of life and love, which even the speaker's cold, imprisoned heart cannot kill? Life has forced the frozen heart back into yet another cycle of suffering. The haven of death or dream is proved a sham, but the analogy of Herbert's "Love Unknown" suggests that the painful process of revival may purge and thus make new. The weed connotes an unconscious, suppressed wish to take the chance of life, to face the unknown consequences of love, even with a divided heart.

Bishop found Herbert's emblematic method a flexible resource. She would continue to explore the emblematic complexity of objects. Her training in the techniques of metaphysical poetry, and in particular, in the compressed plainness and moral balance of Herbert's verse, would stay with her—as would her haunted awareness of love's insatiable claims.

Words
«A House for Thinking In»

The desperate sleep of "The Weed" offers one uneasy haven from life. Another haven, the enclosed world of art, is also seen as both a resting place and a potential snare. Like the "house for thinking in" discussed below, to lose oneself in works of art can bring either self-knowledge or sterile introspection. The narrator of "In Prison" saw how psychic enclosure could foster surreal works of art. A second prose fable, that droll piece of understatement "The Sea and Its Shore" (1937), playfully explores the consequences of submerging oneself in a modernist's continuum of pure language. It begins in the manner of a fairy tale: "Once, on one of our large public beaches, a man was appointed to keep the sand free from papers" (CProse, 171). The curious routine of the hero, Edwin Boomer, a gently simple fellow, almost a divine fool, emerges through carefully amassed details that emphasize the philosophical quality of his existence—for instance, he lives in a tiny house "4 by 4 by 6 feet": "As a house, it was more like an idea of a 'house,' than a real one. It could have stood at either end of the scale of ideas of houses. It could have been a child's perfect play-house, or an adult's ideal house—since everything that makes most houses nuisances has been done away with" (*CProse*, 171–72). One is reminded of the Gentleman of Shallot's "Half is enough." Renunciation discovers in escape from responsibility an avenue toward thought. His house has room only for ideas.

This tiny house offers "shelter, but not for living in, for thinking in" (*CProse*, 172). Boomer refuses life in favor of words. Does his name reflect the hollow resonance of a world of pure sound? In pursuit of his job, he walks the beach collecting scraps of paper—newsprint, torn pages of books, etc. Then he gets drunk and pores over them by the light of a trash fire. His drunken reading excites the fires of imagination. "On nights that Boomer was most drunk, the sea was of gasoline, terribly dangerous" (*CProse*, 174). His un-tempered imagination makes nature itself frightening, but like "the third rail, the unbroken draft of poison" that unnerves the Man-Moth, the sea poses no immediate danger. Oddly, though barely literate, "Edwin Boomer lived the most literary life pos-sible." Like an Eliot or a Pound, Boomer persistently tries to jux-tapose his random scraps, quite literally "fragments shored against his ruin," assuming that they must refer to *him* or form coherent stories about others. He is perplexed when they fail to resolve themselves. His lonely life of "study" assumes that hard reading will lead to understanding. But: "The more papers he picked up and the more he read, the less he felt he understood. In a sense he depended on 'their imagination,' and was even its slave, but at the same time he thought of it as a kind of disease" (*CProse*, 177–78). Like Bishop's other slaves of imagination, for Boomer the "disease" is both exciting and enervating; it cuts Boomer off from actuality. At last: "Either because of the insect-armies of type so constantly besieging his eyes, or because it was really so, the world, the whole world he saw, came before many years to seem printed, too" (*CProse*, 178). Print obscures nature. Thus the story spoofs not just modernist poetics but the writer herself. She entertains the temptation of Boomer-like immersion in a world of words, of building a house as empty of the nuisances and joys of life as his is, with amused detachment, but also with real sadness. This story suggests a frustration with symbolist and modernist poetics (and with her own mental barriers) that would soon send Bishop off in a fresh direction.

Edwin Boomer unwittingly chooses a vicarious, "literary" life over an engaged life. He is repaid with an existence that is barren of real content and makes no sense. The choice between art and travel is more ambivalent, and cuts closer, in one of Bishop's most tensely balanced early poems, "The Imaginary Iceberg" (1935). The stakes are higher here because she finds an image that can bear the full weight of her inquiry. David Kalstone aptly labels the iceberg "that tempting self-enclosed world, a frosty palace of art."[21] But it is more than this—it is an emblem of all that is alluring yet fatal, of the cold emptiness of the isolated human soul.

> We'd rather have the iceberg than the ship,
> although it meant the end of travel.
> Although it stood stock-still like cloudy rock
> and all the sea were moving marble.   (CP, 4)

An unmoved mover, the iceberg stands "stock-still" in a transfigured sea. It demands sacrifices. "This is a scene a sailor'd give his eyes for," but without his eyes the sailor cannot see—and thus loses the iceberg as well! The iceberg's intoxicating rhetoric, which sways the viewer to take action, even action of a painful kind, recalls the rhetorical quality of love in "Casabianca." Here sacrifice is not self-serving—may even prove fatal.

> This is a scene where he who treads the boards
> is artlessly rhetorical. The curtain
> is light enough to rise on finest ropes
> that airy twists of snow provide.
> The wits of these white peaks
> spar with the sun. Its weight the iceberg dares
> upon a shifting stage and stands and stares.

The iceberg lures one towards a drama of beautiful emptiness. Will the brilliance, will the "wits of these white peaks," lead to any conclusions? Unconscious of its powers, the iceberg merely "stands and stares." It pleases but cannot instruct.

The poem answers the questions the iceberg poses in its final stanza.

> The iceberg cuts its facets from within.
> Like jewelry from a grave
> it saves itself perpetually and adorns
> only itself.

The vast, apparently solid iceberg reveals itself as another strangely hermetic island, another emblem of self. One must tear oneself away from this dazzling, wasted beauty. The contest between the opposing claims of art and travel, which would remain central to Bishop's work, shows her affinity to Wallace Stevens, a poet she had been reading closely since college.[22] Yet the voice is recognizably her own, a voice much less given to the positing of abstractions than even the Stevens of *Harmonium*. Significantly, Bishop's emblem of art is motionless and hermetic—it is a fatal point of terminus, as Stevens emblems of imagination rarely or never are. It is "imaginary," not "imagined," and thus carries implications of artificiality. But like a real iceberg it is to be feared; seen too close it is a killer of ships and sailors, and its physical coldness betokens moral coldness. The poem, for all its high-spirited rhetoric, is grimly earnest at heart. The choice it implicitly makes seems more decisive and more painful than Stevens's choices, since Stevens usually manages to have his cake and eat it too. The passengers call "Good-bye . . . good-bye" and "the ship steers off" for warmer waters. The iceberg's ultimate appeal is to the soul.

> Icebergs behoove the soul
> (both being self-made from elements least visible)
> to see them so: fleshed, fair, erected indivisible.

Bishop has captured the delicate, vaporous sources of the immense iceberg, as well as its curious inwardness. A real iceberg is a sight a traveler might journey to see, but this *imaginary* iceberg, this emblem of the symbolists' artificial paradise, either cancels the will for real voyages or is left behind. One's poems will be as cold and isolated as the imaginary iceberg unless one discovers a kind of art that will not mean the end of travel.

"The Map" (1935), published in the same year as "The Imaginary Iceberg," explores an inward realm that is both more concentrated and vaster. Here was the first of many explorations into ordinary objects, uncovering their latent potential to be worlds in themselves. To study a map is to reveal the will to travel, but here, in keeping with the spirit of her early work, travel is imagined and vicarious rather than actual. Maps are emblems of the world that compete in detail and complexity with the world itself. The poem turns on the fact that although a map can be a practical guide to travel, it may also serve as an abstracting "island of the Imagination." The suggestive conclusion, "More delicate than the historians' are the map-makers' colors," has retained its fascination for Bishop's readers over five decades. Many critics incautiously regard it as the key to all of Bishop's writing, treating an ambiguous line from a tensely balanced early poem as if it were a bold sign pointing down a straight road. These critics tend to overstress Bishop as "mapmaker" and to understress Bishop as "historian." I will argue that the poem is really poised ambivalently between the attractions of the abstracting, fiction-making functions of the map-maker and the more matter-of-fact observation and judgment of the historian. This early poem may lean toward mapmaking, but as her career unfolded, the weight shifted toward history. The poem opposes two elements: the representational intention of the map and the beauty of pure form ("map-makers' colors"). The tension between these elements emerges through the presence of a third: the persistent allusion to actualities that the map recalls, exciting the mind to imaginative, almost surrealistic, sallys beyond the map's frame. The poem's first clause, "Land lies in water," suggests representation. Its second clause, "it is shadowed green," shows that Bishop may also refer to a printed world with a form and beauty of its own. This delicate balance initiates us into an ever-shifting environment:

> Shadows, or are they shallows, at its edges
> showing the line of long sea-weeded ledges
> where weeds hang to the simple blue from green.   (CP, 3)

A term that might be from drawing ("shadowed") contends with glimpses of nature ("shallows, weeds") while the noun "shadows" remains ambiguous. It could refer to art *or* nature. "Edges" may denote either the "long sea-weeded ledges" of a natural coastline or a map's borders. The map becomes a vicarious means of travel, which only partially satisfies the urge for experience itself. Still, although it is a framed world, the map (unlike the iceberg) may open outward. Bishop told interviewer Alexandra Johnson: "my mother's family wandered a lot and loved this strange world of travel. My first poem in my first book was inspired when I was sitting on the floor, one New Year's Eve in Greenwich Village, after I graduated from college. I was staring at a map. The poem wrote itself. People will say that it corresponded to some part of me which I was unaware of at the time. This may be true."[23] Might the poem have grown out of that special sense of estrangement one feels when one is home alone on New Year's Eve? Maps may not be intended to express emotion, but the viewer—not unnaturally—keeps responding emotionally to the map. That response draws forth its potential beauty. It is too rich an alternative world to forgo. One's response imposes life on the picture, but the response is not wholly subjective. It is conditioned by experience as well as human need.

The concluding line, "More delicate than the historians' are the map-makers' colors," must be weighed with care. Mention of the historian pits actuality against the delicate and arbitrarily chosen colors on paper. The mapmaker is treated as an abstract colorist, fashioning a vivid but unreal reconception of sea and land. Certain critics have seen this line as a refusal to confront reality. For example, Edwin Honig called it a "deliberate anticlimax" because: "the line states the poet's aim; a scrupulous representation of the world reduced in scale and line to something like a cartographer's depiction of geographical area. It is a plan for suppressing rather than compressing contours, dimensions, tonality, emotion."[24] Bishop's conclusion does suggest nostalgia for art's subtle, refined abstractions, but the map is not lacking in dimension, tonality, or emotion. Aren't these what the poem finds? She was working along lines that would soon enable her to bring together abstract, immutable creation and transient fact. "The Map" sets the conflicting claims of purely vicarious travel, winged by the mapmakers' art, against the claims of real travel in the historians' none-too-delicate realm. Does the poem's final preference (and still more, in the end, Bishop's own) really rest with mere delicacy? Implicitly, the poem feels the confinement of the mapmakers' framed plane. It keeps expanding the range of reference, out toward actualities that are at once homely and surreal, as when:

> These peninsulas take the water between thumb and
>   finger
> like women feeling for the smoothness of yard-goods.

Geography can be humanized. Bishop might linger over the map-maker's delicate colors, while only alluding to the material facts, but the material facts remain unchanged. Implicitly, she needs them, and they await her attention.

Surrealism and Everyday Life

There *is* a surreal flavor to Bishop's map—it counterpoints versions of nature until one wonders which is which. Bishop's fascination with surprising perspectives led her to seek the point of juncture between dreams and everyday life. She studied surrealistic poetry quite deliberately, encorporating some aspects of the surrealist aesthetic into her style while rejecting others. In 1935, the summer after graduating from Vassar, Bishop made a trip to France, first soliciting from Marianne Moore the names of the modern French poets.[25] Having lingered for a month in a small fishing village on the coast of Brittany with a little library of French books, she then spent several months in Paris. She made a second visit to Paris in the late summer of 1937. During these visits she made herself acquainted with the French avant-garde. Bishop later told Ashley Brown, "I was much interested in Surrealism in the '30's" adding that, when in France, "I had read a lot of surrealist poetry and prose."[26] She came upon surrealism earlier than most American writers of her generation, but it would be a mistake to label her an orthodox surrealist. She had no interest in psychic automatism, and Breton's manifestos proclaiming the coming liberation of the human spirit must have left her cold. Richard Mullen has rightly suggested that while a fascination with dream-like states is the main interest Bishop and the surrealists have in common, there are some fundamental differences in the way Bishop handles dreams. According to Mullen, "She does not seek to subvert logical control and she refuses to accept the 'split' between the roles of conscious and unconscious forces in our perception of the world."[27] This observation can be extended to four poems (not discussed by Mullen) that might seem most likely to follow the orthodox surrealist program, that quartet of lyrics she wrote in France between 1937 and 1938: "Paris, 7 A.M." "Quai d'Orléans," "Sleeping on the Ceiling," and "Sleeping Standing Up." In these poems, logical control *has* been subverted, or nearly so, but the perspective reflects disquiet and disorientation rather than psychic freedom. The conscious mind struggles uncomfortably to reassert itself.

Characteristic of these is "Paris, 7 A.M." (1937), one of Bishop's most difficult pieces. It presents a troubled observer trying to distinguish what is actual and what is imposed. Not even time seems to hold steady.

> I make a trip to each clock in the apartment:
> some hands point histrionically one way
> and some point others, from the ignorant faces. (*CP*, 26)

Of course, it is the observer, disturbed already for unspecified reasons, who finds the clocks' hands histrionic, the faces ignorant. Because literal time and place have been established in the title, one knows what *ought* to be, but one's perceptions won't cooperate. The clocks spin off in a dizzy parody of the orderly cycle they are intended to measure.

> Time is an Etoile; the hours diverge
> so much that days are journeys round the suburbs,
> circles surrounding stars, overlapping circles.

The hours, discrete atoms careening off in intricate patterns of dreamlike motion, suggest the mind's own desperate search. Bishop knew how a surprising simile could drive the picture home. Here, however, precise similitude gives way to the shockingly disjunct.

> The short, half-tone scale of winter weathers
> is a spread pigeon's wing.
> Winter lives under a pigeon's wing, a dead wing with
>   damp feathers.

In this poem's strange mood-painting, perception of the exterior world is shaped by emotion and memory.

> Look down into the courtyard. . . .
>   It is like introspection

to stare inside, or retrospection,
a star inside a rectangle, a recollection.

These lines state a central problem of Bishop's early work. Looking outside, at the clocks or the courtyard, ultimately reveals only the inside, is only another sterile form of introspection or retrospection. Actuality cannot be reached. The viewer is doubly enclosed, isolated from the outer world by the walls of her apartment—and by the usurping force of recollection. In attempting to escape chaotic time *inside,* the viewer finds, not a broad world *outside,* but heaviness, death, and enclosing artifice, "a star inside a rectangle" that only reiterates time's enclosing "Etoile." The framed courtyard leads on to further frames; there is busy motion, but no escape. The wall of buildings provokes memories of a brighter past: the walls of "childish snowforts, built in flashier winters." But recollection proves false.

This sky is no carrier-warrior-pigeon
escaping endless intersecting circles.
It is a dead one, or the sky from which a dead one fell.

The star, a whisper of radiant hope and permanence in a pattern of unmeaning, seems also finally lost, one can't tell quite how or when. Here, truly, a "theory of absence" dominates as it will not in later frame-poems.

When did the star dissolve, or was it captured
by the sequence of squares and squares and circles,
    circles?
Can the clocks say; is it there below,
about to tumble in snow?   (*CP,* 26–27)

Even the star is entrapped and dissipated by ambiguous time. Language that in itself is almost circular depicts a grey world of psychic imprisonment. Bishop's experiment with surreal disjunctions, set in the surrealists' favorite city, creates the reverse of liberation. To split the unconscious from the conscious is, for Bishop, to set in motion a near-fatal vertigo effect.

Each of Bishop's Paris poems treads upon quicksand. For example, "Sleeping Standing Up" (1938) explores the promise and the frustration inherent in dream journeys. Like Hansel and Gretel, the speaker searches the forest of memory, but unlike "the clever children's" search, hers is imprisoned in "the armored cars of dreams" (*CP,* 30). These may lead one to perform "so many a dangerous thing," but they are unwieldy enclosures when on the track of emblematic crumbs or pebbles that might guide one on a devious course to an understanding of the past. They cut one off from touching the forest. Hence:

> How stupidly we steered
> until the night was past
> and never found out where the cottage was.

The past remains dead, one's former home unreachable. The poem expresses doubt about the central surrealist doctrine that the unconscious, once tapped, will lead one toward the essential—toward home. In fact, Bishop's past only came to life in poetry written after long immersion in foreign experience. She had to discover how to bring the present to life before the past could speak, and that past could only speak through the same minute, emblematic details that informed her present.

The pattern of search and frustration is typical of Bishop's early dream poems. They are enigmatic because they present a writer grappling with the enigma of self. Their irony is often, in a veiled way, self-directed, because she longs to get outside herself but can't escape. Nevertheless, her later work makes continual reference to the unconscious, capturing a substantial exterior world while recognizing how deeply interpenetrated are reality and dreams. The surrealist's way of looking got in the bone. For one kind of surrealist search she substitutes another. Bishop declared for a quality she loved in Herbert, "the always-more-successful surrealism of everyday life."[28] Hers would be a casual, consciously controlled revision of surrealism based on freshly seeing the unlikely features of ordinary things. Rather than concentrating exclusively on the strange but telling associations discoverable by turning inward, she would travel, as well, in the quotidian.

Bishop knew a good deal about surrealism before there was any widespread response to the movement in America. As my introduction suggests, she was one of the very first writers who could be called postsurrealist. One reason the current generation of American followers of surrealism, poets like John Ashbery and Mark Strand, are so vocal in their praise, is because Bishop's later poetry demonstrated how, in English, to conjoin the dreamlike with the everyday. But she did not do so very joyfully in her most orthodox surrealistic experiments.

Ambiguous Miracles

As we have seen, in Bishop's early poems imagination is trapped in a box. However, two poems written toward the end of her early phase demonstrate possible avenues toward faith in the miracles of everyday life. Although Bishop was herself an unbeliever in traditional Christianity, she grew up steeped in the verities of small-town Baptist religion. In "The Unbeliever" (1938) questions of belief have been restated. It is a tour de force, a penetrating fable on the psychological dangers of both faith *and* doubt. In this exploration of different unsatisfactory visions, three contrasting characters dwell emblematically within dreams or delusions, never connecting with facts. As in "The Man-Moth," Bishop erects a complete world from a scrap of prose ("He sleeps on the top of the mast"). Here the source, Bunyan, suggests the poem's concern: justification by faith. As was Bunyan's Pilgrim, the Unbeliever is a man in danger. But the form of unbelief (and source of danger) has been secularized. This Unbeliever disbelieves in reality itself.

> He sleeps on the top of a mast
> with his eyes fast closed.
> The sails fall away below him
> like the sheets of his bed,
> leaving out in the air of the night the sleeper's head.
>
> (*CP*, 22)

He is at once enclosed and exposed, static and moving, a vivid emblem of displacement. This sleeper is opposed to two believers, gull and cloud; their fatuous security is as mistaken as the sleeper's insecurity. For example, the cloud fancies himself "'founded on marble pillars.'" He boasts, "'I never move,'" and he assumes that he can prove it with the remark "'See the pillars there in the sea?'" However, the next line reveals that he has merely pointed to his own image mirrored in the water.

> Secure in introspection
> he peers at the watery pillars of his reflection.

The ironic rhyme and the wicked pun on "reflection" deftly exposes the pomposity of those who imagine themselves securely in contact with life, yet cannot see how self-absorbed (and self-satisfied) they truly are. The watery pillars of his faith are mere reflections of his cloudy self. Of course, the cloud's position *is* secure, but his sense of *what* supports him is fallacious. Similarly, the gull errs when he asserts:

> "Up here
> I tower through the sky
> for the marble wings on my tower-top fly."

He is arrogantly mistaken, of course, in ascribing his loft to the marble tower. Their reiterated confidence in marble may suggest the (illusory) support of the pillars of the traditional church.

Bishop satirizes the emotional smugness of the self-righteously religious. But this is not where the poem is really telling, for Bishop is saving her keenest irony for a subtler target. If the gull and cloud err in locating the source of their security, which they want to attribute to something solid, the Unbeliever judges even less usefully. These two believers may be wrong, but they can at least function. Instead of responding to life, the fearful Unbeliever:

> sleeps on the top of his mast
> with his eyes closed tight.
> The gull inquired into his dream,
> which was, "I must not fall.
> The spangled sea below wants me to fall.
> It is hard as diamonds; it wants to destroy us all."

The poem's understated humor helps us accept its curious premise. At the same time, one can empathize with the Unbeliever's anxieties—his paranoia, directed against a supposedly threatening world. In a scene in which mental barriers are remarkably permeable, the Unbeliever refuses to wake up; all that penetrates *his* barriers are fear and beauty. In repeating the opening lines, Bishop varies them pointedly. A mast becomes *his* mast, his possession, and he seems to hold his eyes closed willfully. The Unbeliever chooses neither to see nor to act, but to dream. He knows life in terms of his dream alone. Where someone else might see only indifferent—if dangerous—water below, he *knows* the spangled sea's malevolence: it "wants me to fall." Like the frozen heart of the Imaginary Iceberg, the sea is jewellike—hard, precious, perilous. The danger of an imagination directed solely inward is that it will lead either to the fatuous security of gull and cloud or to the displacement and fear of the Unbeliever. Both impose a spurious vision.

Bishop implicitly rejects the dreamer's abject dependence on dreams along with the delusive vision of the self-righteously faithful. Paradoxically, it is their unexamined faith that renders all three unbelievers. Failure to respond responsibly to natural fact supports both the cloud's and gull's silly self-satisfaction and the Unbeliever's apocalyptic terror. As do "Love Lies Sleeping" or "The Weed," this fable dramatizes the necessity of waking up. The Unbeliever's fear prevents him from opening his eyes onto a world he considers too terrible, yet awakening is literally the act most likely to save him from rolling off his perch. Not nature's malice but his own timid self-absorption cuts him off from action and security. Bishop has phrased the problem in its full, paradoxical complexity, and its solution remains but a step away.

The sestina "A Miracle for Breakfast" (1937) explores literal and figurative awakening. The word *miracle* might refer to the surrealists' concern with the marvelous, but the poem's frame of reference is specifically Christian, alluding to the well-known miracle of the loaves and fishes. A modern and ironic quality surrounds that miracle's present tokens—coffee for fishes and the "charitable crumb" for loaves. And the world of the poem is in need of a modern miracle. The speaker is not the only one waiting in the cold morning light. The poem was written during the Depression, and Bishop called it "my 'social consciousness' poem, a poem about hunger."[29] She is part of a needy community, a more scattered and lonely one than the crowd waiting for Jesus, because each sits isolated on a balcony. The sestina form within which Bishop achieves such marvels of colloquialism (she is the only poet I know of who can give the impression of easy storytelling in this archaic, difficult form; she did it again in "Sestina") serves well because of the ambiguity surrounding the repeated end words. These keep acquiring and losing symbolic value, particularly *crumb, coffee,* and *miracle.* Such changes reflect the fact that the nature of the miracle remains uncertain. Are we concerned with the simple matter of breakfast or the simpler matter of salvation?

When at last a man appears, bearing, to everyone's disappointment, "one lone cup of coffee / and one roll," the miracle appears
to have failed.

> Each man received one rather hard crumb,
> which some flicked scornfully into the river,
> and, in a cup, one drop of the coffee.
> Some of us stood around, waiting for the miracle.
>
> (CP, 18)

In a material sense, the miracle does not take place. But the real
importance of miracles lies outside the material. Alert to this, the
poet, at least, attends to her gift. She pushes beyond the question
of breakfast and testifies to the reward of the unworldly.

> I can tell what I saw next; it was not a miracle.
> A beautiful villa stood in the sun
> and from its doors came the smell of hot coffee.
> In front, a baroque white plaster balcony
> added by birds, who nest along the river,
> —I saw it with one eye close to the crumb—
>
> and galleries and marble chambers.   (CP, 18–19)

This opulent earthly vision, discovered by a dramatic shift in perspective, was theologically no miracle. Its source is the imagination, turning upon the sharpest observation of common, even
disappointing things; growing, in this case, from the optical distor-
tion that occurs when one looks very closely at an object. The
vision is made credible by its unforeseen detail. An uncanny feature is that the vision in most respects, even to the plentiful coffee,
anticipates Bishop's years in an eighteenth-century house in Ouro
Prêto, Brazil, several decades in the future. Was this her choicest
fantasy even in 1937?

>   My crumb,
> my mansion, made for me by a miracle,
> through ages, by insects, birds, and the river
> working the stone.   (CP, 19)

The miraculous mansion is "made for me" by the age-old process
that pollinated the wheat and milled the grain and baked the roll

that gave the crumb. For a moment, at least, the miracle stands
forth, with a vision of life that seems both durable and fun.

> Every day, in the sun,
> at breakfast time I sit on my balcony
> with my feet up, and drink gallons of coffee.

But this boisterous image of continuity and luxury is abruptly discarded in the terse envoy.

> We licked up the crumb and swallowed the coffee.
> A window across the river caught the sun
> as if the miracle were working, on the wrong balcony.

The vision created by the imagination is a secular kind of miracle.
Its duration, which seemed endless, was just a moment in the
mind.

Bishop's secular miracle has no divine sanction or permanence.
In substance, if not in tone, the conclusion recalls the critical
awareness of the limits of imagination expressed in the final line of
Keats's "Ode to a Nightingale." "Fled is that music;—Do I wake or
sleep?" Like Keats, Bishop is alive to the inherently deceptive potential of imaginative vision. One's experiences of it are so compelling that they amplify our being in ways that we are at a loss to
document afterwards. Nonetheless, the experience is there. Emotional rewards derive from careful attention to ordinary detail. And
this is the discovery. An enclosure has been bridged—a kind of
communion has been experienced—by fixing the eye on an object
of seemingly little importance. Even here, however, the debt to
Herbert is greater than the debt to Keats. I'm not thinking of Bishop's deft reworking of traditional Christian symbols, impressive as
that is, so much as of the poem's constantly shifting tone and frame
of reference, its subtle exploitation of what she called "poetic psychology." Herbert and his contemporaries (e.g., Donne and the baroque prose writers) were valued by Bishop because they offered
an escape from Wordsworth's formula of "emotion recollected in
tranquility," which makes poetry chiefly retrospective. Bishop's effort would increasingly be "to dramatize the mind in action rather
than in repose." Her appropriation of this technique, which she
considered "baroque," is foreshadowed in early poems like "A Miracle for Breakfast," but receives its full development in the poems
of her middle phase. She found that "switching tenses always gives

effects of depth, space, foreground, background, and so on," and these effects, first tested in poems like "A Miracle" (where the tense shifts tellingly to the present in the penultimate stanza) would be at the heart of her technique from then on.[30] "A Miracle for Breakfast," written two years after "The Imaginary Iceberg" and "The Man-Moth," suggests a young writer overcoming radical doubts about valid perception. She discovers that—leavened with irony—imagination can make a crumb a loaf.

Bishop's early work captures isolated souls baffled before the crisis of awakening. Her later work confronts the same crisis but with more confidence and in her own person or in the persons of people she knew. Because her early poems do not constitute an obvious personal history, they may perplex readers who have acquired an appetite for more direct confession. The function of Bishop's early poems within her own career closely parallels that of the tales of another writer in the New England Puritan tradition, Hawthorne. In both, a personal ambivalence about the introspective life is objectified, that is, projected outside the self in fables with universal implications. It is worth noting that both were Massachusetts natives with Puritan roots and a skeptical turn of mind who suffered the early loss of a father and spent much of their youth in isolation. But Bishop's tales are never anchored in anything like Hawthorne's sturdy historical settings. Rather, they float precariously through a sharply visualized realm of idea. These fables return again and again to the limitations of art and imagination; reversing Blake, Bishop seems to say, "If only these doors of perception could be cleansed—by actuality!" Her later work turns toward the ordinary in search of just this. She would not allow dreams or a theory of absence to erect a bulwark against nature. Instead, Bishop would exploit symbolist technique for her own ends, bringing its irony, its distrust of rhetoric, its linguistic adroitness, to bear upon the actual.

For one to escape the fate of the Unbeliever, one must apprehend what is miraculous in one's daily bread. But daily bread *can* grow monotonous, even stultifying, and the cities she lived in throughout the mid-thirties seemed to spawn only claustrophobic fables. With her first visit to Florida, she found natural facts equal to her imagination's cry for the exotic.

MIDDLE PHASE: TRAVEL

1939–55

Images of Florida

NORTH & SOUTH II

Florida
One Version of Pastoral

In January of 1937, searching for relief from asthma, a disease that had contributed to her isolated childhood, Bishop began a stay of several months in Naples, Florida. She would soon turn twenty-six, and her adult life lay ahead.

She would spend most of her remaining years near the edges of the tropical zone. Her poetry began to explore and record tropic life and to establish the South as a counterpoint to a symbolic North. Travel emerged as an alternative to enclosure. The dull, "rock-like book" from which the narrator of "In Prison" would draw surrealistic marvels gives way to the tangible "surrealism-of-everyday-life"[1] offered by mangrove keys and pelicans and the odd, courageous lives of the plain folk who lived among them. Despite staking claim to a compelling exterior world, she remained in her way an introspective traveler. But while her observation speaks to, and is inevitably shaped by, the inner being, it is also a response to independent life.

In her first letter from Florida to Marianne Moore she wrote, "From the few states I have seen I should now immediately select Florida as my favorite. . . . It is so wild."[2] Reacting against her early years of isolation, she sought visual wildness. Writing from Europe two years before, Bishop had complained to Moore that the French fishing village where she happened to be staying was "too PICTURESQUE for much longer than a month—maybe even for that."[3] By contrast, the brilliant sun and exuberant detail of coastal Florida, Key West, and later Brazil, was more satisfying. Of Key West she said, "I liked living there. The light and blaze of colors made a good impression on me, and I loved the swimming."[4] The imaginary iceberg had promised mysterious, imaginative riches, but its chill solitudes exacted the sacrifice of nature. It offered the hard, the bare, the eternal. Here, she could readily enjoy the transient things she saw and touched. The naturalist in her found as much scope as the surrealist.

Bishop has sometimes been called a tourist among poets, and she herself applied the word self-deprecatingly in "Arrival at Santos" (1951), but these poems are too elegantly and freshly composed to be mere snapshots. The term *tourist* implies a degree of superficiality that is foreign to Bishop's poetic practice. Typically, Bishop lived for months and sometimes years in a place before she began to compose poems about it, and when she had not, as in "Arrival at Santos" or "Over 2,000 Illustrations and a Complete Concordance," the inevitable superficiality of the tourist's viewpoint became an object of irony. More often, her observations balance the outsider's capacity for surprise with some of the background and understanding of an insider. Characteristically, the poems of her middle period embody a process of discovery, what might be called the drama of transition from a tourist's to a native's point of view.

During her Florida years, Bishop evolved a technique that would become her trademark—she composed poems out of a succession of linked images, usually without supplying explicit connectives. These create a serial effect that is different from Pound's method of kinetic juxtaposition because each image is sufficiently related to the next in place and time to achieve a primary effect of continuity rather than of dislocation. Even more than in Pound's verse (or, for that matter, Marianne Moore's), which is in fact full of assertions, Bishop's verse leaves much unstated that the reader must supply, for if the poem's continuity is never in doubt, the significance of its arresting imagery often is. These poems contain the lowest density of generalization that it is possible for poems to contain, yet through the selection and arrangement of their pictures, they remain richly significant and almost infinitely re-readable. By no means a retreat from modernist principles of composition, Bishop's verse, at its vivid, impersonal, mysterious best, represents a significant and influential development of imagism's stress on the clear-eyed observation of fact that would have a significant impact on the work of Lowell, Merrill, and Ashbery, among others. Her new stylistic approach, which attempted to pre-

sent the mind thinking, allowed her to capture transient moments
in all their unlikeliness and bring them back alive. This technique
grew out of Bishop's reflections on what she considered a baroque
approach to composition, while incorporating related ideas derived
from other sources. She renounces the satisfaction of moral-
pointing, but the absence of explicit moral judgment does not
mean that her work lacks moral conviction. As Marianne Moore
phrased it, "At last we have someone who knows, who is not didac-
tic."[5] Her conviction and her significance are reflected in her refusal to extract more from her material than is really there. But
she distills all that *is* there, down to the last gram.

The subjects of these poems seem small—a fish, roosters, ordinary pictures and toys, tropical seascapes, a few impoverished Flo-
ridians and Cubans. Bishop's choice and handling of simple,
apparently innocent subjects places her poems firmly in the pastoral tradition: in particular, that complex, American version of
pastoral defined by Leo Marx in *The Machine in the Garden.* In
Marx's view, what raises the great works of American pastoral,
such as *Huckleberry Finn,* above the banal and sentimental pastoral
that pervades American culture is the confrontation of elements
that disturb tranquillity. For Marx, the pastoral Garden is most
often disturbed by Technology, the Machine. He states more generally that: "Most literary works called pastorals—at least those
substantial enough to retain our interest—do not finally permit us
to come away with anything like the simple, affirmative attitude we
adopt toward pleasing rural scenery. In one way or another, if only
by virtue of the unmistakable sophistication with which they are
composed, these works manage to qualify, or call into question, or
bring irony to bear on the illusion of peace and harmony in a green
pasture."[6] Bishop's poems are unmistakably sophisticated treat-
ments of simple subjects. What qualifies the illusion of peace and
harmony in *her* poems, however, is not the intrusive presence of
technology but the flaw in the soul (and hence the eye) of the
observer—that original sin, that taint of egotism, lurking even in
the best of us. For Bishop, what mars the purity of simple objects
and settings is never someone else's fault, but one's own fault: it is
one's own condescension, one's own willful misreading of natural
fact, one's own pride, that may upset the harmony of things. *North
& South* as a whole studies opposing avenues toward radical simplicity. Her early protagonists were compelled by an egocentric de-

sire to shed the complexities of life abroad and to linger, safely enclosed, at home. The pastoral poems of Bishop's middle phase go beyond the early works by discovering a chance of redemption: by purging away pride. As a poem like "Roosters" suggests, Bishop restates a familiar Christian formula in secular terms, directing devotion towards transient things. She differs from her contemporary Theodore Roethke in that her urge to empathize never tempts her to submerge her identity in the other. Her encounters with exterior things nearly always include a barrier, a physical or psychological distancing element, that, one might say, defines the encounter as devotional or pastoral rather than romantic. An external object has virtue and that virtue may be coolly appreciated, but it is not necessarily subsumed into the self. Rarely do the poems explicitly attempt to understand or reshape the self in terms of something exterior. The element of distance allows Bishop's observed objects autonomy, independent existence, in spite of the soul's implicit desire to appropriate them. In this sense, at least, Bishop's poetry may be seen as running contrary to the contemporary avatars of romanticism.

When *North & South* appeared in 1946, it marked a milestone in Bishop's career. She was thirty-five and had been publishing a few poems annually in prominent magazines for twelve years, but this was her first book. With letters of support from Edmund Wilson and Marianne Moore, it won the Houghton Mifflin Poetry Award, chosen ahead of almost eight hundred other manuscripts. (Thereafter each succeeding book would appear only after a decade, and most would win a prestigious award.) More valuable than any prize, *North & South* also won the attention and advocacy— and even the affection—of a number of distinguished readers, including Robert Lowell, Randall Jarrell, and the young John Ashbery. Lowell praised the "splendour and minuteness of her observations" and her "large, controlled and elaborate commonsense," calling her "one of the best craftsmen alive." Jarrell was equally impressed with her craft, pointing to the "restraint, calm, and proportion . . . implicit in every detail of organization and workmanship," while declaring that "She is morally so attractive because she understands so well that the wickedness and confusion of the age can extenuate other people's wickedness and confusion, but not, for you, your own."[7] Jarrell's early definition of the moral perception underlying Bishop's work was characteristic of his critical savvy. Both Lowell and Jarrell hailed qualities of organization and control that they themselves were striving for, as well as a freshness and mystery that they found unique and moving. Ashbery, only nineteen when *North & South* appeared, later testified to the book's enduring effect on him, describing himself as one who "read, reread, studied and absorbed Miss Bishop's first book."[8] Not all readers were equally impressed. Edwin Honig and Oscar Williams, for example, had only faint praise for Bishop's elegance and restraint. They felt these qualities more as defects than virtues in the presence of what they considered an insufficient decisiveness.[9] The lines of debate that have since governed Bishop criticism were already being drawn. Were her elegant surfaces laid over a foundation of moral toughness and artistic control, or were they merely a hollow facade, erected to charm and dazzle while avoiding commitment and responsibility? I hold that the evidence suggests the former. And the best place to begin a discussion of that evidence is with "Florida" (1939), which inaugurates her exploration of pastoral.

"Florida," Bishop's first poem about the tropics, is also, and not accidentally, her first poem whose imagery is drawn directly from nature. Its rich, exotic color does not shine, as before, through the prism of the inward gaze. The arrangement of the poem resembles a string of beads: a succession of surprising facts hung together. The earlier Northern poems are tightly conceived and intricate meditations that have the hard integrity and inwardness of the chambered nautilus. The poems of the South are freer, looser, more prodigally detailed, more imagistic, less obviously narrative. Bishop was among the first of a cadre of poets including Roethke, Adrienne Rich, and James Wright to follow a path from early formal tightness to greater stylistic freedom. That she did so within the covers of a single book has tended to confuse some critics. The coiled intensity of the earlier poems was congenial to their achieved quality of inwardness. The Florida poems suggest a more relaxed openness to sensuous fact. "Florida" bursts with startling detail, with the exultation of discovery.

> The state with the prettiest name,
> the state that floats in brackish water,
> held together by mangrove roots
> that bear while living oysters in clusters,

and when dead strew white swamps with skeletons,
dotted as if bombarded, with green hummocks
like ancient cannon-balls sprouting grass.
The state full of long S-shaped birds, blue and white,
and unseen hysterical birds who rush up the scale
every time in a tantrum.
Tanagers embarrassed by their flashiness,
and pelicans whose delight it is to clown.   (CP, 32)

The echo of Marianne Moore in the first line is unmistakable.[10] It is almost as if Bishop were announcing her debt to Moore in the first poem in which, like Moore, she sets up shop as a naturalist. The verse has the rhythm of easy breathing. The prevailing four-beat, end-stopped controlled-free-verse line expands and contracts, gaining or losing beats gracefully in keeping with the requirements of each observation. Each long sentence holds together a string of loosely related, startling individual images. The scene's comic exuberance, its constant, understated personification, evoke pleasure, fascination, horror, as each pregnant detail is impartially rendered with offhand exactitude. Coleridge's insightful observation that "The presence of genius is not shown in elaborating a picture. . . . The power of poetry is, by a single word perhaps, to instill that energy into the mind which compels the imagination to produce the picture," is relevant here.[11] Bishop's images gain force from single words, the *skeletons* of the mangrove roots, the *tantrum* of the *hysterical* birds, the *clowning* of the pelicans, each of which compels the imagination to produce a picture. They have an energy, an effect of surprise, that Bishop would call baroque. She insisted that she learned more from metaphysical poetry than from her contemporaries, and her work does have its parallels with the work of Donne (as well as Herbert). Recalling Samuel Johnson's famous definition of the metaphysical conceit, Bishop's similes yoke "the most heterogeneous ideas" together, but their joining rarely creates the effect of "violence" described by Johnson, because the single point of similitude is so easy to see. Rather, they excite a surprised recognition and acceptance. Bishop's comparisons embody the risk-taking ambiguity and irony of metaphysical poetry, while conveying an air of only slightly tense gracefulness foreign to the metaphysical conceit, with its deliberate and self-conscious cultivation of strain.

Here is an old chaos of the sun where hysteria and clowning go on side by side; growth and death roll along on contrary courses with perfect indifference to one another. Bishop's Florida has its parallels to Stevens's famous celebrations of tropic energy, of which a representative statement is "O Florida, Venereal Soil." Neither poet flinches from what in "O Florida" Stevens calls "The dreadful sundry of this world," since that is part of a context so ample that it can be taken as it is. "A few things for themselves," Stevens's poem's refrain, aptly characterizes the intent of both writers to isolate and to relish sensuous detail.[12] Both recognize the awesome sexual vigor that permeates soil and culture. But for all Stevens's claim to take "a few things for themselves," his phrases are more rhetorically shaped, more shrouded in evocative mystery, more explicitly meditative, more prone to elevating or inflating what they celebrate, than the crystal-clear sentences of Bishop in their colloquial, understated phrasing, without vibrato. Compare the twilight images: Stevens's heavily scented "Donna, donna, dark, / Stooping in indigo gown" and Bishop's equally rich, but more delicately textured, "Smoke from woods-fires filters fine blue solvents" (CP, 32). Both specimens employ alliteration and assonance with telling effect, but Stevens's orotundity intoxicates, his image a broad curve of rich darkness, while Bishop's clipped syllables focus one's attention on fine gradations of observed color. The elder poet is always present as artificer. By contrast, the symbolic value of Bishop's Florida emerges from specific moments and places, speaking for itself in a way that Stevens's Florida never does. For example, the following lines, so surprising in their details, are only implicitly meditative:

> Enormous turtles, helpless and mild,
> die and leave their barnacled shells on the beaches,
> and their large white skulls with round eye-sockets
> twice the size of a man's.

"Florida" realizes the energy of death as prodigiously as the energy of life, but Bishop would never state this outright. David Kalstone may be only half right when he observes of Bishop's scene-painting: "Landscapes meant to sound detached are really inner landscapes. They show an effort at reconstituting the world as if it were in danger of being continually lost."[13] Though her turtles certainly point toward an aspect of the inner being, they are, first of all, turtles, and their force comes from a presence and integrity that the observer cannot simply preempt. "Florida" reveals Bishop's unwillingness to go on writing what she had called "horrendous fable ideas,"[14] to go on creating exclusively amid inner landscapes, continually "reconstituting the world" in the manner of the Gentleman of Shalott or the narrator of "In Prison," even if imagining their strange lives was needed training for seeing Florida. Rarely after "Florida" will Bishop's landscapes be *only* inner ones. If the images that constitute "Florida" reveal an inner world, it is fresher and brighter now, and it has more independence, than her early landscapes, and that is the point.

"Florida" is a brilliant poem, teeming with extraordinary detail, but it does not seek dramatic culmination. Kalstone observes, "There is some notion of neat and total structure which the critic expects and imposes, but which the poem subverts."[15] Kalstone implies that the subversion is intentional and characteristic, but I am inclined to read the organization of the poem as instead reflecting a stage in Bishop's development as observer and stylist. The poem's understated schema, which relies chiefly on the movement from daylight to evening, and perhaps implicitly, from splendid life to inevitable death, adumbrates a conclusion that is not completely articulated. Slightly later poems show that she was working toward a fresh approach to form as well as to subject matter: a form that can accrete meaning and symbolic architecture without explicit marks of organization. The importance of "Florida" for Bishop's artistic development resides in the singular vitality of each observed fact. "Florida" demonstrates imaginative contact with nature. At the same time, if all her later poems were like it, that might open the door to questions about Bishop's command of the looser form of her pastoral poems. Can poems made of a succession of images, with no explicit connectives and no stated conclusions, achieve real decisiveness? "Florida" might suggest not. In a thoughtful review of the 1955 volume *Poems,* which includes all of *North & South* as well as the later *A Cold Spring,* Howard Nemerov discussed the potentialities and limits of Bishop's method. His evaluation is mostly praise, but he suggests that Bishop loses as well as gains by her insistence on letting details speak for themselves, her refusal to sermonize. He concludes, "The happiest consequences of this kind of work will be the refreshment it affords the language (which becomes impoverished by the moralizing of descriptive

words) and the sense it gives of immense possibilities opening. . . .
But there are consequences less cheerful as well; one of them is
triviality, or you may call it want of action, where the poem never
becomes so much as the sum of its details and so, in two senses,
fails to move, another, closely related, is the inspired tendency to
believe all things possible to clever precision and a dry tone."[16] Here
one confronts a conflict between distinguished readers. As we have
seen, Lowell calls Bishop "one of the best craftsmen alive." In comparing her to Dylan Thomas, he says Thomas "has greater moments and fewer successful poems." Jarrell, who extolls the
"proportion . . . implicit in every detail of organization," evidently
shares Lowell's admiration for Bishop's poems as unified wholes.[17]
But Nemerov implies that Bishop's poems sometimes fail to come
together and can be more tone than substance, hardly the marks
of a master. It is impossible for both views to be right. As a first
effort, "Florida" does not offer a fair test. In "The Fish," published
only a year later, Bishop showed that she could create poems that
are more than the sum of their details, because they animate potentially static observations with a sense of decisive action.

"The Fish" (1940), one of her best and most familiar poems, is
also a landmark of her development as an artist. In it she achieved
an unstated but more complete closure than "Florida" attempts.
Bishop succeeds by the simple device of injecting an understated
but decisive element of narrative: she details the changing impres-
sions of an observer, on the way to a final, implied recognition.
One might contrast her approach to Auden's, in whose work, increasingly, the narrator's personality and values are a presence in
poems that are, very often, explicitly narrative. Bishop, who made
a point of *not* sounding like Auden, sought a different tone alto-
gether. There is nothing quite like it in the verse of other poets of
the forties. Her narrative technique is subtle in that it has less to
do with outward events, although these are generally present, than
with the quietly changing attitude of the observer as it responds to
the object observed. This is particularly true of the poem before
us, in which the fish, itself unchanging, appears to undergo a
transformation as the observer's eye moves over it. Bishop told interviewer Alexandra Johnson that when she wrote poetry: "The
greatest challenge, for me, is to try to express difficult thoughts in
plain language. I prize clarity and simplicity. I like to present complicated or mysterious ideas in the simplest possible way. This is a

discipline which many poets don't see as important as I do."[18] "The Fish" presents a complicated and mysterious idea in "the simplest possible way." Bishop's argument unfolds through a succession of increasingly charged images, which reflect the observer's growing awareness of inherent moral choices. The reader experiences this awareness vividly without necessarily being able to state it. Bishop's poems yield pleasure immediately, but they yield their inner life only after they have been lived with.

The poem is set in Florida, where Bishop enjoyed fishing. It dramatizes a confrontation with an animal. When her friend Marianne Moore writes about an animal, she meditates upon the characteristics of an entire species: the elephant, the jeraboa. Bishop encounters animals in chance, once-only affairs involving individual creatures. This difference begins to suggest the more dramatic character of Bishop's verse, its greater concern with changing perceptions of an observer. At first, this encounter seems straightforward enough.

> I caught a tremendous fish
> and held him beside the boat
> half out of water, with my hook
> fast in a corner of his mouth.   (CP, 42)

The tone at the beginning is dispassionate. The fish is very big, but no other points of interest are noted. The playing and landing of it, the usual source of excitement in fish stories, is not the issue here. Indeed his lack of fight is the first thing that provokes attention, so that instead of gloating over one's catch, one begins to study it.

> He didn't fight.
> He hadn't fought at all.
> He hung a grunting weight,
> battered and venerable
> and homely.

The adjectives with which the observer describes him—"grunting," "battered," "venerable," "homely"—show that one instinctively perceives this creature dangling on the end of one's line in terms of human analogy. It is critical to take note of this, because one key to the secret of Bishop's form is provided by Moore's observation that for Bishop, "The adornments are structural."[19] Moore is thinking about matters of sound, but the statement applies with equal force to Bishop's uniquely vivid, apparently ornamental imagery. Each detail is part of a sequence of varying emotional charges that lead the reader unconsciously but inexorably toward a specific response. Here is one of the most important parallels between her work and the art of the baroque. In this way, Bishop's poetry has the capacity to "move" in both of Nemerov's senses, despite the appearance of being dispassionate and statically descriptive.

> Here and there
> his brown skin hung in strips
> like ancient wallpaper,
> and its pattern of darker brown
> was like wallpaper:
> shapes like full-blown roses
> stained and lost through age.

Each short line contains a beat of meaning, a significant glimpse. The natural pause at the end of each line suggests the slight cadences of speech rhythm, which animate the controlled, three-stress free-verse line. The tone is matter-of-fact, the subject plain, the imagery startling. In the passage above, each two-line phrase constitutes a distinct image—a distinct, complex response to an aspect of the fish. The ruined elegance of the fish is accurately presented, but, many critics to the contrary, this treatment cannot be called objective. Richard Moore rightly observed, in a most penetrating early study of the poem, that "perhaps the apprehension of a character in things is an essential part of seeing them as real at all."[20] The analogies continue to discover beauty amid decay. Its "barnacles" are "fine rosettes of lime"; the "green weed" that hangs from his body is in "rags." One is kept from sentimentalizing by reference to gross natural fact: the fine rosettes are "infested / with tiny white sea-lice." Balancing human connotation are images insisting upon the fish's alienness.

> While his gills were breathing in
> the terrible oxygen
> —the frightening gills,
> fresh and crisp with blood,
> that can cut so badly—

The fish can never be a friend. Despite barriers, the observer has begun to empathize, but empathy does not delude her, because she avoids the naive anthropomorphism that would imagine a response from the fish's eyes. "They shifted a little, but not / to return my stare" (*CP*, 43). Bishop's language lends the fish a personality while respecting his autonomy.

E. H. Gombrich has stressed in *Art and Illusion* that no eye is innocent of learned responses, and Bishop's thinking is close to his. Although the poet cannot see the fish uncolored by human association, her eyes remain fixed on natural facts. The order in which these facts are observed take us closer and closer to the fish's central achievement. When the observer finally notices the five fishhooks embedded in the fish's jaw, the poem begins a decisive transition from alert observation to moral action. As in "A Miracle for Breakfast," this persistent observation eventually yields an almost religious vision: an icon of a saint with his martyr's scars upon him?

> and then I saw
> that from his lower lip
> —if you could call it a lip—
> grim, wet, and weaponlike,
> hung five old pieces of fish-line,
> or four and a wire leader
> with the swivel still attached,
> with all their five big hooks
> grown firmly in his mouth.

The fish makes his mark on the poet, but fishermen have left their own marks in the fish.

> A green line, frayed at the end
> where he broke it, two heavier lines,
> and a fine black thread
> still crimped from the strain and snap
> when it broke and he got away.

The mood, until this point calmly inquisitive, now grows impassioned. The fish takes on emblematic overtones. The fishlines now seem:

> Like medals with their ribbons
> frayed and wavering,

a five-haired beard of wisdom
trailing from his aching jaw.

Discovering in the fish, so alien, so sullen under scrutiny, a bemedaled, venerable hero, helps one to know him: not only in the
ways fish are like people (their tenacity, their courage, their loneliness) but also in the ways fish remain different. The fish's barbed
decorations are never simply symbolic, since (as fishhooks) they
afflict him with an "aching jaw."

This coming to terms with the fish is, in a sense, a spiritual
achievement. As far back as Virgil, pastoral has been a genre that
calls for moral understanding of things overlooked and under-
valued. Here, the potential to overlook lies with the observer and
(implicitly) with the audience. The observer has so controlled egotism, in particular the arrogant tendency to see blindly and judge
superficially, that elation ennobles the oily bilge at the bottom of
the boat until one sees *its* overlooked beauty, which is analogous
to the overlooked beauty of the fish. It, and everything else, *is*
"rainbow, rainbow, rainbow!" That "I let the fish go" need not be
explained, because it is the inevitable consequence of this recognition. One might not let the next fish go, but this particular act
of observation has recognized this fish's uniqueness and has
lead to a decision. For Bishop, observation is a moral act, since
whether it is done carelessly or scrupulously bears moral fruit.
"The Fish" achieves culmination within an apparently loose structure in ways that "Florida" did not attempt. What thinking lay
behind this sudden mastery of an elusive form, in which a succession of images suddenly lock in on a decisive recognition? This
approach, which makes new structural use of the principles of
imagism, has yet been largely unappreciated by literary historians,
but it has had widespread influence on poets, both directly,
through Bishop's own example, and indirectly, through the development of the technique by Robert Lowell, who, some sixteen
years after "The Fish" had brought the basic style to life, applied
its formal principles to "Skunk Hour" and the *Life Studies* poems
that followed it. In a letter to Bishop he confessed that in writing
"Skunk Hour" he felt "a petty plagiarist" of "The Armadillo," the
poem of hers that most directly influenced him.[21] Maintaining
Bishop's understated narrative pace, her reliance on a succession
of dramatically progressive imagistic details, and even, to a degree,

her impersonal surface, Lowell added a dimension of confessional revelation bursting through that surface that sent shock waves through the world of poetry that have been felt ever since. This implicitly narrative technique, in its various forms, some more like Lowell, some more like Bishop, has become one of the common tongues of contemporary verse. This is sufficiently appreciated among poets themselves that the poet / editors of the *Morrow Anthology of Younger American Poets* could casually say of the typically adroit young poet of today that, "He speaks Williams as fluently as he speaks Eliot, Neruda and Milosz as quickly as James Wright or Elizabeth Bishop."[22] In a later chapter I will discuss the specifics of Lowell's response and explore the ways in which each friend influenced the other. My concern for the moment is to trace the intellectual and artistic roots that nourished Bishop's method.

Essentially indifferent to her standing among critics, Bishop was not much concerned with articulating the theory behind her practice. But she *had* a theory, and it can be pieced together by an effort of critical reconstruction. It will be necessary to discuss several of Bishop's remarks about earlier poets, specifically Moore, Poe, and Hopkins, in order to get her own understanding of this method into perspective. These remarks, widely scattered and mostly off the cuff, reveal a highly personal understanding of her masters and show that she had a very clear idea of what she was doing and why she was doing it.

«The Mind in Action»

In "As We Like It," a 1948 essay honoring Marianne Moore, Bishop lets one see how she approached nature. She compared Moore's tact in describing animals with the wrongheaded anthropomorphism of "our greatest poet" in *As You Like It*. There, Jaques, transplanted to Arden, considers deer to be "native burghers of this desert city," an inferior sort of men, "poor dappled fools." Bishop argues for Moore's more scrupulous method: "It was perhaps consoling and popular to think that the animals were just like the citizenry, but how untrue, and one feels Miss Moore would feel, how selfish. There are morals a'plenty in animal life, but they have to be studied out by devotedly and minutely observing the animal, not by regarding the deer as a man imprisoned in a 'leath

ern coat.'"[23] Bishop's fish, like Jaques' deer, is understood by analogy to people, but its essential difference is respected. Minute
observation of the fish is precisely what Bishop devotes before she
can uncover its meaning: a recognition that can only derive from
close scrutiny and need not be expressly stated, since it resides in
what was seen.

Fish are alien, and a hero among fish should remain in its element. But the "victory" that fills up "the little rented boat," and
the rainbow that spreads

> from the pool of bilge
>   . . . until everything
> was rainbow, rainbow, rainbow!   (CP, 43–44)

could not come from recognizing this alienness. With alienness
comes the recognition of kinship, and this recognition depends on
fictions that uncover in the fish a human analogy. Ruskin rightly
insisted that "the spirit of truth must guide us in some sort, even
in our enjoyment of fallacy."[24] The spirit of truth guides this victory, even to the discovery of the rainbow in a pool of bilge among
rusted bailers and sun-cracked thwarts. A subjective view discovers the fish's meaning for us—and saves him! Attributed human
qualities precipitate a moral decision by teaching something. The
"fallacy" actually penetrates a barrier. The fish, an emblem of the
mysteriously separate, can be understood. But now Bishop's
understanding of mystery and separation reaches beyond the inner
corridors of self.

In her essay on Moore, Bishop speaks of parallels between
Moore and Edgar Allan Poe. While the surface resemblance is not
obvious, the parallels are even closer between Poe and herself.
They arise as Bishop examines Poe's aesthetic theory. She points
with approval to Poe's claim in "Philosophy of Composition" that
"it is not until the last two stanzas of 'The Raven' that he permits
himself the use of any metaphorical expression."[25] The subtle, delayed effects sought by Bishop's own method are implicit in her
discussion of a further remark of Poe's: "that such expressions 'dispose the mind to seek a moral in all that has been previously narrated.' Poe has already stressed the importance of avoiding the
'excess of the suggested meaning,' and said that metaphor is a device that must be very carefully employed."[26] Analogies between
Poe's restraint in "The Raven" and Bishop's restraint in "The Fish"

reveal Poe as a source for the constraints she imposed upon herself, as well as suggesting what she hoped to gain from them. Although she uses numerous similes throughout, she deliberately reserves *symbolic* overtones, which "dispose the mind to seek a moral in all that has been previously narrated," until the end. The old fish with his medals comes to represent the silent, lonely struggle of the quietly desperate. Bishop's praise of Moore can be applied even more directly to herself: as Bishop said of Moore in "As We Like It," Bishop's own controlled handling of symbols "gives her poetry its steady aura of both reserve and having possibly more meanings 'in reserve.'"[27]

That Bishop's observations about Poe may be applied directly to herself is confirmed by a comment to Moore written ten years before this essay, and two years before "The Fish" itself. In a letter from Key West in 1938, the year she began working toward her new style, Bishop spoke of her attempts to write: "according to a *theory* I've been thinking up down here—and of a combination of Poe's theories and reading 17th century prose!"[28] What Poe meant to her should now be clear. What seventeenth-century prose meant to her requires explanation. The clues lie in a student essay she wrote for the *Vassar Review* four years earlier, "Gerard Manley Hopkins: Notes on Timing in His Poetry" (1934). This essay, which Moore called, in a letter, the best thing she had seen on Hopkins, studies the way Hopkins's poems unfold. What Bishop found significant was the way Hopkins "times" the articulation of his idea, the moment he chooses to stop his movement toward "the poem; unique and perfect" which "seems to be separate from the conscious mind, deliberately avoiding it, while the conscious mind takes difficult steps toward it."[29] According to Bishop, Hopkins chose "to stop his poems, set them on paper, at the point in their development where they are still incomplete, still close to the first kernel of truth or apprehension that gave rise to them." Bishop's own determination "to catch and preserve the movement of an idea—the point being to crystallize it early enough so that it still has movement" is not only apparent in the way "The Fish" unfolds but can be found in most of the poems that follow (and a few that precede) it. Although Bishop concedes the importance for Hopkins of seventeenth-century baroque or metaphysical *poetry*, she makes a special case for the relevance of the timing of baroque *prose* to Hopkins's poetic practice. She quotes several lengthy passages from

M. W. Croll's famous essay "The Baroque Style in Prose." Most significant is this: "Their purpose was to portray, not a thought, but the mind thinking. . . . They knew that an idea separated from the act of experiencing it is not the same idea that we experienced. . . . They . . . deliberately chose as the moment of expression that in which the idea first clearly objectifies itself in the mind, in which, therefore, each of its parts still preserves its own peculiar emphasis and an independent vigor of its own—in brief, the moment in which the truth is still *imagined*."[30]

To capture this moment would remain the essential goal of her technique. The 1966 interview with Ashley Brown showed Bishop had not forgotten the example of baroque prose. She mentioned that Vassar essay, recalling "a phrase that impressed me in 'The Wreck of the Deutschland,' where Hopkins says, 'Fancy, come faster.' He breaks off and addresses himself. It's a baroque poem." Although Bishop did not herself use such overt devices as abrupt self-address (except, memorably, in the late poem "One Art") her new style is designed, as was Hopkins's, "to dramatize the mind in action rather than in repose."[31] After a succession of details have been absorbed, truth is *just* being recognized, still tingling in the surprised discovery of "rainbow, rainbow, rainbow!" She can embody moral insight in action, without sermonizing. "Florida" had attempted no drama of thought. In "The Fish," observations gain in emotional charge until they culminate in a shock of recognition. The moral necessity behind scrupulous observation she found in Moore. The dramatically delayed recognition of symbolic value she found in Poe. The psychological dimension, the drama of the mind thinking, she found in Hopkins and his baroque forebearers. It took Bishop to fuse them in a style that resembles her sources almost not at all. When Bishop told interviewer Johnson, "I simply try to see things afresh,"[32] she was putting it modestly. To achieve such simple freshness required a fresh conception of the way to set a series of distinct images into motion as a complexly unfolding narration.

Bishop's method dramatizes an observer unconsciously defeating the sin of pride. Instead of exulting in the victory of catching a tremendous fish, as most of us would do, the observer overcomes this kind of egotism, and the subtler egotism that would see the fish only in human terms, and thus achieves greater victories: she achieves self-knowledge and the knowledge of something other, finding outside the self an unforeseen courage, persistence, and beauty. To make the moral struggle explicit would betray the unconscious level on which that struggle is fought. Presenting a complicated and mysterious idea in the simplest possible way, she lures one inward from the simple and engaging surface, until one has made the poem's pattern of knowing one's own.

This technique underlines the distinction between Bishop and her mentor, Marianne Moore. Like Moore, Bishop characteristically presents a crisp series of images. But Bishop's discoveries are deeply rooted in the act of observation; they take place in real time. In Moore's verse the mind must nimbly follow the implicit logic, but the mood is reflective and time stands still. Moreover, the convictions behind Moore's observations are rock-solid. For all their purported objectivity (even anonymity), the modernists were a contentious lot, and Bishop's closest friend among them is no exception. Take, for example, the decisive opening of Moore's "Critics and Connoisseurs": "There is a great amount of poetry in unconscious / fastidiousness."[33] Although the tone is impersonal, it reflects rooted personal belief. Bishop never begins a poem this way. Moore sets off with a proposition to prove; Bishop arrives at a surprised recognition. (Of course, Marianne Moore's methods of demonstration were unique, which may distract one from the fact that a proof is being presented.) Moore lays down the law, in a way that Bishop never cared to. As Croll had said of the baroque writers, Bishop's "progression adapts itself to the movements of a mind discovering truth as it goes, thinking while it writes."[34] John Ashbery characterized the relationship shrewdly when he said, "the two poets couldn't be more different; Miss Moore's synthesizing, collector's approach is far from Miss Bishop's linear, exploring one."[35] Baroque writers had dramatized the act of *writing*. Bishop's linear structures dramatize the act of *seeing*. Pound and Moore extended imagism in *space*, sifting together a kinetic field of objects and remarks. This tradition, as explored in the *Cantos* and in the work of Olson, Creeley, Levertov, and others, has long been the object of critical attention. By contrast, the formal implications of Bishop's work, with its more traditional appearance, have been generally overlooked. Her poem's spaces are almost always one particular place, but she extends imagism in *time* by melding a succession of related images, each in itself a Poundian "intellectual and emotional complex in an instant of time," into a story.[36] She re-creates the process of conscious, deliberate perception, in all its double-edged intensity. M. L. Rosenthal observed that in her verse Bishop "extends the Imagist instant," but he was not much impressed with the potential of that achievement. Rosenthal found her to be merely "remolding, improving, getting the nuances not of a new artistic problem but of an established tradition." The recurrence of Bishop's name on the tongues of a host of younger poets would suggest that they disagree, that they find in Bishop's work much that is fresh, daring, and technically relevant. Her style reflects, among its other achievements, an expansion of the possibilities of imagism that merits as much attention as Olson's method of composition by field. Rosenthal, who spoke in 1960 of the "revolutionary breakthroughs" of *Life Studies,* appears to have little suspected that Bishop's supposedly old-fashioned techniques were one of the handful of vital discoveries that lay behind them.[37]

« Roosters »

One of the challenges facing her technique and sensibility was whether it could respond to the violence and complexity of what would become the central event of the time, World War II. The case can be made that the war daunted her creatively; she published nothing at all in either 1942 or 1943, and her production throughout the war was limited by even her own standards. In "Roosters," however, which was first published in *New Republic* in April 1941—when war only threatened at home but had begun elsewhere—Bishop wrote a contemplation of the motives for war that begins with characteristic indirectness but evolves into an extraordinary meditation on human violence and cowardice and on the possibility of being forgiven for one's casual betrayals of responsibility, if not by God, then by oneself. She produced not only one of the great modern considerations of the causes and effects of war but one of the great modern meditations on guilt, spiritual poverty, and the consolations that come with facing the facts.

The poem addresses the guilt and dismay faced by those who, while not themselves barbarous, sin by omission, acquiescing to the barbarism of others through deliberate inaction (symbolized here first by sleep, later by Peter's three-time denial of Christ). Roosters have a mysterious, double-edged symbolic value. This emerges in a veiled way at first, but it leads at last to a decisive recognition. The brutal roosters are presented as symbols of fascism's empty, vainglorious delight in intimidation and combat, but they are also presented as the bringers of bitter truth to reluctant hearers. Roosters rouse the modern moral sleeper, just as a rooster reminded Peter of his oath of fealty, prompting him to acknowledge and repent the evil of his betrayal. In awakening us to our failures, they also point to the possibility of forgiveness and redemption. The rooster's double significance is not as contradictory as it may seem, since both meanings depend on what is commonly known about roosters: they *are* pugnacious, and they *do* wake up reluctant sleepers. This poem, like "Florida" and "The Fish," is set in the South. The "little wooden northern houses" referred to (*CP*, 36) are houses built in Key West by transplanted northerners. The poem's surface looks tight, with its packed, witty, triple-rhymed stanzas, but the stanzas are in controlled free verse, with a beat added to each succeeding line, and its overall structure has the apparent looseness, the calculated digressions, the freedom within constraint, that typifies Bishop's best work. The waker is greeted by a simple—but forbidding—setting:

> At four o'clock
> in the gun-metal blue dark
> we hear the first crow of the first cock
>
> just below
> the gun-metal blue window (*CP*, 35)

Pastorally uncluttered, this world is nevertheless charged with danger. The "gun-metal blue" shading darkens both outside and in. The cocks' cries have a "horrible insistence" that

> grates like a wet match
> from the broccoli patch,
> flares, and all over town begins to catch.

The waker, who had been safely enclosed in sleep, is now prey to the roosters' cries and the audible conflagration they excite. Roosters emblematize the harsh reality they wake one into. In their masculine meanness, they revel in sordid dominance over a "dropping-plastered henhouse floor." For there, in:

> the blue blur
> their rustling wives admire,
> the roosters brace their cruel feet and glare

> with stupid eyes
> while from their beaks there rise
> the uncontrolled, traditional cries.

> Deep from protruding chests
> in green-gold medals dressed,
> planned to command and terrorize the rest.

Has Bishop abandoned the principle of reserving symbolic meaning until the end? Not at all, for, as I have already indicated, the symbolic significance of roosters is due for a reversal that is already being subtly prepared. These lines are charged with violent revulsion. Bishop told Moore, who attempted to bowdlerize the poem before it was published: "I cherish my 'water-closet' and the other sordidities because I want to emphasize the essential baseness of militarism."[38] Bishop's exploration of the motives for war was oblique but telling. The analogy between roosters and men, each sporting emblems of vainglory, contrasts with the fish, also manlike and bemedaled, but with honorable trophies of the struggle to live free.

If the poem deplores militarism, it also deplores the females' fatuous acceptance of it.

> the many wives
> who lead hens' lives
> of being courted and despised.

Hens, called wives, are compared to—hens! Aren't human wives who allow their husbands to strut and crow vaingloriously also like hens?

As roosters and men come to seem more and more alike, Bishop's pastoral barnyard grows dense with analogies to grim contemporary history. Like the Fascists in Europe, roosters resemble oneself but are also different. Their justification lies in their dominance, which they achieve by brutal self-assertion:

> deep from raw throats
> a senseless order floats
> all over town. A rooster gloats
>
> over our beds
> from rusty iron sheds
> and fences made with old bedsteads.   (CP, 36)

Theirs is a "senseless order" because it relies on force and routine and the supineness of others, rather than on reason and observation. As in "Love Lies Sleeping" and other early poems, the effort of awakening requires an act of affirmation that seems difficult in the face of the inevitable conflict and surrender the day will bring. The roosters' cries shock one back into consciousness ("Each screaming / 'Get up! Stop dreaming!'"); they seem to own the morning. Their gloating dominion encourages a reluctance to relinquish the protection of dreams, for to relinquish dreams is to enter necessity. Throughout the long tradition of dawn poems, the necessities of morning are not welcomed with joy. As in Donne's "The Sun Rising," "Roosters" objects to a power that thrusts one back into the waking world. However, love—the familiar theme of the aubade—is not the experience that one is being torn away from. Instead, it is part of what one hates to face.

> what right have you to give
> commands and tell us how to live,
>
> cry "Here!" and "Here!"
> and wake us here where are
> unwanted love, conceit and war?

The surprising juxtaposition of public and private—of war, conceit, and "unwanted love"—suggests that brutal roosters, in their contemptuous exploitation of the female as in their warlike posturing, exemplify a world in which even love can be unwanted. When they fight, "with raging heroism defying / even the sensation of dying" (CP, 37) their "heroism," for all its energy, is pointless. Although they sing, they are not poets and their songs are not remembered; when one is killed, his songs are done,

and what he sung
no matter. He is flung
on the gray ash-heap, lies in dung

with his dead wives
with open, bloody eyes,
while those metallic feathers oxidize.

So much, it seems, for roosters! Associated with excrement and
rusting machinery—that is, with the effects of human civilization—they externalize man's baseness. Their shrill cries only
summon one to a scene of unwelcome necessities, brutality, boredom, and pain. The poem has reached its nadir.

The uniqueness of "Roosters" lies in the fact that it can discover
in roosters themselves, the very creatures who have symbolized so
much that is evil in human nature, a source of reassurance. Without apparent transition, the poem shifts toward a new subject, the
magnitude of Peter's sin in betraying Christ. Apparently a digres-
sion, this is really leading toward unlooked-for connections.

St. Peter's sin
was worse than that of Magdalen
whose sin was of the flesh alone;

of spirit, Peter's,
falling, beneath the flares,
among the "servants and officers."

A calm meditative pace succeeds the earlier intensity, as the central emblem slowly emerges. The sin of the spirit explored here
resembles Peter's cowardly refusal to rise and take action against
the sacreligious cruelty of others. To deny once is inevitably to
deny again, to become paralyzed by guilt. In "Lapis Lazuli," another poem about emblems that was written in response to war,
Yeats turns away from the tragedy of the modern scene to examine
a carven figure embodying tragic joy. Bishop turns from live roosters, symbolic of contemporary brutishness, to discover a piece of
"Old holy sculpture" that could set "all together / in one small
scene, past and future," the drama of Peter's betrayal and repen-
tance. But their informing emblems are as different as they are
similar. Yeats chose, for his part, an emblem marked by exquisite

form and by exotic remoteness from Western artistic and religious traditions, implying a rejection of the cultural phenomena that had led to the world war. His piece of lapis lazuli symbolizes a pure art that subsumes tragedy and rises above it to a gaiety fierce and beyond sorrow. Bishop seeks, not to rise above tragedy, but to face it, and her emblem is chosen, not for its remoteness from the Western tradition, but for its centrality, though she arrives at this emblem from the oblique perspective of a Key West barnyard. Where Yeats (and many another modernist) would turn ecstatically to the mystical retreat of art, Bishop is pragmatic and moral, alert in a hardheaded—and, in the end, cheerful—way to realities that must be endured because they cannot be altered. The poem is frank in its yearning to retreat from unpleasant facts, and just as straightforward in its refusal to do so. Carven roosters redefine the import of their living counterparts: these emblematic fowl suggest the possibility of redemption.

> carved on a dim column in the travertine,

> explained by *gallus canit;*
> *flet Petrus* underneath it.
> There is inescapable hope, the pivot;

> yes, and there Peter's tears
> run down our chanticleer's
> sides and gem his spurs.   (CP, 38)

"The cock crows; Peter weeps." This rooster emblematizes human cowardice in the face of arrogant challenge and the inescapable frailty of all future popes, but he also enshrines Peter's weeping, the remorse that pierces him like a rooster's spur. The commitment to remember this central betrayal in Western spiritual history, by the very successors of the betrayer, reasserts the Church's capacity to forgive this frailty. The rooster's weapon is now beautiful, gemmed for greater awe and terror, and it drives home Peter's painful realization of his need for (and fear of) forgiveness. The obtrusive rooster shocks one into unwelcome consciousness each morning, but he also serves to pierce Peter's pride, shocking him into self-knowledge:

> those cock-a-doodles yet might bless,
> his dreadful rooster come to mean forgiveness.

Here is another case of "love unknown," of transfiguration through the process of suffering and redemption, in a context that secularizes Christian iconography. The two pieces of the emblematic puzzle snap into a surprising fit. Roosters are now paralleled as an emblem accepted by both the Church and the common man, providing

> a new weathervane
> on basilica and barn.

This emblem atop the roof was mentioned early in the poem, but there it only suggested the rooster's hideous power to "gloat:"

> over our churches
> where the tin rooster perches,
> over our little wooden northern houses.   (CP, 36)

Then the tin rooster seemed a minor detail, but its place there is significant because the rooster has been erected atop the churches and houses in this Catholic community to remind the pope and "to convince"

> all the assembly
> that "Deny deny deny"
> is not all the roosters cry.   (CP, 38)

Like their popes, the congregation must accept the fact that they will transgress and must accept also the somewhat discomfiting necessity of grace. Roosters insist on necessity: literally on the necessity of waking up; figuratively on the necessity of pain and failure, but also on "inescapable hope, the pivot." One may wish to hug the blanket of despair, but, like the light of dawn or the rooster's cry, hope pursues.

One test of this poem is that it stands up well against one of Yeats's best. In "Lapis Lazuli" Yeats established his carven figure as a symbol for tragic joy and then ended, magnificently, with an image of gaiety at the center of contemplative repose:

> There, on the mountain and the sky,
> On all the tragic scene they stare.
> One asks for mournful melodies;
> Accomplished fingers begin to play.
> Their eyes mid many wrinkles, their eyes,
> Their ancient, glittering eyes, are gay.[39]

These lines satisfy as image and symbol; they resolve conflict by presenting a means, at once practical and mythic, of transcending unhappiness through tragic art. Bishop's poem might rest at a similar height of transcendence, but instead, characteristically, it goes on, returning to the barnyard again, coming down to ordinary reality to test its emblem. Here, as elsewhere in her work, Bishop insists shrewdly on the limits of her own achieved moments of spiritual discovery. If the poem has a weakness, it is that it exists almost entirely on an analogical and emblematic plane. We never have direct access to the situations and emotions that inspired it. Its thesis is that one must confront rather than evade unpleasant truths, but it confronts them only at an allegorical remove. Roosters are just barely able to sustain the weight that the poem asks them to carry. But the poem succeeds because it is presenting something everyone has experienced, the *struggle* to confront unpleasant truths. Here is the work of a writer for whom such confrontations were necessary but not easy, and Bishop made the effort they cost her the grist for many of her best poems. Of course, such hard and thankless confrontations are the stuff of human life. As she once observed, "Surely there is an element of mortal panic and fear underlying all works of art?" (*CProse*, 144). "Roosters," which she later called "the most ambitious poem I had up to then attempted" (*CProse*, 145), should be read, in the context of her artistic development, as a crucial step on the path to the more direct and historically centered later style. Bishop's declaration about one of her earlier creations, "What the Man-Moth fears most he must do," seems, as in so many other contexts, to apply to the writer herself.

In the delicately beautiful concluding section, the original scene is touched by newfound pastoral calm.

> In the morning
> a low light is floating
> in the backyard, and gilding
>
> from underneath
> the broccoli, leaf by leaf;
> how could the night have come to grief?   (*CP*, 39)

The effect of the dawn's early light has rarely been described with such touching precision. "The cocks are now almost inaudible." However, the world remains the old scene of tragedy.

> The sun climbs in,
> following "to see the end,"
> faithful as enemy, or friend.

The sun enters the scene with effort, "climbs in," surrounded by ambiguous foreboding. Peter, too, followed Christ's trial "afar off" and (as Bishop reminded an interviewer) "sat with the servants *to see the end*" (Matt. 25:58). Life is an ambiguous gift, a gift the sun proffers faithfully each morning. Peter's following of Christ was ambiguous, a mixture of betrayal and faithfulness, the act of both enemy and friend. The roosters, themselves our enemies and our friends, will return, faithfully crowing one into experience.

One's poverty at the poem's beginning is profound. One does not even want to wake up. Carven roosters, emblems of brutality, cowardice, *and* forgiveness, provide a quietly enduring response to the "senseless order" the worst part of our nature would impose. The most deeply wrought emblems recall old heroisms that can lend one, in the face of a world "where are / unwanted love, conceit and war," the courage to accept and endure.

Florida's Poor

Despite its sensuous richness, Bishop's South, like her North, is melancholy. Bishop was moved by the simplicity and poverty she found among the black and Cuban inhabitants of coastal Florida and Key West. Describing Key West as she had known it in 1939, the year she first settled there, she said, "The town was absolutely broke then. Everybody lived on the W.P.A. I seemed to have a taste for impoverished places in those days."[40] Herself the beneficiary of a small inherited income, she found in the graceful courage of certain poor individuals an example at once sobering and encouraging. Bishop praised Marianne Moore and John Dewey (whom she knew at Key West) for being completely democratic, for their "instinctive respect for other people," no matter what their social level. These were qualities she not only admired but shared. A very shy woman, she felt at least as comfortable among the Cuban cigar makers of Key West as among members of the artistic elite. Bishop's poems of the Florida poor extended her exploration of pastoral, of an existence simpler, more elemental, than that of the urban intellectual. For either, in his or her own way, it comes down to "what will suffice," spiritually as well as materially. In search of what might suffice, "Jeronimo's House" (1941) catalogues the possessions that the house contains. All the tiny house *has,* really, is the affection Jeronimo breathes into its few objects.

> My house, my fairy
> > palace is
> of perishable
> > clapboards with
> three rooms in all.   (*CP,* 34)

His tone is gentle but it is also tough. The song's short lines bounce along airily, but bitterness almost chokes affection in the phrase,

> my gray wasps' nest
> of chewed-up paper
> > glued with spit,

lines that cannot be spoken without an angry sputter. "My home, my love-nest" is fragile, temporary.

> When I move
> I take these things,
> > not much more, from
> my shelter from
> > the hurricane.

Bishop's Jeronimo was based on a real person, yet because of differences in class, she was not able to be on intimate terms with this man.[41] His house was evidently one of the tiny, identical, unpainted board shacks that had been erected in close-packed, identical rows for workers in the cigar factories, yet he has stamped it with his personality. Bishop's letters tell us that she was one of those onlookers the speaker imagines who, at night, thought

> my house abandoned,
> Come closer. You

                    can see and hear
         the writing-paper
                    lines of light
         and the voices of
                    my radio

         singing flamencos
                    in between
         the lottery numbers.

The life the house offers to the outsider is ghostly, disembodied, yet Jeronimo beckons one to observe that what goes on inside has color and intensity. One imagines Bishop leaning in, straining to pursue her acquaintance with Jeronimo, a man who answers poverty with bitterness *and* love.

Fronting barriers of social class, Jeronimo shyly exposes his deeper feelings. Bishop knew how to take artistic advantage of the distance separating her from the objects of her curiosity. These barriers did not prevent her from relishing the vitality and humor of observations such as this one (described in a letter to Moore): "We have an old Negro fish-man who has a cart that should have been in the surrealist show—a red wheelbarrow fitted with a huge rusty pair of scales, and six American flags and four small mirrors nailed to it, also two large tin alligators on top with their mouths open—a good deal of fanciful lettering, cakes of ice, and large shiny fish draped in the barrow-post."[42] Bishop appreciates endurance, imagination, and good will wherever she can find them. Where wit or comic energy or beguiling singularity are found, they must be appreciated. "The Monument," a strange, rich poem about a mysterious, battered old monument constructed from crates, concludes: "The crudest scrollwork says 'commemorate.'" This speech illuminates Bishop's own art. Very often, she wishes simply to commemorate "the little things, small plants and weeds and animals," and the humble people, that she, along with John Dewey, loved.[43] For Bishop, as she told Alexandra Johnson, the function of art is to "surprise." This was the most important quality a poem could have: "The subject and language should surprise you. You should be surprised at seeing something new and strangely alive."[44] One of the ways to achieve surprise is to seek out "the little things," and these surprises often led to poems. Miss

Lula ran the boardinghouse in Naples, Florida, where Bishop stayed on her first trip. Miss Lula's black servant Cootchie told Bishop: "That's why I like colored folks—they never commit suicide."[45] Bishop quoted this surprising remark to Moore admiringly, even though she knew it was not literally true. Bishop remained attracted to figures who would never commit suicide, who maintain their countenance and grace in the face of unpleasant necessity.

Two years later, when Miss Lula's servant died, she became the subject of the brief but penetrating "Cootchie" (1941). It pictures the peculiar intimacy between servant and master, black and white, that persisted in Florida alongside cruel distinctions in race and status:

> Her life was spent
>   in caring for Miss Lula, who is deaf,
> eating her dinner off the kitchen sink
> while Lula ate hers off the kitchen table.　　　(CP, 46)

Miss Lula's deafness implies a moral deafness to the gratitude she owes Cootchie for a life devoted to her service. "The skies were egg-white for the funeral / and the faces sable." The strange pallor of nature provides the only touch of whiteness. Oblivious to the ceremony's unpleasant ironies, Miss Lula didn't even go, "but who will shout and make her understand?" Insulated by her assumptions, Miss Lula is not even aware that she has failed. Meanwhile, the personified lighthouse appears to share the indifference of its white builders.

> Searching the land and sea for someone else,
> the lighthouse will discover Cootchie's grave
> and dismiss all as trivial; the sea, desperate,
>   will proffer wave after wave.

Bishop captures the futile closeness Cootchie and Miss Lula shared. Few poets would have taken either Lula or Cootchie seriously enough to bother to write a poem about them. What Bishop recognizes is the dehumanizing effect that a system of discrimination has on those who uphold it. The desperate sea, personified representative of the natural order that is here being violated, can do nothing but "proffer wave after wave" in a futile gesture of atonement.

The most extensive treatment of the poor in *North & South* is in the four "Songs for a Colored Singer," which adopt the personae of frustrated black women. Interestingly, these are the first poems by Bishop to have specifically female speakers, male speakers having been preferred in earlier dramatic monologues. Each of these tells a different story of loneliness and sorrow, and the mood gradually darkens and grows more dreamlike as one moves from song to song. The tone and voice are varied, but always alive to the rhythms of popular song. These poems, first published in 1944, were among the last to go into her first book. Asked if she had written the songs with tunes in mind, Bishop replied, "I was hoping somebody would compose the tunes for *them.* I think I had Billie Holiday in mind. I put in a couple of big words just because she sang big words well— '*conspiring* root' for instance."[46]

The "Songs for a Colored Singer" cannot be numbered among Bishop's finest efforts. Although the poems contain some deft strokes of characterization, they seem to require the additional lyric pulse of music. The tendency to seize and dramatize a social issue with journalistic directness that often marks good song lyrics is evident, however, and this comparatively unguarded directness is worth studying in a writer usually so *un*journalistic. Each song offers insight into the way Bishop looked at male-female relations. The perspective of the songs, written some forty years ago, is not very far from a contemporary feminist viewpoint in its exploration of the limitations men place on women's lives. It is as much for the way these songs reflect Bishop's views about women as for their intrinsic merit as poetry that I propose to discuss them in some detail. Each of the women brought to life in these songs is dramatically realized in her own terms, but each explores concerns of the poet's recognizable from other contexts. The first song presents a wife's clear-eyed disenchantment with a husband devoted, significantly, to a life of travel and risk. A series of ironic couplets opens the poem in which long initial lines that make apparently neutral observations are rhymed with short, deflating lines that betray the wife's frustrated longing for comfort and stability.

> A washing hangs upon the line,
>> but it's not mine.
> None of the things that I can see
>> belong to me.

> The neighbors got a radio with an aerial;
>   we got a little portable.
> They got a lot of closet space;
>   we got a suitcase.   (CP, 47)

The wife tries to stifle these frustrations, but they keep slipping out. Her husband, Le Roy, has blithely chosen the rewards of travel over the rewards of home, and as a result, their home is impoverished, spiritually as well as financially.

> What have we got for all his dollars and cents?
> —A pile of bottles by the fence.

The poem's sympathy is evidently with the patient, long-suffering woman, but there is an infectious, if naïve, vigor in the husband's curiosity that makes him appealing. The cost of travel, however, must be paid by wife more than husband, and travel calls for the acceptance of uncertainty and the neglect of home.

> He's faithful and he's kind
>   but he sure has an inquiring mind.
> He's seen a lot; he's bound to see the rest,
>   and if I protest
>
> Le Roy answers with a frown,
> "Darling, when I earns I spends.
> The world is wide; it still extends. . . .
> I'm going to get a job in the next town."
> Le Roy, you're earning too much money now.

Evidently, this family's problem is not so much lack of cash as the inability to agree on how to use their limited resources. The poem externalizes an opposition between home and travel that Bishop more often presents as being fought out within her own consciousness, and by doing so it is able to dramatize anxieties about the toll travel takes on personal life. The husband's cruelty is unconscious and unintended, but his decisions are peremptory and their effects keenly felt. By extension, every traveler, in eager pursuit of knowledge, runs the risk of wounding those he drags along or leaves behind.

In the second song, the speaker's situation is more desperate, although she too strives to be balanced and fair. Her circumstances force her to abandon home and seek salvation in travel, whether she wants to or not. Her husband has been neither faithful nor kind. He has taken up with another woman, and, in choosing to leave him, his wife enters the unknown.

> I'm leaving on the bus tonight.
>   Far down the highway wet and black
>   I'll ride and ride and not come back.
>   . . . . .
> I've borrowed fifteen dollars fare
> And it will take me anywhere   (CP, 48)

The understated anxiety and the tranced rhythm of this passage betray a deep hurt, even a desperation, that contrasts with the earlier rueful tone and petulant rhymes ("Varella / umbrella"). The imagined "highway wet and black" anticipates a dark, uncertain future. But the petulant note returns in other rhymes ("bus / monogamous"). The woman seems to feel awkward with her newfound anger and independence. Her husband, meanwhile, is bathed in security.

> Through rain and dark I see his face
> across the street at Flossie's place.
> He's drinking in the warm pink glow
> to th'accompaniment of the piccolo.

Brazenly enjoying himself in the flattering pink light before his wife's very eyes, the husband betrays not only his insensitivity but his awareness of the power residing in his mere masculinity, which seems to insulate him from the "rain and dark" his wife must enter. As in the first song, the speaker voices a quietly resentful protest against a dominating man, whose behavior undermines the home and forces travel on the unwilling.

Neither the language nor the action of the final two songs insists upon a specifically black context, but each is dark and moody enough that one can readily imagine Billie Holiday singing it. The third is clearly a response to the world war; it reflects the irony of giving birth to a child when surrounded by death. An opposition is drawn between the danger of travel and the safety of home. But is any home really safe from the threats faced by a traveler?

Lullaby.
Adult and child
sink to their rest.
At sea the big ship sinks and dies,
lead in its breast.   (CP, 49)

This opening stanza, full of significant doublings, suggests that
the same dangers lurk everywhere. Like the big ship, the adult and
child "sink," if not toward death, then toward rest, that temporary
form of extinction. The ship, maternally heavy, "sinks and dies, /
lead in its breast." War may have made a travesty of reproduction
and motherhood, but in another light, the power and violence of
warring nations is transient and unimportant in the face of the
inevitable and eternal bond joining mother to child. That this bond
can be tender is suggested by the reassuring, wavelike rhythms,
themselves so like a lullaby. But these rhythms are ironic and re-
inforce the irony that motherhood is itself a kind of prison for
mother and child alike.

Lullaby.
Let nations rage,
let nations fall.
The shadow of the crib makes an enormous cage
upon the wall.

The numbed calm of this lyric contrasts with the near hysteria
of the fourth song, which returns to the strange, enclosed atmosphere of the early poems, particularly "The Weed." The relentless
repetitions, the hammering rhythms, and the enigmatic vision of
an army of faces growing from small black seeds "in a dark and
dreary place," like some nightmarish transformation of the myth of
Cadmus and his dragons' teeth, takes the introspective mood of the
previous songs and projects it deeper, toward some hidden vein of
anxiety or dread. As in "The Weed," one attends to the thoughts
of a dreamer gripped by an ominous, inevitable, increasingly terrifying process, and as in that earlier poem, there is some uncertainty here as to what is dreamed and what is real. But in this
poem the ending is more disturbing still—and harder to interpret.
Can these dark faces—which, one recognizes in dread, are "too
real to be a dream" (CP, 51)—be the faces of those one has deserted or wronged in the past? At any rate, they have the power to

make one want to jump out of one's skin. In this song, Bishop seems at her closest to Poe and at her farthest from pastoral. Her brooding, introspective side has asserted itself emphatically and enigmatically in verses that make of absence a forceful, unnerving presence. They serve to remind that the cool and polished surfaces of Bishop's more elegant and descriptive poems mask dark and involuted depths.

The Beauty of the Ordinary

Bishop's fascination with the little things, with the pastoral dimension of the subtropics and the lives of the poor, remained powerful throughout her work. Another recurrent fascination, objects of art, may seem, at first, more elevated. But Bishop's art objects generally share the simplicity and even the poverty she studied elsewhere. She was a distinctive maker of poems about works of art, because—unlike Pound or Williams or Auden or Ashbery, moderns whose poems celebrate works whose quality cannot be questioned—Bishop created poems about ordinary or even failed art objects. This is a harder and more unique task than discovering the poem in a great painting or carving. In Breughel's *Landscape with the Fall of Icarus,* Auden found a powerful realization of the simultaneity of tragedy and routine. When William Carlos Williams looked at Breughel, he found a mastery of the rhythms of common life. These poets discovered in pictorial art satisfying expressions of profound conceptions of life. For each of them, the work of art recreated is recognized as elevated above ordinary experience. This is not true for Bishop. Elizabeth Bishop's poetry responds to the artistic quality of ordinary objects, and to workaday art discovered *within* the texture of ordinary experience. The very banality she contemplates sets her a hard task— she cannot simply translate the contours of a masterpiece from one medium to another but must discover something unforeseen that makes it possible to lift the work to a new level. What makes this effort worthwhile? Why not merely explore art that is unquestionably great? The answer has to do with Bishop's fascination with the scorned or the overlooked.

Bishop was intrigued by the way beauty penetrates ordinary things. In this she is close to Stevens. But as we have already seen

in reference to "The Fish," her work offers a more *dramatic* exploration of the psychology of perception than one can find in Stevens,
whom Randall Jarrell rightly considered the most undramatic of
poets. In Bishop's "Seascape" (1941) a brightly lit Florida coastline
seems so celestial that it must be compared to Renaissance drawing: "this cartoon by Raphael for a tapestry for a Pope: / it does look
like heaven" (*CP*, 40). Nature imitates art, or more precisely, the
mind sees nature in terms of a familiar artistic style. In a later
book, the Portuguese explorers who arrive to conquer a half continent in "Brazil, January 1st, 1502" (1960) cannot help but see the
dense undergrowth of the jungle in terms of the elegant tapestries
they left at home. Bishop calls attention to the way ingrained expectations influence the way we see, feel, and act.

When Bishop explores objects generally written off as utilitar-
ian, such as a map or an illustrated family Bible, she discovers
their beauty, their capacity to excite desire, doubt, elation, surprise: the whole range of emotions we associate with the powers of
art. "Cirque d'Hiver" (1940) observes a wind-up toy, a circus horse
and rider, finding there a complex human drama, an unforeseen
pathos, an unforeseen perplexity. The toy calls forth a response
that its creator may never have imagined but that the features of
the object nevertheless excite. For Bishop, beauty and spirituality
do not exist apart from everyday experience, but are woven into its
very fabric. To reveal them is not an imposition but a discovery.

It was natural, then, for Bishop to gravitate toward aesthetic
objects that do not come from the venerable past (even Williams,
well known for his absorption in common experience, was drawn
to such venerable objects) but from the banal present—such objects as anyone might find in an attic or on a relative's walls. "Large
Bad Picture" (1946) explores a bad work of art painted by one such
relative and in the process dramatizes an aesthetic discovery. Auden's "Musée des Beaux Arts" is announced by a voice that has
already drawn its conclusions about Breughel's *Icarus*. The voice
speaks from a great height, making sweeping pronouncements:

> About suffering they were never wrong
> The Old Masters: how well they understood
> Its human position.

Randall Jarrell slyly chided this know-it-all tone in his "The Old
and New Masters," which begins: "About suffering, about adora-

tion, the old masters / Disagree."[47] Bishop's approach revises Auden's in the following way: she captures the mind at an earlier
moment, long before it is capable of dogmatic statement. As in
"The Fish," she wants the moving response, before it has hardened
into certainty. A good poem, indeed, a sublime piece of high
comedy, can be written about a bad picture because an individual
response may be more complex and powerful than the picture itself. The observer stands before the picture, taking it in, and we
watch as she responds. She accepts its scale and perspective but
ridicules silly and unrealistic details. The poem does *not* scoff at
the painting's intention to capture the spacious harbor's pastoral
tranquillity. The cliffs *do* recede for miles; the sky *is* flushed and
still; the sea *is* a quiet floor. But it isolates false details: the "perfect" waves, the "spars like burnt match-sticks," the birds "hanging
in *n*'s in banks" (*CP,* 11). These fail through ludicrous oversimpl-
icity. The true simplicity of pastoral art cannot be obtained by
technical naïveté. There is not enough reality in this imaginary
garden; the painting has more clumsy artifice, and less art, than it
means to have.

At first, the response remains on technical grounds, with only
hints of latent sympathy. But a decisive transition occurs in the
sixth stanza; the painting springs to life. The poet heeds those
childish *n*-shaped birds:

> One can hear their crying, crying,
> the only sound there is
> except for occasional sighing
> as a large aquatic animal breathes.

Comedy remains alive in the funny rhymes ("crying, crying / oc-
casional sighing" and "is / breathes") and the vague image of a
"large aquatic animal"—evidently it isn't clear *what* animal! But
one also hears the gulls' lament. Here is the mind in action. Because the picture answers one's need for pastoral tranquillity, the
mind helps out, providing a dimension of duration and movement
the painting lacks. The sun comes strangely into motion, and ships
appear; these are almost human, pregnant with thought, the most
intelligent things around.

> In the pink light
> the small red sun goes rolling, rolling,

round and round and round at the same height
in perpetual sunset, comprehensive, consoling,

while the ships consider it.
Apparently they have reached their destination.
It would be hard to say what brought them there,
commerce or contemplation.   (*CP*, 11–12)

This conclusion mocks, and yet it concedes the vision's energy.
The language has grown almost comically resonant—the repeated
"rolling, rolling" echoes the gulls "crying, crying" and resounds
with wryly euphonious *o* sounds, "round and round and round."
The sun, though small and red, emerges from its flat plane, rolling
in eternal motion through a moment of beauty and calm that is
"comprehensive, consoling." Alliteration and assonance balance
this phrase against the closing line: "commerce or contemplation."
Bishop's language achieves the painting's implied artistic intention
by far outstripping it in technical command, and yet that is but
half of its accomplishment. The key word, here, is *perpetual;* almost the whole poem hangs on its two possible meanings. Is the
painting "eternal" in its achievement of pregnant calm? Or is it
frankly "unending," monotonous in a flat vision of impossible
shores?

While sustaining an amused distance, Bishop harkens to the
painting's mute longing. She enjoys playful commerce with the
painting's technical failure while helping it achieve its pastoral as-
pirations. The poem is not an endorsement of bad art. Rather, it
carries its critic into a strange region where amusement and transcendence mingle.

The school of Bishop criticism that sees her work as devoted to
objective depiction of observed fact cannot account for a poem like
this. "Large Bad Picture" shows that no matter how scrupulously
one studies a thing, exact description will not take one far without
subjective participation. Nor is there any real conflict between the
demands of exactness and imagination—in fact, the two comple-
ment any sound observation. One of her infrequent critical essays
(on a minor Cuban painter which she published in 1939, just as
she entered her middle period) demonstrates once and for all that

the exactness she sought was not merely a minutely accurate verbal picture. One must also capture the peculiar life of the thing, its human or animal mystery.

While living in Key West, Bishop came to know the primitive artist Gregorio Valdes, whose work has some of the coolness, simplicity, and pastoral charm of a Key West Henri Rousseau (without one of Rousseau's strangest and most effective features, his sublimated violence). She discovered his work hanging in a barbershop window. Bishop's essay is a posthumous tribute to the painter, who died shortly before the essay was written. She celebrates a shy and gracious man—whose manners were as beautiful as his poverty was profound—admist the quiet tempo of life in Key West. She retells how, after Valdes had belatedly received recognition and a few much-needed commissions, he changed the sign in front of his decrepit studio from "Sign Painter" to "Artist Painter" (*CProse*, 54). Although Gregorio Valdes was simple and untutored, his naïve art in important features resembles that of our sophisticated poet, nor should the resemblance seem surprising.

Although Valdes never mastered one classical feature of illusionist art, three-dimensional perspective, Bishop praises his work for its "exactness." Evidently, the impression of depth is not essential; but then exactness can be of different kinds. She retells a story of how the young Valdes once fooled his uncle by removing the towel rack near the sink and painting another rack, complete with towels, in the old spot. The uncle washed his face and reached for a towel, but "with water streaming into his eyes, he squinted up at it, saw it and clawed at it, but the towel wouldn't come off the wall. 'Me laugh plenty, plenty,' Valdes said." Here was exactness of a sort, but Bishop's retelling of the story concludes with the significant observation that "This classical ideal of verisimilitude did not always succeed quite so well, fortunately" (*CProse*, 58). Although she prized precision, classical verisimilitude was *not* her goal. She implies, indeed, that it can get in the way. Evidently the secret of Valdes appeal for her lay elsewhere. Much of his work, like Bishop's own, involved copying from something else. But as "Large Bad Picture" proved, copying secondhand sources doesn't preclude freshness. Freshness arises from the quality of the artist's response. Valdes lacked discrimination. When he copied from sentimental art, the result was disappointing—"the worst sort of 'calendar' painting"—but when he copied from photographs of "something he knew and liked, such as palm trees, he managed to make just the right changes in perspective and coloring to give it a peculiar and captivating freshness, flatness and remoteness" (*CProse*, 58). Bishop too, makes just the right changes. Her preferred trope is the simile because the comparatives "like" or "as" preserve the act of copying or "changing." When she notes in "Florida," "On stumps and dead trees the charring is like black velvet" (*CP*, 33), two realms of experience mingle. The trees' texture is rendered with uncanny precision, but the connotations of velvet are so different from burnt wood that the wood is changed, achieving a peculiar and captivating remoteness, even as the image stands freshly before one's eyes.

Bishop's imagination was ever alert for moments where two realms of association or experience merge. When she opposes dream life to waking life, the surreal to the everyday, she stands in a mysterious borderground. These are thresholds of decision. Howard Nemerov phrased it well when he said that, in her work, "art and nature, as it were, compare themselves to one another, or stand in such a relation that a remark about one is a remark about the other."[48] Her observation of bad art is enriched by her knowledge of life.

The most mysterious border ground of all is that dividing exact observation from sheer invention. "Little Exercise" reveals a mind in the act of inventing the precise details of an unseen event. Never did Bishop better capture what Croll had called an "idea in the act of experiencing it," because we see the poet in the process of deliberately summoning an invented vision. Titled "Little Exercise at 4 A.M." when it first appeared in the *New Yorker* in 1946,[49] the poem suggests a sleepless author projecting a scene from the seclusion of her room; she composes a calming exercise for the imagination like the little exercises for the keyboard that Bishop played as a student. (A lover of music and a capable amateur musician, she briefly took lessons from Ralph Kirkpatrick and owned a clavichord in Brazil.) Ruskin said that "poets of the second order . . . are generally themselves subdued by the feelings under which they write, or, at least, write as choosing to do so."[50] By contrast, Bishop writes with detachment, deliberately manufacturing compelling images.

Think of the storm roaming the sky uneasily
like a dog looking for a place to sleep in,
listen to it growling.

Think how they must look now, the mangrove keys
lying out there unresponsive to the lightning
in dark, coarse-fibred families,

where occasionally a heron may undo his head,
shake up his feathers, make an uncertain comment
when the surrounding water shines.   (CP, 41)

The mind resolutely conjures up those details that *must* be fleetingly visible outside. This poem echoes Stevens's "Disillusionment
of Ten O'Clock," where events that have not occurred dominate
over events that have, but in Bishop's poem the anxious presence
of the poet is more directly felt, and her imagination creates an
extraordinarily detailed *equivalent* to natural fact, rather than, as
Stevens did, a sprightly and colorful *alternative*.

Think of the boulevard and the little palm trees
all stuck in rows, suddenly revealed
as fistfuls of limp fish-skeletons.

The surprising comparison to skeletons makes the image flash before the inward eye with stroboscopic suddenness, surreal yet actual. In this little exercise at seeing with the memory, the mind
tests the possessions of the mind's eye.

The penultimate stanza brings out the theatrical element latent
in the exercise. The poem is itself theater, complete with vivid
mental props.

Now the storm goes away again in a series
of small, badly lit battle-scenes,
each in "Another part of the field."

As in Shakespeare's battles, one sees, not the whole field of war,
but a series of isolated glimpses, only here there are no Hotspurs,
Falstaffs, or Antonys. The sidewalk and sea have "human"
needs—the "broken sidewalks with weeds in every crack / are re-
lieved to be wet, the sea to be freshened,"—but their relief cannot

hold one's interest long without a human figure, and the drama gradually dwindles out to sea.

But wait! There is a human figure tucked away somewhere; the mind demands it. Although in the storm, he is as unaware of it as the removed author is aware.

> Think of someone sleeping in the bottom of a row-boat
> tied to a mangrove root or the pile of a bridge;
> think of him as uninjured, barely disturbed.

The little exercise has deliberately called up a human figure to fill an emotional and dramatic need. His situation uncannily reverses the lot of an earlier imagined figure, the Unbeliever, who "sleeps at the top of his mast." Both are asleep on the sea as life passes them by, but the differences are more decisive than the similarities. The Unbeliever's insecurity, his nightmare perched on the top of his mast, contrast strikingly with the security of the sleeper in "Little Exercise," who sleeps in the *bottom* of a rowboat tied to the shore. Unlike Stevens's drunken sailor in "Disillusionment" or Bishop's Unbeliever, he does not dream of an unreal and thereby heightened kind of experience, of "tigers in red weather" or a malevolent sea that "wants to destroy us all." He does not dream at all, as far as we know. He offers himself trustingly to the elements; the warm rain handles him gently. He emblematizes sensuous openness: his mind shrouded in sleep, his body exposed to the storm. Stevens's search for the never-quite-achieved absolute, for a "Supreme Fiction," for an intensity surpassing ordinary experience, is something Bishop was putting behind her. From now on, although her work would often entertain dream and fantasy, it was fully engaged by everyday life, by its humorous surprises, its quietness, its "always-more-successful surrealism,"[51] finding there an arena for entertainment and moral contemplation that was rich enough to last a lifetime. Ordinary experience contains what Stevens called "what will suffice," if it exists anywhere.[52] Its mystery and beauty may even exceed the mystery and beauty that belong to islands of the imagination. Imagination would still find stimulus behind protective shields, but most often in the process of reaching out into the risky domain of travel.

The creator, shaping the "Exercise" through an effort of will, remains physically apart. Mentally, however, she is in it. The poem has reversed the flight depicted in "In Prison"; enclosure no longer means the refusal of tangible experience, nor is imagination to be released only by a desperate turning inward. The landscape imagined here is no surrealistic abstraction, but a pastoral vision, a product of memory and desire, of the conscious exercise of the mind. After moving to Florida in 1939, whether Bishop wrote of South or North, she wrote of a large and complex geography—of "unwanted love, conceit and war"—but also of surprising compensations. Detachment need no longer mean alienation nor introspection the end of travel.

«Infant Sight»

A COLD SPRING

«Old Correspondences»
The Link with Nature

My story is Elizabeth Bishop's persistent artistic growth. Was *A Cold Spring,* her second book, something of a deviation from this pattern? So thought John Ashbery, whose praise of the earlier *North & South* had been unqualified: "As one who read, reread, studied and absorbed Miss Bishop's first book and waited impatiently for her second one, I felt slightly disappointed when it finally did arrive nine years later. . . . Some of the new poems were not, for me, up to the perhaps impossibly high standard set by the first book. Several seemed content with picture making. . . . And in several, the poet's life threatened to intrude on the poetry in a way that did not suit it."[1] Ashbery makes an exception for one masterpiece, "Over 2,000 Illustrations and a Complete Concordance," and I would argue for a second, "At the Fishhouses," perhaps her finest nature lyric, a large and nearly perfect poem. But many other examples are almost as good. I find many poems of observation that are not content with picturemaking: "Faustina or Rock Roses," "Invitation to Miss Marianne Moore," and "The Prodigal," to name several very different ones, are not only irresistibly fresh but the pictures they make are alive with thought and moral awareness. *A Cold Spring* does contain a handful of comparatively slight poems, such as "View of the Capitol from the Library of Congress," "Letter to N.Y.," and "The Shampoo," and Ashbery is rightly cautious about a half-dozen less-than-fully-achieved love poems, in which "the poet's life" uncomfortably "threatened to intrude." But in the book's five or six finest poems, at least, Bishop attacks with wit, grace, and cogent insight some of the unsettling questions posed by her earlier work. I'm thinking primarily of lyrics like "A Cold Spring" and "The Bight," which display growing confidence and sophistication in defining meaningful correspondences between poetry about nature—and of ambitious poems like "Over 2,000 Illustrations" and "At the Fishhouses," in which Bishop demonstrates how history can add moral and emotional depth to the delicate, abstractly colored world of the mapmaker. This book is best understood as an extension of Bishop's middle phase, tending toward a consolidation and expansion of the artistic ground gained after the achievement of more direct access to nature in "Florida" and "The Fish" in 1939 and 1940.

The book certainly did not harm Bishop's reputation when it first appeared in 1955, along with a reprinting of *North & South*, in a volume called *Poems* that was, in fact, her collected verse. It won the Pulitzer Prize. As a record of nine years work, *A Cold Spring* is not long: eighteen poems in the first edition. ("The Mountain" was dropped from later collections, and "Arrival at Santos" was shifted to the lead-off spot in *Questions of Travel*, so the book is now even shorter.) During those nine years her career as a poet was quietly advancing. She won several important awards and fellowships (including a Guggenheim); she served as Consultant in Poetry at the Library of Congress (in 1949–50); she developed close friendships with Robert Lowell and Randall Jarrell; she became a friend of Pauline Hemingway's and lived briefly in the Hemingway guesthouse at Key West (in rooms below Ernest's former study); and in 1951, she settled in Brazil with her friend Lota de Macedo Soares, an act that would have a profound impact on her future writing—an impact not easy to measure, though, until the appearance of her next book in 1965. What had begun as a brief visit to an old friend, a tourist's stop on a long-dreamed-of freighter cruise around South America, would extend into a stay of eighteen years. But Brazil makes itself little felt in *A Cold Spring*, although she had lived there for four years when it was published. Only "Arrival At Santos" (deleted from later collections, as mentioned) and "The Shampoo" have a Brazilian setting. The opposition between North and South nonetheless remains alive: many poems return to the North, recreating seascapes of Nova Scotia seen through the eyes of a returning adult. (Her stories "The Farmer's Children" and "The Housekeeper" (both 1948) and

"Gwendolyn" and "In the Village" (both 1953) anticipate the emphasis of her later poetry on the remembered Nova Scotia of her childhood.) Other poems continue to explore the South, through the exotic paradoxes of Key West.

Although she was publishing an average of only two poems a year, their yield of artistic excellence was high. Throughout her life, Bishop suppressed, or, more often, left uncompleted, dozens of poems (drafts of which are preserved at the Vassar College Library) that a less scrupulous craftsman might have finished and published. Her working methods are worth discussing in this regard. Rarely did she produce a draft of a lyric at one sitting, as many poets do, and then rework it, searching for more colorful and precise language. Bishop tended to find the words for her poems in fragments, sometimes virtually perfect ones, although adjacent segments of the poem continued to be blanks. Subsequent drafts show evidence of slight rephrasing of existing material, but, more significantly, they record the gradual discovery of language for the remaining blank sections, again often in virtually final form. The process is fascinating to watch. "The Moose," which was twenty years in the making, remained for years with many stanzas virtually perfected while others (numbered in one version) were completely blank, or existed only as fragmentary images or scraps of dialogue. Bishop must have had the entire scheme visualized and outlined almost from the start, as her arrangements of the fragments strongly suggests, but she would not put a word on the page until it had matured in her mind. Poems with tempting titles like "The Owl's Journey" or "Suicide of a Moderate Dictator" were abandoned after one or a few drafts, presumably because they failed to complete themselves. One test of a poem's genuineness, then, was a simple one: Could she finish it? Her craft was based not so much on skillful and painstaking rewriting, a process so important to her friend Robert Lowell, as on simple patience, the art of waiting (or groping) for what the unconscious mind was maturing within it.

In her Vassar essay on Hopkins (1934), Bishop showed that she was already familiar with this method of achieving a poem, a method that relies on the conscious tapping of unconscious mental resources. The essay speaks of a process that "anyone who has ever tried to write a single poem because he felt he had one in his head will recognize. . . . The poem, unique and perfect, seems to be separate from the conscious mind, deliberately avoiding it, while the conscious mind takes difficult steps toward it. The process resembles somewhat the more familiar one of puzzling over a momentarily forgotten name or word which seems to be taking on an elusive brain-life of its own as we try to grasp it."[2] This conception of the poem as having an objective existence, separate from the self, helps to explain two of Bishop's most pronounced tendencies as a poet: first of all, her relatively small production, and second, the fact that she never significantly revised a poem after she published it. Yeats said that when he rewrote an already published poem, "It is myself that I remake."[3] Lowell, who often revised published poems extensively and whose poems are always versions of himself, would have agreed. Bishop produced little because each poem, elusively preexistent in the unconscious, could not be summoned into being by a mere act of will, and because only a perfect realization of that poem was adequate. But, because a poem's existence was independent of the self, once the poem had been perfected it need not be changed to reflect a changing self. It was for his tendency to *"revise, revise, revise"* that Bishop chided Lowell in her elegy "North Haven" (1978):

> . . . And now—you've left
> for good. You can't derange, or re-arrange,
> your poems again. (But the Sparrows can their song.)
> The words won't change again. Sad friend, you cannot
> change.   (CP, 189)

Lowell's penchant for rearrangements is seen as one more evidence of life's transience. His poems find permanence (and whatever perfection they will have) only after their author loses his own capacity to change.

To speak of finality and perfection in reference to Bishop's poems is not to say that they were always perfectly realized. Nearly half of A Cold Spring's eighteen poems, all published by 1951, the year she settled in Brazil, are lyrics of frustrated love; these are the ones into which Ashbery felt "the poet's life threatened to intrude." They display an unresolved tension surprising in a poet known for cool restraint. In North & South, impersonal poems like "The Weed" and "Love Lies Sleeping" speak of the frustration of love with grand, sad eloquence. The more personal note struck here sometimes releases a querulousness that the poems do not completely absorb. A few even border on self-pity, an emotional temptation so elegantly refused elsewhere. Although these love poems require attention, I will look first at two representative poems of travel, "A Cold Spring" and "The Bight." They are remarkable, like so many of Bishop's lyrics, for the way apparently unsorted and even disorderly observation lures one toward unstated but artistically inevitable conclusions. In this regard, they are even more elusive than "The Fish," because they rely on only the slenderest of narrative threads. The key to these poems' organization is their sly commerce in correspondences, that is, in the analogies between nature and the human spirit that she studied in two quite distinct but not entirely unrelated sources, the poetry of Christian devotion and the poetry of French symbolism.

One way to answer Ashbery's concern that mere "picture making" is too present in Bishop's second book is to define the questions it implicitly asks. The quiet allusions to Christian belief and ritual that permeate Bishop's poetry are particularly significant in A Cold Spring, which contains examples close in spirit to two devotional poets she admired all her life: Hopkins and Herbert. For both of them, the loveliness of this world acquires value from the analogy between the seen reality of earthly beauty and the unseen reality of God's power and care. In Hopkins's words, "He fathers-forth whose beauty is past change: / Praise him." The book's title poem, "A Cold Spring," takes its epigraph, "Nothing is so beautiful as spring," from Hopkins.[4]

But as a reading of that poem suggests, Bishop finds no immanent Godhead fathering and giving meaning to the transient procession of spring. In her poem, spring itself is the enormously powerful but latent force that one attempts to recognize and celebrate, in surroundings of chilly incompletion. Verbs subtly personify and humanize the setting but with accents of failure or uncertainty.

> A cold spring:
> the violet was flawed on the lawn.
> For two weeks or more the trees hesitated;
> the little leaves waited,
> carefully indicating their characteristics.
> Finally a grave green dust
> settled over your big and aimless hills.

One day, in a chill white blast of sunshine,
on the side of one a calf was born.   (CP, 55)

Bishop calls the hills "aimless," a term Hopkins could never use
in the same way, because she discovers in their starkness no hint
of purpose. She is a searcher for correspondences, but skeptical,
not easily satisfied. The free-verse lines, with their irregular
lengths and unexpected rhymes on key words ("flawed on the
lawn," "hesitated / waited") embody spring's uncertain progress.
The imagery carries quiet surprises. Instead of the accustomed
dust of snow, these lines make one see "a grave green dust" of
sparse grass and foliage. Here is a slightly unsettling, incomplete
correspondence between human expectation and natural fact.
These correspondences flirt ironically with the traditional reassur-
ances of nature poetry. Birth, accomplished "in a chill white blast
of sunshine," seems a tenuous affair at best.

The success with which Bishop has washed her diction clean of
romantic encrustation appears in the deliberate modulation toward
flat prose rhythms.

Greenish-white dogwood infiltrated the wood,
each petal burned, apparently, by a cigarette-butt.

The seemingly accidental repetition of *wood* in the first line imitates the flat, unpremeditated repetitions of ordinary speech, but
that casual, prosaic quality, which persists in the diction of the
second line, is reversed by a precise but completely unexpected
image ("burned, apparently, by a cigarette-butt") which makes one
visualize dogwood petals according to an entirely new and unsentimental set of associations. The word *apparently*, which seems like
another prosaic intrusion, is the key to the line's effect, since it
puts the poet in the implicit position of an only-just-arrived, not-
quite-convinced observer, seeing the flower as if for the first time.

Time moves in uneven waves, meandering from early spring
mornings through the first sultry dusks of summer. As the climate
changes, so does the tone, which relaxes from clipped austerity
and begins to revel in sensuous profusion. Subjective interpretation ("The hills grow softer") stands next to stark, objective no-
tation ("Tufts of long grass show / where each cow-flop lies"—
CP, 55–56). These are counterpointed by striking metaphor

("The bull-frogs are sounding, / slack strings plucked by heavy thumbs"— *CP*, 56). No one tone or mode of perception is allowed to dominate. But while each contributes to a complex picture, they are all building towards the poem's most delicate passage, an intimate display of word-painting:

> Beneath the light, against your white front door,
> the smallest moths, like Chinese fans,
> flatten themselves, silver and silver-gilt
> over pale yellow, orange, or gray.

Note the caesura dividing each line, so that each fragmentary image will be savored separately, whereas the opening lines had each marched briskly to a final stop. The comparison to Chinese fans is not only precise and surprising; it carries associations of feminine warmth, of Oriental fragility and elegance, that contrast pointedly with the chill starkness of early spring. The time of austere uncertainty having passed, objects may now be relished merely for themselves. The poem's meaning rests on its gradual evolution in tone. The recognition that the rising fireflies are "exactly like the bubbles in champagne" suggests an almost frivolous desire to celebrate. Rather than a devotional hymn to God's providence, Bishop offers a kind of toast to the Maryland hillside. She can even speak, in words that mimic the glib toastmaster, of "glowing tributes." These "tributes," however, refresh the cliché because they really *do* glow—on the tails of fireflies. The poem comes lightly to rest on an analogy between natural and human celebration that is presented both sincerely and ironically. Bishop's devotions are unquestionably temporal, yet, in her own lightly skeptical way, her commitment to the fresh discovery of a landscape's latent analogies parallels Hopkins's keen exploration of the analogical beauty and transience of nature.

Bishop omits Hopkins's doctrine, but she retains his humility. The beauty she devotes herself to is transient, without guarantees of redemption—like the "Sweet day, so cool, so calm, so bright" which excites the constant reminder "For thou must die" in Herbert's "Virtue," without Herbert's saving alternative of eternal life. Bishop was not exploring nature romantically, to elevate her own ego in the grand Wordsworthian manner. *Disciplining* the ego, devoting it to the study of external appearance, permits self-forgetfulness and surprise. In this sense, her observations are spiritual exercises. To state it simply, her approach is devotional rather than romantic. By incorporating a modern skepticism and irony, Bishop suggests how a devotional attitude may be rescued from this most secular and cynical of centuries.

A second source that spoke to Bishop on the doctrine of correspondences was symbolist poetry, particularly that of the father of symbolism, Baudelaire. He is subjected to good-humored irony in Bishop's "The Bight." Baudelaire's faith in correspondence rested on a long tradition with parallels to the devotional poetry of Hopkins. As Octavio Paz points out in *Children of the Mire,* an imaginative study of the concepts underlying modern poetry: "The belief in correspondences between beings and worlds predates Christianity, crosses the Middle Ages, and, through Neoplatonism, illuminism, and occultism, reaches the nineteenth century."[5] Baudelaire and Hopkins agreed on the need to search material things for their analogies to the human soul. But while Bishop recognizes that such analogies can be found, she does not treat correspondences as articles of faith. This is particularly clear in her ironic treatment of Baudelaire in "The Bight." The great French poet was transforming a devotional tradition when he said: "Imagination is an almost divine faculty which perceives immediately and without philosophical methods the inner and secret relations of things, the correspondences and the analogies."[6] For Herbert the belief, stated in "Man," that

> All things unto our flesh are kind
> in their descent and being: to our mind
> In their ascent and cause

has absolute sanction.[7] As an unbeliever, Baudelaire had to transfer the divine source that justifies the system from God to the human imagination. Hence, it inevitably becomes "almost divine" and he *must*, it seems, dispense with "philosophical methods," which were essential to Herbert. Baudelaire's perceptions might seem emotionally true, but they are simply intuitions. Symbolist poetry has been criticized for creating moments of symbolic communion that are, in the words of Irving Howe, "sacraments without faith," since they "cannot survive in daylight or the flatness of time."[8] Because Baudelaire was an honest writer, he could sustain only *dark* sacraments of blasphemy. T. S. Eliot, retracing Baudelaire's footsteps, sensed the instability of an aesthetic maintained "without philosophical methods"; when he turned to the Anglican church, he found what was, for him, a more absolute sanction for the correspondence between himself and the rose, the sanction of divine grace. Bishop took a humbler route, asking for neither the transcendence sought by Baudelaire nor Eliot's longed-for certitude. The correspondences she discovers are often funny, sometimes accidental. Octavio Paz observed, "Modern poetry is awareness of [the] dissonance within analogy."[9] Bishop's strength comes from her arabesques on this "dissonance," which permit her to explore transience through irony, with what she called "knowledge of necessity" in the early story "In Prison" (*CProse*, 191). She has a kind of tough, cheerful resignation to metaphysical uncertainty that allows her to see through all kinds of pretensions.

Even "The Bight," one of Bishop's most loosely descriptive poems, can wryly intimate this philosophy. Critics have noted the apparently random character of this portrait of an unglamorous tropical bay, but the poem implicitly questions one's footing among externals, amidst Emerson's "not me," but with a difference, since this "not me" seems devoid of transcendental possibilities. It takes an ironic look at Baudelaire's temptation to find (possibly) inflated analogies between nature and the human soul. When Richard Howard, translator of the complete *Les Fleurs du Mal*, called Elizabeth Bishop "one of our most profound Baudelaireans," he had in mind this modest poem.[10]

Howard Nemerov first noted the poem's essential feature, its intention to discover analogies between human and natural activity. Birds seem strangely human: pelicans "going off with humorous elbowings"; workboats seem canine: "frowsy sponge boats keep coming in / with the obliging air of retrievers." Bishop's homely correspondences, which reveal unawed but delighted attention, are intended to deflate Baudelaire's more haughty analogies for "the inner and secret relations of things," as the following lines make more or less explicit.

> Absorbing, rather than being absorbed,
> the water in the bight doesn't wet anything,
> the color of the gas flame turned as low as possible.
> One can smell it turning to gas; if one were Baudelaire,
> one could probably hear it turning to marimba music.
>
> (*CP*, 60)

Bishop suggests that, facing the same scene, Baudelaire would
have been alert primarily to the chance for synesthetic transformation: alert, not to the scene itself, but to its exotic possibilities.
Wouldn't he have forgotten that the dark, romantic marimba music
was really evoked by a muddy dredge? But doesn't Bishop's more
low-key approach refuse not just loftiness but aesthetic unity, in
favor of deflating irony? Wickedly, Bishop puns on Baudelaire's ex-
alted notion of transcendental correspondences:

> Some of the little white boats are still piled up
> against each other, or lie on their sides, stove in,
> and not yet salvaged, if they ever will be, from the last
>   bad storm,
> like torn-open, unanswered letters.
> The bight is littered with old correspondences.

The grammatically unnecessary plural, "correspondences," clues
one in—it is not just unanswered letters that concern her. Bishop
would generally accept another poet's discovery of correspondences; her own imagery is full of them. But she employs them
wryly. Bishop's "correspondences" are "old" and plain, not "secret"
or "almost divine." They emerge with a dry and self-effacing clarity
that wears well.

"The Bight" seems at first a mere grab bag, but in its offhand
way it defines one of Bishop's deftest and least noticed achievements: her transformation of symbolist absolutes into something
moderate and useful by uniting them with the precise delineations
of imagism. Exploiting what Charles Feidelson calls the modern
symbolist's "preoccupations with the medium,"[8] she creates a casual and convincing transcription of an ordinary afternoon. Hers
is not a "timid reaction to Symbolism" (as Paz felt imagism was).[12]
Unifying "The Bight," in spite of its random look, is a consistent
sensibility that sifts through each image—feeling, comparing,
judging. The bight becomes a symbol, but it is first of all just what
is seems, an open bay. As an imagist, Bishop expands imagism,
making it a medium for complex philosophical investigation. As a
symbolist, she draws her symbols back toward rigorously observed
natural fact. She is not calling for the symbolist's *paradis artificiel*
by any means, as Eliot and Pound, in their own ways, may still
have been. Because Bishop dies *not* "protest against nature," as
Baudelaire did, she can calmly conclude:

Click. Click. Goes the dredge,
and brings up a dripping jawful of marl.
All the untidy activity continues,
awful but cheerful.   (CP, 60–61)

Making no attempt to *predetermine* what the response must be,
Bishop creates an apparently random surface, while expressing
pointed observations about the world. Correspondences—between
pelican and pickaxes, stove-in boats and unanswered letters—
arise naturally, even inevitably. But why do these correspondences
matter? The epigraph "On my birthday" points obliquely toward
the answer. On birthdays one assesses one's progress so far. What
the poet has achieved is the scene itself, no mean feat if one considers the inwardness of her early work. She turns from image to
image and drinks it all in. That this scene was specifically observed
on her birthday is actually itself a fiction (which supports the con-
tention that reference to her birthday is an artistic calculation).
Bishop was born on 8 February, but a letter to Robert Lowell from
Key West dated 1 January 1948 includes observations that contain
the gist of the poem: "The water looks like blue gas—the harbor is
always a mess, here, junky little boats all piled up, some hung with
sponges and always a few half sunk or splintered up from the most
recent hurricane—it reminds me a little of my desk." Elsewhere
in the same letter she tells Lowell, "When somebody says 'beautiful'
about Key West you should really take it with a grain of salt until
you've seen it for yourself—in general it is really *awful* & the
'beauty' is just the light or something equally perverse." She continues, "I like it very much."[13] Although the arrangement of the
poem appears, like this harbor, unsorted, it is actually building
toward a meditative conclusion: life can be awful but cheerful. In
fact, this poem actually enjoys the "awful," just as it relishes the
rather awful rhyming of *awful, jawful,* and *cheerful,* which lend its
final lines a droll, off-key sort of conclusiveness.

The achievement of this birthday is its capturing of the vitality
and color of a place—a place that needs all kinds of untidy effort if
it will thrive. Where Baudelaire and Eliot and many postmodern-
ists tend to explore their exclusion from scenes dominated by stu-
pidity and materialism—a response hinted at, as well, in some of
Bishop's early work—she can now take these elements in stride as
she savors a place rife with crude energy. Her new correspon-

dences are fictions, but they work. Bishop deftly knocks the pins out from under more elevated attitudes. This pragmatic sacrament cannot be erased by "daylight and the flatness of time," because it is made of flatness and daylight.

Love
«A *mirror on which to dwell*»

Bishop's correspondences succeed because of their humor and common sense. In the love poetry of her middle phase, the tone is one of almost numb intensity. Later love poems like "Song for the Rainy Season" or "Electrical Storm," both written in Brazil in 1960, are controlled and understated celebrations of satisfying, if never unthreatened, love experiences, but the love poems grouped in the latter half of A *Cold Spring* betray frustration and even bafflement. These return to the mirrored inwardness we found in the early fables, and their reliance on more formal kinds of rhetoric and more intricate and extended lines of reasoning, approximating the metaphysical conceit, resembles the early work as well. But the ironic detachment that gives the early fables their cool reserve and their capacity to amuse as they unsettle is often wanting here.

The self-contained intensity of Bishop's middle-phase love poetry can be seen in the lyric "Insomnia" (1951). Even the sentences turn inward, looping back upon themselves. She writes, it seems, out of bewilderment, as if she is trying to grasp experience whole and wring some crumb of comfort from it.

The poem's point of departure is its curious reason for admiring the moon: not for its beauty but for its power to broadcast its own presence, yet see itself only. The moon has, in its enviably inhuman way, left behind any need for rest or fellowship.

> The moon in the bureau mirror
> looks out a million miles
> (and perhaps with pride, at herself,
> but she never, never smiles)
> far and away beyond sleep, or
> perhaps she's a daytime sleeper.   (CP, 70)

The sentence winds intricately through a maze of suppositions. Its nervous, oblique quality is teasing—very unlike the blunter directness Lowell's personal poetry would soon achieve. But the very simple diction retains an air of childlike wonder and uncertainty. The moon possesses an invulnerable detachment.

> By the Universe deserted,
> *she*'d tell it to go to hell,
> and she'd find a body of water,
> or a mirror, on which to dwell.

Significantly female, the moon can live, it seems, on self-contemplation alone. She can "wrap up care in a cobweb / and drop it down the well," through the water's mirrored surface to a place beyond, where all relationships, physical and personal, are inside out:

> into that world inverted
> where left is always right,
> where the shadows are really the body,
> where we stay awake all night,
> where the heavens are shallow as the sea
> is now deep, and you love me.

Like the moon, the speaker suffers from insomnia and thus lives an inverted life, staying "awake all night." Only in the inverted mirror world is the speaker loved. A surprise is reserved for the last line. The poet has not mentioned her own desertion until then, and at that only indirectly. By confessing her pain, she surprises one with the reason for her own sleeplessness and her longing to emulate the moon's aloofness. At this moment she might like to tell the universe to go to hell. But the urge to look only at a mirror is set off by the emptiness of an extraordinarily visualized place where "the shadows are really the body."

The moon corresponds exactly to the unattainable loved one: cool, remote (yet all pervasive), self-sufficient, unsmiling, indifferent. The poem's inverted method has its source in two influences: Bishop's shyness and her own sexual orientation. Although Bishop did have affairs with men, she never married, and her serious love relationships were always with women. Given the times and her own temperament—she admired the "sexual courage" of Auden but could not emulate it—she could not speak freely.[14] The poem draws a veil over facts that may be central to it, although the language offers covert indications. As I have suggested, the fact that the moon is female in no accident. This moon / beloved is an icy, modern version of the virginal huntress Diana, and it betrays spiritual kinship with the alluring but fatal inwardness of the imaginary iceberg. Alan Williamson finds in these poems "a kind of ground-conviction that reciprocal love is, almost metaphysically, impossible."[15] The combined effect of the early loss of both parents and a sexual orientation that, judging from the poems, appears to have contributed to an innate disposition toward shyness, anxiety, and loneliness, must have made it almost impossible (at this time) for her to produce poetry about love that reveals the same balance, humor, and grace found nearly everywhere else in her work. The period between 1946 and 1951 was, by all evidence, a very trying one. Other explorations of loneliness and separation such as "Argument" (1947), "Varick Street" (1947), and each of the group called "Four Poems": "Conversation," "Rain Towards Morning," "While Someone Telephones," and "O Breath" (1949–51) make it clear that failed love troubled Bishop deeply. These poems, with their strange, almost surrealistic, patterns, breathe pain and—in their tense, fragile beauty—acknowledge love's dangerous but compelling force. In "Varick Street" a sleeping couple is surrounded by a threatening Manhattan, pulsing with nocturnal activity, whispering of inevitable betrayal. The mechanical city is gruesomely personified.

> At night the factories
> struggle awake,
> wretched uneasy buildings
> veined with pipes
> attempt their work.
> Trying to breathe,
> the elongated nostrils
> haired with spikes
> give off such stenches, too.
> *And I shall sell you sell you*
> *sell you of course, my dear, and you'll sell me.*   (CP, 75)

Like the gross odors that smother their embrace, the lovers are themselves both hapless and dangerous, and selling others—in this commercial environment—seems a harsh but inevitable necessity. "Varick Street" lacks the grand, sorrowing tenderness of the earlier "Love Lies Sleeping." Instead, the refrain is coolly (but transparently) insouciant. But this breezy, knowing tone, which, as Anne Stevenson notes, is too much like Auden's, cannot disguise the recognition that mutual betrayal is all love has to offer.[16] The poem, for all its lurid force, doesn't quite earn its cynicism. A significant advance of the last two books lies in their greater ease and conviction in treating personal emotion, even when that emotion is painful. For this her friend Lota de Macedo Soares, with whom she shared many years in Brazil, no doubt deserves some credit, for helping Bishop toward a more secure idea of herself and the possibilities of human relationships. While poems like "Varick Street" or "Insomnia" are not quite dominated by the emotions they explore—and although their artistic resources are impressive—they seem to lack that intelligent reliance on humility and that capacity for measure, wit, and calm in the face of the unfathomable that distinguishes so much of Bishop's poetry.

Bishop's least personal poem about love, "The Prodigal," is perhaps her best. Parallel in form to the early work, it is a parable concerning parental and filial love, an aspect of love less freshly painful and therefore easier to control artistically than amorous love. This is not to say that "The Prodigal" (1950) makes love seem easy. The prodigal knows that even offers of generosity and forgiveness can be frightening, because in accepting them one confesses one's need and lays oneself open. Although Bishop had virtually abandoned the overt reliance on fable that predominated in her early verse, here the form remains effective because she treats a voluntary incarceration, the central theme of her early fables. The poem alludes to Herbert, of course, in its (somewhat freer) use of one of his favorite forms, the double sonnet. Unlike the Gospel according to Luke, this contemporary parable spotlights, not the triumph of forgiveness and reconciliation, in which the affronted father gladly celebrates his wastral son's return, but the crippling period of doubt before he returns home. It details the prodigal's peculiar life in an apparently modern barn, the home he has chosen. A sensuously overwhelming place, in one essential it serves him well, keeping thoughts at bay.

> The brown enormous odor he lived by
> was too close, with its breathing and thick hair,

>   for him to judge. The floor was rotten; the sty
>   was plastered halfway up with glass-smooth dung.
>
>   (CP, 71)

Adopting the moon's posture in "Insomnia," this prodigal has, in effect, deserted the universe and told it to go to hell. But his isolation is neither cool nor remote. He has cosied so close to this oddly familiar haven from parental love, so intimately obscene, so almost lovely in its "glass-smooth dung," that he need never admit its awful inhumanity. He lives "by" the enormous odor in two senses: he lives near it, of course, but, horribly, he also lives *on* it. He must be desperate if he can find beauty and companionship here, but, even so, images of the humanity he fears cannot be escaped. The "cheerful stare" of the sow "that always ate her young—/ till, sickening, he leaned to scratch her head" suggests the danger of arbitrary parental power and hints at the young man's unspoken terror. Still, the sty is almost a satisfactory home.

>   But sometimes mornings after drinking bouts
>   (he hid the pints behind a two-by-four),
>   the sunrise glazed the barnyard mud with red;
>   the burning puddles seemed to reassure.
>   And then he thought he almost might endure
>   his exile yet another year or more.

Despite the scene's strangely reassuring beauties, his return is (implicitly) inevitable and delay a matter of endurance, because enclosure in this haven / prison cannot last forever even though the exile is self-chosen.

Subhuman physical intimacy almost, but not quite, replaces human love. The prodigal's barn is "safe and companionable as in the Ark." His bedfellows the pigs, in gross parody of human sleep, "stuck out their little feet and snored." What frightens him, however, is not this grossness but the moments he must face alone. Even this haven, where so much is "too close . . . for him to judge," cannot hold thought or need at bay forever.

>   Carrying a bucket along a slimy board,
>   he felt the bats' uncertain staggering flight,
>   his shuddering insights, beyond his control,
>   touching him. But it took him a long time
>   finally to make his mind up to go home.

The "bats' uncertain staggering flight" terrifies because it re-sembles—in its dark, lonely, furtive passage—his own curious destiny. The prodigal—who, in his retreat from love, parallels the Man-Moth—has clung to a strange thread of freedom. Rather than protest nature, he has flung himself into it. Physical hunger does not make his mind up, as in Luke. The anguish of isolation, like the bat's wing, touches him "beyond his control." That he does leave his haven and return to face the harrowing challenge of parental affection shows the prodigal's latent courage and implies that, in the last analysis, Bishop would be unwilling to accept Williamson's suggestion that "reciprocal love is, almost metaphysically, impossible."

Bishop's best work is a heroic overcoming of the enclosure imposed by early traumas. Much of its value derives from her ability to push beyond potentially paralyzing demands for sheltered safety. Her best poetry tends to emerge when she is considering risks, in the instant of shying off from them. Throughout her work the safety of enclosure and the love of permanence counterpoint the transience and danger of travel. This reflects a genuine ambivalence in her character.

«Over 2,000 Illustrations and a Complete Concordance»

Frustration with the transient rewards of travel is voiced in the opening lines of one of Bishop's finest poems, a searching exploration of the opposition between inward and outward life: "Over 2,000 Illustrations and a Complete Concordance." This is Bishop's one poem in the high modernist mode and appropriately so, because she critiques one of the great themes of modernism, the necessity of discovering what Ezra Pound called a "live tradition" as a means of ordering and giving value to experience. But Bishop's poem, after beginning with modernist assumptions, discovers the emptiness of much of that past culture that was supposed to supply coherence and value. One then must resort to fictions of another kind. It begins on a note of disappointment with the ordinary that colors all that follows:

Thus should have been our travels:
serious, engravable.   (CP, 57)

The poet sits looking at the page, wishing that past travels had the lucid seriousness and the order of this Bible's engravings. The poet's posture recalls the situation of "The Map": she pores over a representation of nature, comparing it to actualities. The map-makers' colors were "more delicate than the historians'" (CP, 3). Here, memories of one's travels insist upon being sordid, vagrant, irrelevant. Having tasted the world, she wants to reject its dismaying randomness and vacuity. Like the earlier imaginary iceberg, the engraved Bible is a tempting alternative to real travel, offering remoteness, permanence, and perhaps the respite of annihilation.

"Over 2,000 Illustrations and a Complete Concordance" may be divided into three movements: the first examines the Bible's engravings; the second recalls disjointed glimpses of the poet's travels; the third returns to the Bible, finding an "old Nativity," a fiction whose warm, concentrating power stands against the disconnection, flatness, and fearfulness of travel. The three movements oppose three different ways of knowing, through artifacts, travel, and fictions. Transitions between these perspectives constitute the action of the poem.

After insisting that our travels should have been engravable, the observer begins to see the emotional deadness of the steel engravings of her Bible, and thus the limitations of *vicarious* travel. There may be the merit of variety in foreignness, but these so-called wonders lack surprise, they are "tired / and a touch familiar." Bishop never made much of the authorized wonders, anyhow. There is even something sinister about many of these "innumerable" images.

Often the squatting Arab,
or group of Arabs, plotting, probably,
against our Christian Empire,
while one apart, with outstretched arm and hand
points to the Tomb, the Pit, the Sepulcher.

The capital letters lent to Tomb, Pit, and Sepulcher suggest historic or religious significance, but their emphasis rests uneasily on death, on what is "sad and still." The sardonic reference to age-old religious conflict between Christians and Arabs reminds one of historic displacements, suspicions, and hatreds in the Holy Land, suggesting, one surmises, the failure of history to fulfill religious vision. As in "Large Bad Picture," Bishop now begins to analyze the limitations of the pictorial technique and artistic achievement of these engravings:

> The branches of the date-palms look like files.
> The cobbled courtyard, where the Well is dry,
> is like a diagram, the brickwork conduits
> are vast and obvious, the human figure
> far gone in history or theology,
> gone with its camel or its faithful horse.

The dry "Well" suggests spiritual dryness, as in Eliot. The cobbled courtyard, with its emptiness, cannot be personified ("the human figure / far gone") because of Moslem rejection of representation in art. These scenes lack the vivid incongruities, the "awful but cheerful" correspondences relished in "The Bight."

Paradoxically, although vicarious travel was intended to lead one toward serious, engravable *meaning*, spiritual emptiness pervades these images. One's disillusionment with the engravings excites scrutiny of the limits of the engraver's technique: his incised lines begin to seem fake. Instead of entering the picture, as one wants to do and as one did in "Large Bad Picture," the viewer pulls back. This signals a gradual withdrawal from and refusal of the engraver's illusion.

> Always the silence, the gesture, the specks of birds
> suspended on invisible threads above the Site,
> or the smoke rising solemnly, pulled by threads.

Ghostly, unspoken meanings pervade these pictures, but they have grown oppressive. The "threads" that suspend the birds in air and pull the solemn smoke, incongruously break the intended illusion. How can one lose oneself to such a blank, unconvincing world?

Bishop begins to follow the incised lines themselves, losing the larger image in frustrated pursuit of inlying value, until her vision begins to blur under the strain:

> The eye drops, weighted through the lines
> the burin made, the lines that move apart

like ripples above sand,
dispersing storms, God's spreading fingerprint,
and painfully, finally, that ignite
in watery prismatic white-and-blue.

One "reads," literally, between the lines. Eyed that way, the engraving's hoped-for order collapses into a "dispersing" sandstorm, while "God's spreading fingerprint" covers all in a manner not wholly reassuring. The God whose "fingerprint" it is is a fearful being whose fat finger mars his creation. When the lines blur together and "ignite / in watery prismatic white-and-blue," the image becomes a photonegative of real experience: a smeared white-and-black inversion of the tear-streaked "Rainbow, rainbow, rainbow!" epiphany in "The Fish." The engravings can no longer claim meaning or permanence. One's expectations were wrong.

From this moment there is a subtle transition into the second movement: recollections from actual travels in many lands. Seven vignettes, each ripe with connotation, unfold with no more transition than "and" and "and." Although some are set in the Middle East, it is necessary to distinguish these real-life travels from the engravings, but more than one critic has confessed the difficulty of doing so. Bishop indicated the division by placing a typographical break in the text between the first movement and the second; some scenes in the second movement are drawn from a visit to Morroco, a parallel world to that of the biblical engravings, but these are remembered events. Unfortunately, this section break was lost at the bottom of the page in *Poems* and was erroneously dropped from *The Complete Poems* of 1969. It was restored (through the care of Frank Bidart) to the definitive *Complete Poems: 1927–1979*. The mistake made in the 1969 *Complete Poems* has been disseminated through a number of anthologies, however, and has no doubt confused many readers. Without the typographical break, the division between the first movement's preoccupation with vicarious travel and the second's with real memories is much harder to catch.

These memories offer color and vitality missing in the Bible's 2,000 engravings, but, like the engravings, they fail to point toward coherence or significance.

Entering the Narrows at St. Johns
the touching bleat of goats reached to the ship.

We glimpsed them, reddish, leaping up the cliffs
among the fog-soaked weeds and butter-and-eggs.
(CP, 57–58)

Here are vivid images, but nothing "serious, engravable." In Rome, at St. Peter's, where one might have hoped to find exaltation or, at least, meaningful order,

the wind blew and the sun shone madly.
Rapidly, purposefully, the Collegians marched in lines
crisscrossing the great square with black, like ants.
(CP, 58)

The Collegians' "purpose" is subhuman, instinctive. It mocks the implicit search for spiritual purpose. Throughout, Bishop's memory sets past glories against present emptiness. But what if even the great relics of the past have lost human value? By contrast, the bleat of goats touches a sad chord. But it does not soothe a longing for seriousness, for graven truth.

And at Volubilis there were beautiful poppies
splitting the mosaics; the fat old guide made eyes.

Bishop counterpoints the beautiful, decaying site with the lovely, ruinous strength of nature and the seaminess of human nature— the fat old guide. Even the "little pockmarked prostitutes" of Marrakesh are sad reflections of corrupted innocence and decadent culture as they:

balanced their tea-trays on their heads
and did their belly-dances; flung themselves
naked and giggling against our knees,
asking for cigarettes.

But it is not this debased girlishness that "frightened me most of all." (By implication much in her travels *has* frightened her.) It is the shocking decay of a nearby tomb, a relic of this same culture: "A holy grave, not looking particularly holy." The narrator shifts from the first person plural to the singular "me." The other experiences were, in a sense, universal. This recognition is disturbingly personal. The erosion of the old relic and symbol, which now pays tribute only to the random murders of time, affronts innocent yearnings; the tourist's expectation of something significant melts before this gruesome parody of meaning.

An open, gritty, marble trough, carved solid
with exhortation, yellowed
as scattered cattle-teeth;
half-filled with dust, not even the dust
of the poor prophet paynim who once lay there.

Despite chilling imagery, the tone of the last line is detached and
bantering, as if the poet would mock her own terror. A worldly
Arab guide is inured to the response this "holy grave" provokes and
finds the observer's shock funny. "In a smart burnoose Khadour
looked on amused." One is not even allowed the dignity of one's
anguish. The religion of a tomb "carved solid / with exhortation"
may seem too fervid. But here even the old fervor is lost.

The final scene before the tomb echoes the one in Mexico where
"the dead man lay / in a blue arcade." More significantly, it recapit-
ulates the disillusioned contemplation of "The Tomb, the Pit, the
Sepulcher" engraved in the Bible. By emphasizing parallels between two planes of experience, the poem indicates the limitations
of both vicarious and direct exploration. But the reader must discover this thesis through close attention. No explicit connections
are drawn.

The third movement begins: "Everything only connected by
'and' and 'and.'" Both in one's experience and in the poem, no
*since*s or *therefore*s indicate causal or symbolic links. Reality is not
always "serious, engravable." Nor is it always possible to impose or
discover connections, although the longing for them persists.
Bishop may be alluding to the difficulties of her own style of narration by accretion of detail, as well as protesting the limits of
these parallel worlds. The Bible is also a book in which, literally,
everything is "only connected by 'and' and 'and.'" Still, the Bible
conveys, to many, a satisfying and complete meaning. The third
movement returns to that heavy book, all explorations apparently a
failure. The poem has engaged in a search for meaning and has
tested two modes of seeing: vicariously through art and directly
through travel. Now it explores a third mode—imaginative vision.

Open the book. (The gilt rubs off the edges
of the pages and pollinates the fingertips.)
Open the heavy book. Why couldn't we have seen
this old Nativity while we were at it?

The search for graven truth is a failure, and the monuments and wonders observed in one's travels are corrupt, bewildering, or in decay; but one still has the imaginative strength to summon a vision that will answer, if only momentarily and conditionally, one's most pressing spiritual needs. This image-making power, which is fully aware of the value of irony, does not retreat from experience, but acts in response to it. The result, as seen in the conclusion of this poem, is one of the miracles of contemporary verse. Why couldn't we have seen:

> —the dark ajar, the rocks breaking with light,
> an undisturbed, unbreathing flame,
> colorless, sparkless, freely fed on straw,
> and, lulled within, a family with pets
> —and looked and looked our infant sight away.
>
> (CP, 58–59)

Ashbery's characterization of this conclusion's effect would be hard to improve on:

> Description and meaning, text and ornament, subject and object, the visible world and the poet's consciousness fuse together to form a substance that is undescribable and a continuing joy and one returns to it again and again, ravished and unsatisfied. After twenty years . . . I am unable to exhaust the meaning of its concluding line: "And looked and looked our infant sight away," and I suspect that its secret has very much to do with the secret of Miss Bishop's poetry. Looking, or attention, will absorb the object with its meaning."[17]

Bishop defines as she goes the dimensions and limitations of the experience. The flame must be a pictured flame because it breathes no air (or it may, after all, be a miracle). The colloquial language emphasizes not so much the divine qualities of the holy family as the domestic—"lulled within, a family with pets." If we could have found this experience on our pilgrimage, it would have been satisfying—we could have regained and fed "infant sight" instead of losing it to disillusionment.

Evidently, we *can't* see "this old Nativity" in the course of real travel. Balancing triumph and despair, the poem confronts a problem: How does one reconcile this private exaltation (which is real enough on its imagined plane) with one's mundane and frightening travels? Although an "old Nativity" offers a fiction of miraculous rebirth, it does not unify a dismaying array of incidents, just as ancient orders do not necessarily unify the modern world. "Over 2,000 Illustrations" suggests that a determination to find permanence and seriousness on one's secular pilgrimage is doomed to frustration—while exalting visionary moments are hard to apply in the outer world. But despite these limitations, one can still devote oneself to the freshness of "infant sight." To see with infant sight is not to return to childhood, but, far more difficult, to see, through the eyes of experience, with a child's curiosity and wonder.

Bishop works on the margin of Christian statement. As in so many of her best poems she takes a central Christian symbol and experiments with it in a secular context: her demands are those of a modern agnostic with a religious education and the spiritual expectations created by that education. Her New England Baptist background, with its lingering imperative to work out an individual accommodation with God, and to read God's providential message in the landscape, underlies the poem and lends it urgency. Travel, symbolic of mundane experience, needs something beyond itself to give it meaning. With this intent in mind, many of the poems in this book, especially "Cape Breton" and "A Cold Spring," can be interpreted as modern, ironic responses to religious imperatives.

These ideas could not have been presented in the form of a personal myth, for unlike so many of Bishop's modernist predecessors—Pound, Yeats, Eliot—Bishop is not seeking a myth so much as a way to see freshly. From her viewpoint, a myth is an inhibition. In this she is closer to William Carlos Williams than to other modernists. In fact, her work is even freer from myth than his. When Ashley Brown asked, "Do you think it is necessary for a poet to have a 'myth'—Christian or otherwise—to sustain his work?" she replied, "It all depends—some poets do, some don't. You must have something to sustain you, but perhaps you needn't be conscious of it. Look at Robert Lowell: he's written just as good poetry since he left the Church. Look at Paul Klee: he had 16 paintings going at once; *he* didn't have a formulated myth to look to, apparently, and his accomplishment was very considerable."[18] Bishop's lack of interest in personal myth is as characteristic as her refusal to impose her approach on others. She employed those exact words, "It all depends," as a blanket response to a battery of questions on poetic craft and creative psychology submitted by

John Ciardi for his anthology *Mid-Century American Poets*. Bishop's work stresses the value of *finding* beliefs rather than imposing them; refusing to commit oneself to dogma is an avenue to freedom. Like Keats, she would not "let go by a fine isolated versimilitude caught from the Penetralium of mystery, from being incapable of remaining content with half-knowledge."[19] However, Bishop's capacity for negative capability did not restrict her, anymore than it did Keats, to fine, isolated versimilitudes, despite the judgment of a few critics. Like Paul Klee, whom she deeply admired, she had a talent for discovering shape and order in a complex visual field. Many of her poems describe the unbeautiful or the awful, and yet her perceptions find a kind of asymmetrical permanence.

Bishop said that "perhaps you don't need to be conscious of what sustains you." I submit that what sustained her was devotion to the rewards of "infant sight," to what she called, in a letter to Anne Stevenson, "a self-forgetful, perfectly useless concentration."[20] This humble, unworldly intensity has surprising strength. It cuts through toward mystery, toward the supernatural significance (if you will) of ordinary domestic scenes, providing something to set against her Bible's meaningless engravings and the busy square of St. Peter's and the brothels of Marrakesh and the open graves of the desert. The material world offers objects for an almost religious self-abandonment.

Later in her interview with Ashley Brown, Bishop pointed out that "Some people crave organization more than others—the desire to get everything in its place."[21] Preserving the casual and disorderly aspect of experience usually led, she felt, to a more convincing kind of artistic order; this belief is mirrored in poems that quietly seek surprising yet convincing form. Nemerov noted in his review of *Poems*, "At her best she moves by means of accumulated details, and needs a good deal of space if the details are to connect without forcing.[22] Her best poems are comparatively long, and they may at first appear to be her loosest and most digressive, because they are also her most inclusive. Unengravable travels may seem random and even squalid, but they press on toward the ecstatic or melancholy consolations of mature understanding. She is able to sustain simultaneous awareness of the world's flatness and vacuity and of its fullness and wonder. As Ashbery phrased it, in Bishop's poetry, "The power of vision, 'our infant sight,' is both our torment and our salvation."[23]

«At the Fishhouses»

"At the Fishhouses" (1948) has an important place in Bishop's development quite apart from its extraordinary artistic merit, because it defines the vital role of history in Bishop's work, a role that numerous critics have dismissed too lightly. Stephen Stepanchev's evaluation is shared by others: "Unlike many of her Auden-influenced contemporaries, she distrusts history, with its melodramatic blacks and whites, and prefers geography, with its subtle gradations of color."[24] In support he quotes the famous concluding lines from "The Map" (1935), Bishop's first poem from her first book: "Typography displays no favorites; North's as near as West. / More delicate than the historians' are the map-makers' colors" (CP, 3). What Stepanchev had in mind is that Bishop's work, unlike that of friends and contemporaries like Lowell and Jarrell, rarely confronts the major turning points of history, and that is correct as far as it goes. But there is another kind of history, whose study is very much the trend among contemporary historians, that is vital to her work: that history reflected in what Braudel calls "The structure of everyday life." Poems like "At the Fishhouses" reflect on the quiet but decisive effect of history on ordinary people and the places they live in. "At the Fishhouses" closes with the recognition, subtly prepared, that "our knowledge is historical, flowing and flown" (CP, 66), a conclusion supported not only by this poem but by the bulk of her writing after 1939. There is a confusion in Stepanchev's formulation, one widely shared by other critics, that needs to be cleared up before discussion can proceed. This confusion turns on the difference between a mapmaker (or cartographer) and a geographer, a distinction that he (and many others) treat casually, as if they were equivalent. A mapmaker simply makes maps; he drafts a scaled-down abstraction of a charted world; he may even, as in "The Map," place arbitrarily chosen colors over the various countries in the interests of design. In her early work, Bishop might well be called a mapmaker—if one understands the mapmaker as an emblem for the symbolist artist—abstracting, coloring, and shifting the scale. But even her early work suggests a longing to move from cartography to geography. A geographer is a scientist who studies different places in terms of such elements as climate, soil, vegetation, population, industries, and national and political entities. The geographer has a much broader range of interests than the cartographer, and he can never ignore history, since history has placed its signature on the land and people. In her mature work, while Bishop retains a talent for abstraction and design that is felt in every line, she has deliberately shed the role of cartographer and adopted the role of geographer, a role that demands something like "total immersion"—as "At the Fishhouses" puts it (CP, 65)—in a place and its history. The poems of her middle phase, and to an even greater degree of her later, are devoted to reading the signature of history, not in terms of its dramatic events but in terms of its drifting accumulations.

That signature is evident in every detail of "At the Fishhouses." It explores a Nova Scotia seascape, a place worn by age and decline. Although the images are impressively lifelike, Bishop claimed in a letter that the donnée of the first verse paragraph came "in a dream,"[25] and dreamlike touches appear throughout. This is not simply history, but history transformed. An old man sits netting in the twilight, "his shuttle worn and polished," (CP, 64); she assembles the scene: the cold, the overpowering smell of codfish, the sky's uncertain light. Its queer lambent quality unifies and curiously elevates this rundown setting where "All is silver." But what is the poem's thrust—where is this vivid rumination taking us? Seeking an answer, the reader is forced to look closely at things—the sea, the tools, the light itself. Here:

> the heavy surface of the sea,
> swelling slowly as if considering spilling over,
> is opaque.

Implicitly, it appears to have some choice, though that choice is exercised indecisively. Time's signature on this place is ambiguous. Marked by losses, weathered by age, undermined by uncertainties, the setting can still be seen as imbued with an indefinable nobility, as well as sadness. Silver burnishes the gear that combs the sea:

> the silver of the benches,
> the lobster pots, and masts, scattered
> among the wild jagged rocks,
> is of an apparent translucence
> like the small old buildings with an emerald moss
> growing on their shoreward walls.

Each of these images discovers traces of sublimity in the weathered, the dull, the rough, the overgrown, the decayed. The silver of herring scales plasters iridescent wheelbarrows "with small iridescent flies crawling on them." Loveliness blends unnervingly with putrefaction and the parasites that thrive on it, in an atmosphere of nostalgia and loss. Here is history written visibly on surfaces.

This human world seems enervated, though briefly ennobled by fading light. Nor is the sea yet recognized as a source of life—rather it is the chief adversary; the chief source of wear; the dull, unwearying foe of those who live by it. The old man, like the "ancient wooden capstan," suggests the passing of more vigorous times. Small talk is casually but significantly of local decay: "the decline in the population." The old man, a destroyer of loveliness as well as an upholder of traditions, "has scraped the scales, the principle of beauty, / from unnumbered fish" (*CP*, 65). He is epitomized by his "black old knife, / the blade of which is almost worn away." The melancholy fatality of the scene reminds one of death and of the sweetness of passing things.

Then the poem moves abruptly away from the shore and turns toward the sea. A central opposition is implicit: the decaying human world set against the frigid, impenetrable (and alluring) North Atlantic. By comparison with the sea, the fishhouses are safe and homey, despite the smell of codfish and the aura of decay. The sea, when one looks down on it, is "Cold dark deep and absolutely clear, / element bearable to no mortal." Industries decline, men die, but the sea remains. Again we find Bishop ambivalently drawn to an image of icy beauty, but this one, unlike the imaginary iceberg, is clear, moving, a source of life as well as death. She seeks an intermediary and finds a playful one.

> One seal particularly
> I have seen here evening after evening.
> He was curious about me. He was interested in music;
> like me a believer in total immersion,
> so I used to sing him Baptist hymns.

The seal, a mammal, is both responsive and elusive—not held on the end of a fishline, as in "The Fish." The barriers are less extreme and the tone lighter, turning on the two meanings of "total immersion." Of course, Bishop was not a believer in the literal sense. Bishop *does* believe in total immersion in experience, but despite her yearning for immersion in this sea, she cannot enter it.

The seal will not leave his element; nor can one talk about the seal in other than human terms: *his* "interest" in music or the "sort of shrug" he gives while watching, "as if it were against his better judgment." So one turns at last away from the seal to repeat, with fresh emphasis, the characterization of the sea that holds one separate.

> Cold dark deep and absolutely clear,
> the clear gray icy water.

Here is a lucidity and depth that, earlier, the "opaque" sea, seen from a more landward angle, would not reveal. The observer glances back to the familiar land with its "million Christmas trees . . ./ waiting for Christmas." But it is not with the familiar—beautifully silvered, yes, but wearing out and dying—that one would remain. Bishop presses toward the unfathomed source. The observer has long stared at the cold sea, but no familiarity will render it comfortable or tame. The language takes on unlooked-for incantatory magnificence, created by telling repetition, assonance, and alliteration, as the mind drifts from observation toward meditation.

> I have seen it over and over, the same sea, the same,
> slightly, indifferently swinging above the stones,
> icily free above the stones,
> above the stones and then the world.

The startling turn in the final phrase takes one to a new dimension, broader and more deeply meditative. To personify the sea, to feel what we call its grand indifference, its immutability, culminates in discovering in the sea a hidden metaphor for knowledge, which emerges, at last, as the theme of these observations. Each perception, one now begins to recognize, has spoken of the heterogenity, mystery, and pain that is human knowing.

One knows the decay on land, and the transfiguring beauty of the light, but most of all one seeks to know the otherness of the sea: foreign, challenging, essential. The poem implicates the reader by referring for the first time to "you," inviting one to share

a recognition, in lines that are as hypnotically eloquent as any
Bishop ever wrote.

> If you should dip your hands in,
> your wrist would ache immediately,
> your bones would begin to ache and your hand would
>   burn
> as if the water were a transmutation of fire
> that feeds on stones and burns with a dark gray flame.
> If you tasted it, it would first taste bitter,
> then briny, then surely burn your tongue.
> It is like what we imagine knowledge to be:
> dark, salt, clear, moving, utterly free,
> drawn from the cold hard mouth
> of the world, derived from the rocky breasts
> forever, flowing and drawn, and since
> our knowledge is historical, flowing, and flown.
>
> (CP, 65–66)

Silver has given way decisively to gray. The sea, once hidden by a
temporary but blinding gloss, is now recognized for what it has
been all along, the chill gray milk of earthly knowledge, distilled
by harsh facts into an elixir of shocking clarity. Knowledge, like
the sea "dark, salt, clear, moving, utterly free," is desirable, but
numbing and frightening as well. You crave to "dip your hand in,"
to suckle at the "rocky breasts" of that stern mother. The same salt
sea that cracks the equipment of the old fisherman, whose cold
bars one from knowing a seal at firsthand, supplies a metaphor for
bitter knowledge drawn from history. Like all history, this knowledge can be distorted, lost, misinterpreted; it is "flowing, and
flown." To bear that awareness, even for a moment, is to stand firm
amidst uncertainties. Bishop admits that her construct is a trope;
the sea is *not* knowledge but "like what we imagine knowledge to
be." Even bitter truths can only be perceived metaphorically. This
symbol yields not pain only but tragic joy: joy at the knowledge of
and resignation to necessity. Like the narrator of "In Prison," the
poet seeks a form of "total immersion," but unlike him, she seeks
immersion in the chill and shifting sea of history. In Bishop's early
work she had celebrated the mapmakers' colors; now she calls for
the historians' in poetry that makes emblem and history come together.

Bishop compels the reader to follow the subtle turns of the eye (and mind) on the way toward this complex recognition. Her method makes her meaning. It was in the shifting realm of history that Bishop would choose to move and write. While she relished the delicate colors of the symbolists' introspective kingdom, and continued to employ them with masterly skill, her commitment to poetry based on history, both private and public, was reaffirmed and expanded in her next book, *Questions of Travel*. There she contemplated, and finally made, the artistic transition to Brazil that *A Cold Spring* had postponed. And she returned to her own past. The faith underlying present and future work was not the faith in God that sustain Gerard Manley Hopkins and George Herbert. Rather, it was a commitment to "the torment and salvation" of infant sight and to the validity, as the best we have, of historical knowledge.

LATER PHASE: HISTORY

1956–79

«Driving to the Interior»

QUESTIONS OF TRAVEL

«Brazil»
Public History

Conrad's Marlow is the paradigmatic wanderer in modern literature. His journey into the Congo, "one of the dark places of the earth," is a response to the promise of cartography, to the fatal allure of a river uncurling on a map: "The snake had charmed me." In "Heart of Darkness," as Marlow probes the recesses of the African subcontinent, he seems to move ever closer toward horrible knowledge. His journey has been read as an emblem for the homelessness of the modern truth-seeker. Elizabeth Bishop's *Questions of Travel* presents travels of a very different order. Bishop's response to her travels was far from the Conradian paradigm of the modern. For those many modern artists who have, of necessity, been homeless wanderers, expatriates seeking identity or asylum in foreign lands, travel has often symbolized deep and permanent alienation. By contrast, as the poet Charles Tomlinson complains in a review of *Questions of Travel,* "the fact of the matter is, Miss Bishop travels because she likes it, not because she is homeless in the way that Lawrence or Schoenberg were."[1] But, one might reply, what is so wrong with taking pleasure in travel? Bishop remarked in an interview with Alexandra Johnson, "I've never felt particularly homeless, but then, I've never felt particularly at home. I guess that's a pretty good description of a poet's sense of home. He carries it within him."[2] Bishop traveled to experience freshly, and in the process, she twice accidentally found a home, first in Key West, then in Brazil. Bishop's enjoyment did not set a limit on her insight into the cultures and climates she travels to. If anything, she is more alive to the unique character of native Brazilians than Conrad, with his absorption in European concerns, could be to blacks displayed by colonialism, despite Marlow's evident sympathy for the sufferings of the "niggers" who cross his path to Kurtz. To insist that the traveler suffer suggests a kind of cultural masochism, and Bishop, in fact, knew more about homelessness—and suffering—than she readily let on. What matters finally in "Heart of Darkness" is the return to Europe, now seen with new vision. What matters for Bishop are the objects before her eyes. Every place is equally home; each has an equal claim on attention and allegiance.

Bishop's contemporary Delmore Schwartz, in an essay entitled "The Isolation of Modern Poetry" (1941), saw himself inevitably cut off from meaningful commerce. "The modern poet has had nothing to do, no serious activity other than the cultivation of his own sensibility."[3] Schwartz's conviction led to an artistic dead end that served to frustrate a notable talent. Bishop's appetite for fresh experience enabled her to grow artistically while escaping the constriction and self-pity fostered by unrelieved self-contemplation. She settled in Brazil after having abandoned the remainder of a freighter trip around South America. She wrote to Robert Lowell four month's later, from Lota de Macedo Soares's house in the mountain resort of Petropolis, forty miles from Rio: "I'd started out intending to go all over the continent but I seem to have become a Brazilian home-body, and I get just as excited now over a jeep trip to buy kerosene in the next village as I did in November at the thought of my trip around the Horn." She went on to relate: "After a couple of weeks of rain . . . the cook left, and for about a month I did the cooking—I like to cook, etc., but I'm not used to being confronted with the raw materials, all un-shelled, un-blanched, un-skinned, or un-dead . . . Well, I can cook goat now—with wine sauce." Here were experiences to cultivate that took her outside her own sensibility and cultural preconceptions toward the unforeseen and surprising. *Questions of Travel* shifts in the direction of geography and history in the raw, toward aspects of travel once shunned for the more delicate and hermetic realm of mapmaking, that emblem of the symbolist aesthetic. Her readings are in private and cultural history, not political history. She explores the history behind feeling and domestic action, and her observations are made on the scene rather than in libraries—but they are concerned with history, nonetheless. Bishop sees the effects of history freshly and unpredictably—no poem is quite like another. In "At the Fishhouses" Bishop recognized that "our knowledge is historical." History, broadly defined, may be called the overriding concern of her final phase. In *Questions of Travel*, she explores the cultural history of Brazil and her own private history as a child in Nova Scotia. In *Geography III*, her last book, public and private history intersect in poems that are, for me, Bishop's most trenchant and affecting.

For all its implicit stress on the effects of history, there is something appealingly casual about Bishop's exploration of Brazil, and it is fitting that her decision to stay there had its source in an accident. Brazil, first seen in November 1951, when she was forty, was to be the first stop on a cruise around South America. Santos harbor was to be merely the first of many ports of entry. However, an allergic reaction to cashew fruit kept her recuperating for several months; meanwhile, she fell in love with the country, so much so that she canceled the rest of her trip. Of great importance in this decision, certainly, was the intimate relationship that developed between Bishop and an old friend, Lota de Macedo Soares, whom Bishop had known in New York some years earlier. The person to whom *Questions of Travel* is dedicated, Lota Soares was a remarkable woman, an intelligent, witty, talented member of the Brazilian social and political elite; she was able to bring Bishop quickly to the center of Brazilian artistic and intellectual life. They shared an apartment in Rio for many years and designed and built a country house in Petropolis that won architectural awards. After staying in Brazil for more than eighteen months, Bishop wrote to Lowell,

> I don't feel "out of touch" or "expatriated" or anything like that, or suffer from lack of intellectual life, etc—I was always too shy to have much "intercommunication" in New York, anyway, and I was miserably lonely there most of the time—here I am extremely happy, for the first time in my life. I live in a spectacularly beautiful place; we have between us about 3,000 books now; I know, through Lota, most of the Brazilian "intellectuals" already and I find the people frank,—startlingly so, until you get used to Portuguese vocabularies—extremely affectionate—an atmosphere that I just lap up—no, I guess I mean

loll in—after that dismal year in Washington and that dismaler winter at Yaddo when I though my days were numbered and there was nothing to be done about it.[5]

It is evident that in a number of ways, Bishop then felt more at home in Brazil than she did in the States. And there certainly was plenty to *see*.

The "Brazil" poems are mostly impersonal. Bishop does not make the jungle a symbol for inner turmoil. Her symbolic recognitions are both less archetypal and more varied than that. She involves herself in "externals": the manners, character, and history of a place are revealed for her in neglected details. These provide the meanings that move people, and as such they demand the permanence of art. In these poems, as Lowell said, she "makes the casual perfect."[6] In a 1919 essay examining why Ben Jonson's poetry is inadequately appreciated, T. S. Eliot suggested that it is because: "his poetry is of the surface. Poetry of the surface cannot be understood without study; for to deal with the surface of life, as Jonson dealt with it, is to deal so deliberately that one must be deliberate in order to understand. . . . Unconscious does not speak to unconscious, no swarms of inarticulate feelings are aroused."[7] We remain on this kind of surface in Bishop's Brazil. This deliberate attention to life's surface has troubled some readers. Jerome Mazzaro, for example, finds her too "realistic," and overly self-conscious about detail: "the separate observations of her poems do not gain from appearing in concert with one another. An unconscious element which might here serve as the link by way of recurrent, unresolved patterns is minimal. In fact, one has to conclude in the absence of such unresolved, recurrent patterns that Miss Bishop is an inordinately conscious poet."[8] While in early poems of psychic frustration such as "The Weed" unconscious does speak to unconscious as the poet explores "recurrent, unresolved patterns," in these poems the echo of passionate complaint that for many readers *is* poetry is missing. What these poems offer instead is a sensibility so finely tuned that it vibrates to stimuli too delicate and evanescent to be caught by other instruments. Bishop shows that poems can have depth and resonance without emotional turmoil.

Bishop lived in Brazil for eighteen years, from 1951 until 1969. Afterwards, she continued to return, during vacations from teaching at Harvard, to an eighteenth-century house she restored in Ouro Prêto. The poems in the "Brazil" section of *Questions of Travel* constitute a sequence, as Kalstone was the first to notice, creating a narrative of an observer's growing cultural insight and even identification with what she observed. In the first poems a tourist sorts out the perplexities of a new and alien culture. Everything—customs, typography, climate, postage stamps—is charged with odd significance that can't quite be explained. In succeeding poems one begins to imagine one's way into the Brazilian mind, coming alive to the experience and history that helped create it. The book's other section, entitled "Elsewhere," is more personal. It explores Bishop's own past. Life in Brazil evidently provided the distance needed to come to terms with very painful childhood experiences. A crucial event from that past, the moment of her mother's decisive relapse into insanity (which occurred when the poet was five) is explored in the remarkable "In the Village." These works explore private history, the remembered country of Nova Scotia and Massachusetts that shaped the adult writer.

The book begins with a three-poem series that asks (and answers) related questions of travel. "Arrival at Santos," published in the *New Yorker* in 1952 (a year after Elizabeth Bishop actually landed in Santos harbor), dramatizes a supremely casual initiation into a new culture and geography. The poem punctures the tourist's inflated expectations with prosaic, unforeseen facts. The tourist-speaker arrives with heady expectations and with senses starved by an ocean voyage. What is found cannot fulfill those expectations, raising the implicit question: "Can reality ever live up to imagination?"

> Here is a coast; here is a harbor;
> here, after a meager diet of horizon, is some scenery:
> impractically shaped and—who knows?—self-pitying
>   mountains,
> sad and harsh beneath their frivolous greenery,
>
>
> with a little church on top of one. And warehouses,
> some of them painted a feeble pink, or blue,
> and some tall, uncertain palms. Oh, tourist,
> is this how this country is going to answer you

and your immodest demands for a different world,
and a better life, and complete comprehension
of both at last, and immediately,
after eighteen days of suspension?   (*CP,* 89)

Although the poem is composed of rhymed *a b c b* quatrains, they
have the most offhand feeling imaginable. This feeling is achieved
partly through the extremely elaborate punctuation, which ap-
proximates the pauses and starts of speech. Prose rhythms pre-
dominate, and the unusual rhymes (comprehension / suspension)
fall so lightly in mid sentence that they seem almost accidental.
Disappointment shows in the personifying modifiers: "impracti-
cally," "self-pitying," "sad," "harsh," "feeble," "uncertain." These
evoke a setting tinged with overtones of human weakness or failure
that the observer condescendingly imposes. The disappointed tourist does not care to be really precise, as the shrugged "who knows?"
suggests. The setting is considered abstractly: "*a* coast; . . . *a* harbor"; the observer acknowledges that the place fits its genre as a
travel setting, without yet accepting its particularity. As in "Over
2,000 Illustrations," the setting fails to meet an admittedly "immodest" demand for spiritual identification, a demand edged here
by self-mockery. At times one must face much worse than "eighteen days of suspension." At length, the expectant tourist is di-
verted from reverie and is immersed in the business of safely
disembarking, of helping Miss Breen, a fellow traveler, get free of
a boat hook. This Miss Breen, another North American, is odder
and more "real" than anything the tourist has noticed in Brazil
so far:

> Miss Breen is about seventy,
> a retired police lieutenant, six feet tall,
> with beautiful bright blue eyes and a kind expression.

Like a character out of Forster, she startles us with invincible actuality. Continually, mundane concerns like getting one's bourbon
past customs interrupt more elevated contemplation. Of course,
it is just these irritating distractions that introduce one to the
impossible-to-imagine particularities that make up a new place: the
flag, the melting heat, the crates of coffee beans, the twenty-six
freighters waiting to load them.

The tone is offhand, witty, detached, and the traveler's urgent queries are merely deferred:

> Ports are necessities, like postage stamps, or soap,
>
> but they seldom seem to care what impression they make,
> or, like this, only attempt, since it does not matter,
> the unassertive colors of soap, or postage stamps—
> wasting away like the former, slipping the way the latter
>
> do when we mail the letters we wrote on the boat,
> either because the glue here is very inferior
> or because of the heat. We leave Santos at once;
> we are driving to the interior.   (CP, 90)

Although the port seems disappointing, the poem ends abruptly on a note of dark promise. After "driving to the interior," more of one's "immodest demands for a different world" may find answers. But the imagination is not really starved by Santos. It is merely stimulated in unlooked-for ways. The poem's most incisive irony is directed, not at the port, but at the traveler, who cannot be certain what to make of a scene that does not fit one's preconceptions. This irony is heightened when one takes the poem in sequence. The deftly characterized observer, a version of the poet, has not yet recognized the rich background of life that the dull port actually promises.

The second of the initial three-poem series that deals with the shock the expectant imagination receives from unlooked-for actualities is a neglected masterpiece, "Brazil, January 1, 1502." One of Bishop's rare considerations of a big historical event, it contemplates the moment at which the first Portuguese explorers landed on a bay that they supposed the mouth of a great river, the Rio de Janeiro, or River of January. Since January is summer in Brazil, they found the vegetation at its most lush. When creating any scene, Bishop implicitly dramatizes the way an observer's mental set conditions the response. For these Portuguese explorers, the wild life imitates art because their eyes are trained to see it that way. And as she suggests, this mental set of Brazil's conquerors has far-reaching historical consequences.

The epigraph from Sir Kenneth Clark's *Landscape into Art*, ". . .

embroidered nature . . . tapestried landscape," leads into a poem in which landscape is seen as tapestry. Clark refers to the *hortus conclusus*, the enclosed garden of medieval and early Renaissance art.[9] The Christian conquerors view the lush Brazilian landscape in terms of the familiar enclosed gardens so often celebrated in tapestries back home. Here is a wilderness to explore and command, to enclose as art. The opening lines, "Januaries, Nature greets our eyes / exactly as she must have greeted theirs" (*CP*, 91), suggest how little Rio's lush summer has changed since that January when the Portuguese landed. The viewpoint is complex because the landscape is actually seen through "our" modern eyes, while "their" experience is imagined. For them nature is female; by implication, Brazil is a woman approached by bold males. Bishop implies that little has changed, either in terms of what is seen or in the way the viewer responds to it. Modern readers share assumptions with the earlier Portuguese that make them see this landscape as a tapestry to be possessed:

> every square inch filling in with foliage—
> big leaves, little leaves, and giant leaves,
> blue, blue-green, and olive,
> with occasional lighter veins and edges,
> or a satin underleaf turned over;
> monster ferns
> in silver-gray relief,
> and flowers, too, like giant water lilies
> up in the air—up, rather, in the leaves—
> purple, yellow, two yellows, pink,
> rust red and greenish white;
> solid but airy; fresh as if just finished
> and taken off the frame.

This rich piling-on of interwoven color is as luxurious as the newest and most extravagant embroidery. The involuted, "embroidered" syntactical variety of this slowly unfolding opening evokes not only the scene itself but a leisurely way of experiencing a woven world that gains texture from each shred of light and shadow and tonal nuance. The Portuguese discover a landscape corresponding, *not* to any reality they had actually seen, but to "embroidered nature," often dreamed of but never before experienced.

Here again is the mind in action; "our" observations parallel those of the early conquerors. The Portuguese found the summer landscape of Rio, "not unfamiliar," but corresponding to an ingrained iconography. Here are "big symbolic birds;" here "in the foreground" is "Sin: / five sooty dragons near some massy rocks." Here, also (Hell and Eden blending), the moss seems to burn:

> in lovely hell-green flames,
> attacked above
> by scaling-ladder vines, oblique and neat,
> "one leaf yes and one leaf no" (in Portuguese).

The Portuguese read evil into the landscape, employing old sayings and familiar theological terms, while exotic flora suggest analogies to ladders and language. Moreover, to these male viewers, the femme fatale remains in evidence even among the reptiles:

> The lizards scarcely breathe; all eyes
> are on the smaller, female one, back-to,
> her wicked tail straight up and over,
> red as a red-hot wire.   (CP, 92)

Females, even the female scorpion—offering herself yet threatening—are a locus of fascination and danger in the Portuguese mythology.

The response of the European conquerors is in many ways like a modern, "civilized" one. The tendencies to appreciate aesthetically and to see symbolically are still with us, and we still have the knack of shielding our self-esteem while we pursue base ends. While the explorers' response is arrogant, it is also serviceable. It renders an imposing landscape less bewildering and shows them how to behave:

> Just so the Christians, hard as nails,
> tiny as nails, and glinting,
> in creaking armor, came and found it all,
> not unfamiliar:
> no lovers' walks, no bowers,
> no cherries to be picked, no lute music,
> but corresponding, nevertheless,
> to an old dream of wealth and luxury
> already out of style when they left home—
> wealth, plus a brand-new pleasure.

As something already known, as a courtly or Edenic or even hellish dream, as something other than its simple self, the Christian conquerors can understand Brazil. However, these Christians are the victims of quiet irony. They are "hard as nails, / tiny as nails." Their bright polish and culture is really an affront to the landscape they mean to bend to their will, and in magnificence and scope it dwarfs them and makes them seem obdurate and mean. Casual, pious conquerors, humming a bawdy popular air set to a sacred text on their way from Mass, they set about to apply their interpretation of God's injunction in the original Eden to "Be fruitful and multiply, and replenish the earth, and subdue it: and have dominion . . . over all the earth, and over every living thing that moveth upon the earth." For they know exactly what to do! And they seem to feel it will be no difficult task. They pursue that "brand new pleasure" (rape) with a conqueror's gusto:

> they ripped away into the hanging fabric,
> each out to catch an Indian for himself—
> those maddening little women kept calling,
> calling to each other (or had the birds waked up?)
> and retreating, always retreating behind it.

Their will to see foliage as tapestry dramatizes how their educated eyes confront reality. To achieve the brand-new pleasure of rape, which they are free to enjoy when loosed from the controls of home, they must attack that tapestried paradise of their illusions. Like the travelers in the previous poem, they are "driving to the interior," and their demands are surely "immodest," but they are doomed to frustration—they never catch the maddening women! The ripest fruit of conquest eludes them. In Brazil, these conquerors are at once supported by familiar visions and freed of law. Their observations are suavely superficial and, in effect, immoral. The landscape will be reshaped by them, nevertheless. Insofar as one is likely to share their assumptions, Bishop exposes one's unconscious complicity in the rape of a land, a rape performed without remorse or self-consciousness—not explicitly in the name of lust, but rather in the name of art and in the name of God. But the jungle may have the last laugh. The fact that it still remains a lush and vital tapestry, just as it was in 1502, implies that it has never been enclosed or conquered.

As I've suggested before, when critics, taking the conclusion of

"The Map" as their main text, argue that Elizabeth Bishop is always the mapmaker, never the historian, and when, with Jan B. Gordon, they assert that "In her craft, as in her life, geography always triumphs over history,"[10] they overlook two things: that "The Map" is a very early poem, and that poems such as "Brazil, January 1, 1502" demonstrate the interdependence of geography and history. To separate geography from history is a fundamental error. Although the great turning points of history only rarely form the basis for her poems, she successfully evokes the historically conditioned sensibility of those living in a place, as well as how the place has been shaped by its inhabitants. She continued this historical inquiry throughout *Questions of Travel*. Uncovering the causal determinants of local habits of being, Bishop makes the historians' function a part of the poets'.

The third poem in the opening series, "Questions of Travel," begins with the distresses attendant upon life in Brazil: "There are too many waterfalls here." It ends by choosing travel, with its stimulus to the imagination, over the imagination unaided by travel. But to travel is to take risks, to experience shocks and surprises that upset our daydream visions of a place. If the Portuguese arriving in 1502, full of dreams of a verdant Eden, imagined the place "not unfamiliar," the modern North American will find much that is unsettling, an excess of wildness and beauty. The observer will feel the weight of too much experience, too much moving water, too much humidity, too many clouds, excesses that weren't anticipated from the safety of home.

> The crowded streams
> hurry too rapidly down to the sea,
> and the pressure of so many clouds on the
>   mountaintops
> makes them spill over the sides in soft slow-motion,
> turning to waterfalls under our very eyes.   (CP, 93)

These are the excesses of a country whose language, as Bishop told Ashley Brown, has "no word . . . for understatement," yet they have a certain dreamy loveliness. Waterfalls, "those streaks, those mile-long, shiny, tearstains," drive her to "Think of the long trip home," and imply a desire to be at home, away from nature's sadness. The oft-imagined waterfalls of Brazil have proved not disappointing—but *too much*:

> Should we have stayed at home and thought of here?
> Where should we be today?
> Is it right to be watching strangers in a play
> in this strangest of theatres?

Perhaps there is even something immoral in one's hunger to see.

> What childishness is it that while there's a breath of life
> in our bodies, we are determined to rush
> to see the sun the other way around?
> The tiniest green hummingbird in the world? . . .
> Oh, must we dream our dreams
> and have them, too?

In Brazil one's most extravagant daydreams find fulfillment. But if we dream our dreams and *have* them, too, they will no longer satisfy the immodest demands of the imagination, because they will have become realities.

The competing claims of imagination and reality have had, of course, a long tradition in romantic literature. Wordsworth's "Yarrow Unvisited" provides a concise statement of the romantic belief in the superiority of imagination:

> Be Yarrow stream unseen, unknown:
> It must, or we shall rue it:
> We have a vision of our own;
> Ah! Why should we undo it?

Wordsworth later commented regarding his sequel, "Yarrow Visited:" "As I had succeeded in *Yarrow Unvisited,* I was anxious there should be no falling off; but that was unavoidable, perhaps, from the subject, as imagination almost always transcends reality."[11] Up to this point, Bishop's poem seems to agree with Wordsworth. It may have been a mistake to undo that "vision of our own." But as the poem proceeds, it turns Wordsworth's belief inside out. More than a century after Wordsworth's "Yarrow," in "Arrival at the Waldorf," Wallace Stevens felt similarly torn between the "wild country of the soul" discovered in a bare hotel room upon returning "Home from Guatemala" and the reality of the tropics left behind: "that alien, point-blank, green and actual Guatemala."[12] The Brazil that Bishop's poem goes on to detail encompasses much that is simplified out of Stevens's abstract vision of a "point-blank" Guatemala. Brazil here is more than Stevens's stark pole of actuality, symbolically opposed to the wild country discovered by pure imagination in a blank room. It is a place with a history and a social climate, each of which is capable of *commanding* the imagination. Against the claims of pure imagination, the poem recalls a succession of particular observations that could not have been imagined if we had simply "thought of here":

> But surely it would have been a pity
> not to have seen the trees along this road,
> really exaggerated in their beauty,
> not to have seen them gesturing
> like noble pantomimists, robed in pink.   (CP, 93–94)

Such startling facts as these are real surprises that imagination cannot transcend but instead must serve.

These particulars have no obvious usefulness. But they are full of spiritually elevating mystery:

> inexplicable old stonework,
> inexplicable and impenetrable,
> at any view,
> instantly seen and always, always delightful.   (CP, 93)

What cannot be explained can still be savored. Bishop *does* travel because she likes it, and a chief aim is to convey pleasure in the factual world, but much *can* be explained. It would have been a pity:

> —Not to have had to stop for gas and heard
> the sad, two-noted, wooden tune
> of disparate wooden clogs
> carelessly clacking over
> a grease-stained filling-station floor,
> (In another country the clogs would all be tested.
> Each pair there would have identical pitch.)
> —A pity not to have heard
> the other, less primitive music of the fat brown bird
> who sings above the broken gasoline pump
> in a bamboo church of Jesuit baroque:
> three towers, five silver crosses.
> —Yes, a pity not to have pondered,

blurr'dly and inconclusively,
on what connection can exist for centuries
between the crudest wooden footwear
and, careful and finicky,
the whittled fantasies of wooden cages.
—Never to have studied history in
the weak calligraphy of songbirds' cages.   (CP, 94)

These details, far from randomly chosen, bring a culture alive through the senses. One hears the "sad . . . tune" of the wooden shoes in the phrase "clogs / carelessly clacking." The whole passage is a marvel of prosody, with prose rhythms modulating subtly into understated lyricism. The cultural history one studies in "weak calligraphy" reveals why it is less important that the gas pump work than that the unbeautiful "fat brown bird," a source of elegant music, have an elegant chapel for a cage. The intricacies of this culture (as the songbirds' cages attest) are not the intricacies of commerce or technology but the intricacies of devotion—to iconography, tradition, and craftsmanship. Here, the mapmaker's "delicate colors" merge with the historians' careful records, and the smallest details lead to large conclusions. Bishop discovers consolation of a kind that could never have been derived purely from "thinking of here." No cartographer could have conveyed this sort of cluttered richness.

Bishop has responded decisively to the fear troubling her first work, that imagination must impose solipsism. Instead, having sketched unanticipated, unengravable travels, she concludes, with just the hint of a question:

> "Or could Pascal have been not entirely right
> about just sitting quietly in one's room?"

This poem suggests that Bishop would choose Brazil over Pascal's cell or Guatemala over Stevens's room at the Waldorf every time. But the most alert of our tourists may still be homeless:

> "Continent, city, country, society:
> the choice is never wide and never free.
> And here, or there . . . No. Should we have stayed at home,
> wherever that may be?

A significant minority of critics have protested what they consider the moral neutrality of Bishop's work. They point, for instance, to the rhetorical question that concludes "Questions of Travel," and argue, with Gordon, that "Responsibility rarely derives from rhetorical questions."[13] However, the clear point of Bishop's meditation is that one must grasp experience, must make difficult, decisive choices. That this is posed as a question is characteristic of Bishop's lifelong commitment to capture the mind in action. She presents her conclusion as still tentative, phrased in the moment of discovery—here, being jotted in a notebook. The poem implicitly answers the question, *"Is it lack of imagination that makes us come / to imagined places, not just stay at home?"* with a firm NO. The imagery gives abundant evidence that the imagination is stimulated rather than starved by the challenging facts of travel. One must make choices and live with them, make the most of circumstances. By staying "at home"—safe amidst vicarious imaginings; charmed by, say, a printed map—one will surely find consolations and avoid discomforts, but one will miss graphic, inexplicable, exaggerated, consoling realities. Bishop lived her conclusions. By remaining in Brazil and continuing to observe it with fidelity, Bishop chose travel over *"just sitting quietly in one's room."* Implicitly, but clearly, this poem and the work that follows it accepts the responsibility to report the unforeseen and the overlooked with faithfulness, humor, and zest. This may not seem like responsibility to the disciples of gloom and dullness, but for Bishop it was sufficient to inspire her most decisive work.

The opening poems in the "Brazil" section present the observer as foreigner. The next several poems move towards comprehending a new, more native point of view. They describe not merely places but people, creating a well-populated geography. Some offer a shrewd exterior view of Brazilians, while others trace the intimate mental world of their subjects, disclosing, in the process, a growing imaginative command of the land and its inhabitants. Her insight and affection produced not just poetry but also a significant quantity of other writing: the translation of the classic *Minha Vida de Menina* (literally, "My Life as a Little Girl"), which was called in English *The Diary of "Helena Morley"* (1957); a number of fine translations of important Brazilian poets reprinted in *The Complete Poems; An Anthology of Twentieth Century Brazilian Poetry*, co-edited with Emanuel Brasil (1972); and *Brazil* (1962), a travel book for Life World Library. This was a flood of literary production by Bishop's standards. One public recognition of this effort was a medal, the order of Rio Branco, from the Brazilian government in appreciation of her work on behalf of her adopted nation.

Bishop came to know Brazil at every social level; wherever she lived, she always developed acquaintance with people of all classes. She was godmother to village children, addressed by all as "Dona Elizabetchy." This only made her more acutely aware of the difficulties with which her poorer neighbors struggled. "Manuelzinho," for example, examines the barriers dividing two of those neighbors, one rich and one poor. It is told from the point of view of "A friend of the writer" (Lota Soares according to a letter to Moore),[14] presenting that friend's assumptions and perplexities regarding this "Half squatter, half tenant (no rent)—/ a sort of inheritance" (CP, 96). To overlook that this is a dramatic monologue, exploring two specific points of view, the speaker's and Manuelzinho's, both of which are separate from Bishop's, would be, I suspect to dismiss the poem as condescending, with a remark like Tomlinson's, "The better-off have always preferred their poor processed by style."[15] It is worth remembering that Wordsworth, another "better-off" poet, created, in poems like "Michael" and "The Ruined Cottage," some of the finest poems about the rural poor that we are ever likely to have. Like Wordsworth, Bishop admired, wherever she found it, the power of quiet endurance and faith. In "Manuelzinho," Bishop observes a poor man with empathy and humor, but she also implicitly presents her observations of leading characteristics of the Brazilian gentry: their paternalism, their puzzlement at the curious ways of their tenants, and, yes, their condescension. Condescension is the implicit but central issue of the poem. Sympathetic but trapped in an outmoded feudal relationship, Manuelzinho's boss is often distrustful. She expresses affection colored by anger—dutiful protectiveness, even admiration, blend with frustration, vexation, and incomprehension, since by necessity Manuelzinho lives a life whose values are totally different from hers:

> I watch you through the rain,
> trotting, light, on bare feet,
> up the steep paths you have made—
> or your father and grandfather made—
> all over my property,
> with your head and back inside

a sodden burlap bag,
and I feel I can't endure it
another minute; then,
indoors, beside the stove,
keep on reading a book.

The narrator consciously brings out the differences. Her own comfortable superiority receives at least as much irony as her tenant's odd ways. Bishop's vantage point makes it clear that Manuelzinho's curious antics are forced upon him as he attempts to maintain his autonomy under compromising circumstances. Bishop refuses to swath Manuelzinho in a plaster cast of false dignity. We see him warts and all, clinging to what shreds of individuality and pride he can muster.

You paint—heaven knows why—
the outside of the crown
and brim of your straw hat.
        .   .   .   .   .

One was bright green. Unkindly,
I called you Klorophyll Kid.
My visitors thought it was funny.
I apologize here and now.   (CP, 99)

In apologizing, the speaker tacitly admits that the fun she makes is unfair. The poem in certain ways recalls "The Fish." Both begin with the minute examination of a figure from another world through the itemization of attributes, leading to partial understanding and a sense of accommodation. But in "The Fish" the poet had to go to the animal world to identify a creature of sympathy; here she could turn to a complex man living at a definable cultural moment:

You helpless, foolish man,
I love you all I can,
I think. Or do I?
I take off my hat, unpainted
and figurative, to you.
Again I promise to try.

Like the fish, Manuelzinho is a being whose autonomy the poet cannot or will not compromise. If there is ever to be a meeting of the minds, it will not be, the speaker acknowledges, solely on her terms. The poet's basic honesty and refusal to embrace simple slogans are admirable. Underlying the poem is Christianity's radical imperative to "love thy neighbor," which the poem counterpoints against the actual difficulty of doing so. The speaker's acknowledgment of her own unwitting condescension is an achievement on the path to more complete understanding. It is a path that, the poem admits, may never be traveled to the end.

Bishop's staying in Brazil for so long was, as I have said, decisively influenced by her relationship with Lota de Macedo Soares. The beautiful house that the two of them designed and built together in Petropolis, the old imperial summer capital, was one of the "three loved houses" whose loss Bishop would lament in "One Art" (1976). Bishop described it to Lowell as "an ultra-modern house up on the side of a black granite mountain, with a waterfall at one end, clouds coming into the living room in the middle of the conversation, etc." The same letter begins: "Heavens—I started this yesterday & got interrupted & left the typewriter uncovered over night & I have just had to brush off a large thick cobweb."[16] "Song for the Rainy Season" (1960) celebrates this place and the life that Bishop found sustaining for many years. It is one of the finest love poems written in the last three decades. Here was a life tarnished, perhaps, by humidity and fog, and also by guilt, but comforting nonetheless:

> Hidden, oh hidden
> in the high fog
> the house we live in,
> beneath the magnetic rock,
> rain-, rainbow-ridden,
> where blood-black
> bromelias, lichens,
> owls, and the lint
> of the waterfalls cling,
> familiar, unbidden.   (CP, 101)

The tone is complex. For one thing, the "we" is discrete yet important. Rarely, in her earlier poetry, does Bishop even hint at such casual domestic intimacy. The atmosphere of the house is too humid (another letter mentions a Schwitters painting "that has to be watched for termites and mildew constantly")[17] yet the hiding fog is a comfort as well as a trouble. The poem lives on its extraordinary ambiguity of connotation; would anyone else think to call a place "rain-, rainbow-ridden"? One may notice, moreover, a counterpointing of consonance and dissonance, of soothing assonance and smoothly alliterative *l*'s, set against spikey *k*'s and *b*'s. The language and imagery reflect an underlying moral tension, and, even more important, a vivid awareness of transience.

The place is encircled by monotony, lust, and rapacity, like almost anywhere, but here nature, not man, is the repository for these baser elements. At night:

> the ordinary brown
> owl gives us proof
> he can count:
> five times—always five—
> he stamps and takes off
> after the fat frogs that,
> shrilling for love,
> clamber and mount.

A "dim age / of water" holds the house "in a private cloud." The cloud hides one from the outside world, but also opens the house to different forms of life: not only

> to the white dew
> and the milk-white sunrise
> kind to the eyes   (*CP*, 101–2)

but also

> to membership
> of silver fish, mouse,
> bookworms,
> big moths   (*CP*, 102)

who are willy-nilly citizens of this community. (*Membership* is a suggestive word.) Indeed, this hotbed of surprising intimacies, weighted with the heavy air, the pervading fog, secures a life of hermetic closeness:

> darkened and tarnished
> by the warm touch
> of the warm breath,

maculate, cherished,
rejoice!

These lines are the emotional center of the poem and arguably the emotional center of her stay in Brazil. Although her life is "maculate," with traces of guilt or uneasiness, it is also cherished, a product of sensuous intimacy, "the warm touch / of the warm breath" not only of humidity but also of love. The emotional loading of language and imagery implies a very personal symbolism.

Unlike Bishop's earlier love poems, which, though similarly reticent, record the frustration and even the numbness of the isolated self in "Insomnia" "by the universe deserted," "Song for the Rainy Season" depicts a world of love hidden and stained (perhaps by guilt as much as by mildew) and yet to be rejoiced in. It is "small" and "shadowy," like the inner world of so many Bishop fables, but far more imagistically varied. Behind that rejoicing, though, lies the old fear of loss: killing, intimidating loss that will come in "a later / era" when,

> Without water
> the great rock will stare
> unmagnetized, bare,
> no longer wearing
> rainbows or rain,
> the forgiving air
> and the high fog gone;
> the owl moves on
> and several
> waterfalls shrivel
> in the steady sun.

Better "too many waterfalls here" than none at all. Although this is a vision of a universally catastrophic future, with the rock stripped of its garments—fog and rain and "forgiving" air—it betrays fear of coming private loss. Though the private element of the passage is sublimated, an inevitable future that might seem (in geological terms) impossibly remote is made to appear frighteningly close.

"Song for the Rainy Season" echoes the theme of Auden's "That night that joy began," with the significant twist that Bishop's poem reverses the central trope, rejoicing in the forgiveness of the hiding fog, not in the vision of open, guiltless fields. The scope that Auden longs for is (characteristically) inverted in Bishop's poem. But Bishop's instinct for enclosure and safety has led to a more satisfying form of hermeticism, since the (unnamed) beloved is *inside* rather than *outside* enclosure. (Only a mocking mirror-image of the beloved could be found in the bedroom in "Insomnia.") When the exposing sun burns off the "high fog" and the "forgiving air" and "shrivels" the waterfalls, the owl, symbol of lusty vitality, "will move on." In symbolic terms, exposure is a kind of death. It is evidently Lota of whom she writes in "One Art:"

> —Even losing you (the joking voice, a gesture
> I love) I shan't have lied. It's evident
> the art of losing's not too hard to master
> though it may look like (*Write* it!) like disaster. (*CP*, 178)

Evidently "a later / era" did differ from this one. The feared loss occurred, but before it did, there was something to rejoice in. Confident in domestic intimacy, she expressed less and less the sense of inevitable personal and artistic alienation basic to her earlier poetry. Redolent of humidity and imperfection, tinged by presentiments of loss, this poem embraces it all, even while confessing its transience.

Brazil often appears as a tainted wonderland—vibrant, entertaining, surprising, but morally ambiguous and often frustrating or sad. Throughout her Brazilian period, Bishop proved herself able to treat the most intricate philosophical meditations and moral inquiries in poems that are essentially imagistic and almost entirely free of explicit value statements. Her development along these lines would prove important not only for herself but for her friend Robert Lowell and a range of younger poets. One such poem, "The Armadillo" (1957), had a decisive effect on Lowell at a moment in June 1957 when he was attempting to free himself from the elaborate obscurities of his earlier style, a moment when he had begun to feel that "my own poems seemed like prehistoric monsters dragged down into the bog and death by their ponderous armor."[18] Lowell's stylistic transformation culminating in *Life Studies* has often been discussed, but while Lowell repeatedly acknowledged his debt to Bishop, the specifics of that debt have received little critical attention.

In the summer of 1957, Robert Lowell's art had arrived at a pivotal moment. Lowell, who had written hardly a poem in four years, had felt for some time that his old, highly inflected style was impossible, and he turned in 1955 to autobiographical prose as an outlet. His drafts of an unpublished autobiography were to culminate in the remarkable prose memoir "91 Revere Street" that introduces the autobiographical poems of *Life Studies*. Lowell speaks in "91 Revere Street" of the need to recover and reinterpret his past through things, each of which "has its function, its history, its drama. . . . The things and their owners come back urgent with life and meaning—because finished, they are endurable and perfect."[19] Having approached the past through a rhetoric of things in this prose memoir, Lowell wanted to lighten his poetic style toward a spare but resonant directness. One possible model was his older friend William Carlos Williams, a pioneer of object-centered free verse, whose well-known slogan was "No ideas but in things." But, as Ian Hamilton has pointed out, Lowell "knew that the lessons he could learn from [Williams] would always be of the most general kind: loosen meter, abandon rhyme, use ordinary speech, introduce more characters, and so on."[20] As Lowell wrote to Williams in the fall of 1957, after he had achieved several poems in the new style, "I've been experimenting with mixing loose and free meters with strict in order to get [the] accuracy, naturalness, and multiplicity of the prose, yet, I also want the state and surge of the old verse, the carpentry of definite meter that tells me when to stop rambling."[21] For Lowell was not ready to abandon meter or rhyme, at least not entirely. Rather, he wanted to bring such effects into play against the feel of prose. For more specific instruction in the new carpentry, Lowell turned to another friend, Elizabeth Bishop. Bishop, like Lowell, had independently begun to experiment with autobiographical prose—in stories like "In the Village" (1953), which Lowell admired to the point of imitating it in stanzas (see "The Scream") and which predate Lowell's prose experiments by two years, she had recaptured the most painful moments of her past in a language that was "endurable and perfect." In poems like "The Fish" and "Roosters," she had long since mastered a technique of versification balancing prose rhythms against meter and / or rhyme and had found a way of structuring a poem that appears casual but is in fact intensely organized. As Lowell himself would later stress, many of the poems of *Life Studies*, in their rhythmic strategies, in their luminous presentation of things "urgent with life and meaning," and in their dramatic construction, are closely modeled on Bishop's own. Hers is almost certainly the decisive influence on the form and technique, if not the content, of that epoch-making book.

Specifically, it was "The Armadillo" that helped break the logjam. Bishop and Lowell had been exchanging poems in manuscript for a decade, and Lowell was particularly excited by a batch he had just received: "I've read your poems many times. I think I read you with more interest than anyone now writing. I know I do, but think I would even if it weren't for personal reasons. The Armadillo is surely one of your three or four very best."[22] No doubt Lowell liked it so much because the note of moral urgency and indignation to which it rises, after delicate beginnings, is one that he frequently strikes himself and because it pointed toward the solution of specific technical problems. Lowell later acknowledged, publicly and generously, that his reading of Bishop's poetry, and specifically of "The Armadillo," helped to free him from the burden of his old style and precipitate the writing of "Skunk Hour," his first in the new style, which was drafted in September of 1957 and which he eventually dedicated to Bishop. The autobiographical sequence that formed the backbone of *Life Studies* (1959) followed quickly and, it now seems, inevitably. That book's impact on the literary world was anticipated by the reaction of the editor of *Partisan Review,* the exacting Russian-born Philip Rahv, when he read the poems in manuscript. Lowell reported that response in a December letter to Bishop; Rahv said: "'Diss is da break-through for Cal [Lowell] and for poetry. The one real advance since Eliot.'" Lowell then comments: "You guess how my head is turned. But really I've just broken through to where you've always been and gotten rid of my medieval armor's undermining."[23] Lowell's recurrent imagery of heavy, outmoded armor in reference to the old idiom dramatizes his perception of it as a useless, confining defense and highlights the freedom he associates with the new style. In a later letter, Lowell wrote, "I used your Armadillo in class as a parallel to my Skunks and ended up feeling a petty plagiarist."[24] Of course, in creating poems like "Skunk Hour," "Waking in the Blue," and "Memories of West Street and Lepke," Lowell was no plagiarist. Two obvious and important new features of his approach are the elements of autobiographical revelation and of psychological disturbance. These are uniquely his (though Lowell credited Snodgrass's *Heart's Needle* with pointing him toward verse auto-biography). These personal elements undoubtedly contributed to his work's powerful public impact. But he found techniques in Bishop's verse that offered an escape from what he thought worst in his own style, a tendency to "beat the big drum too much"—an effect more surely fatal to autobiographical poetry than to any other kind.[25]

The qualities in Bishop's work that influenced Lowell have influenced others as well, both through Bishop's own poetry and, indirectly, through Lowell's. There are at least four important techniques to be found in "The Armadillo," and elsewhere in Bishop's verse, that Lowell (and others) have put directly to use: (1) a controlled treatment of idiom and voice that is usually conversational and plain but always singing, and that can rise naturally to support moments of eloquence and intensity; (2) a treatment of the details of common life that is understated, yet capable of carrying great symbolic weight; (3) a way of "timing" the unfolding of a poem so that it seems as if the poem was being composed on the spot, with the poet "thinking as he writes," so that the symbolic import of the images presented dawns on both the speaker and the reader only gradually; (4) a modulation through the details of common life toward underground reservoirs of mystery, moral ambiguity, or psychological tension.

Penelope Laurans, in an excellent essay on Bishop's prosody, has described some of the qualities of "The Armadillo" that Lowell would have found technically suggestive. She explains the poem's cool surface and its underlying indignation in the following way, "The distancing that goes on through most of 'The Armadillo' is a way of keeping the poem free of a sentimentality that the depth of underlying feeling might generate." In *Life Studies*, what must be distanced is the intensity of personal involvement; Lowell works to avoid choking the reader on an excess of unprocessed anger or nostalgia. Lowell praised Bishop in "The Armadillo" and elsewhere for "Her rhythms, idiom, images, and stanza structure [that] seemed to belong to a later century." His own sense of control is attained through a new carpentry of image, rhythm, and rhyme. Laurans observes of Bishop's "The Armadillo": "The primary way Bishop manages this control is metrical variation. . . . The habitually shifting rhythms of the poem do not allow the reader to lose himself in its lyric music." The alternately lyric and prosaic rhythm actually works *against* the reader being swept away by feeling, at least until the appropriate moment. Lowell recognized the importance of a technique permitting dry, precise understatement under circumstances of great intensity, a technique in which, as Robert Pinsky has put it, "Bishop tells us surprisingly much in a quiet voice resembling speech."[26] For Lowell's particular—somewhat bitter—sort of autobiographical poetry, the emphatic pulse and fervor of the old lyric voice would have proved fatal. The essential features of Bishop's style may be traced as far back as "The Fish" (1940), which is why Lowell could say in 1957 that "I've just broken through to where you've always been." But Bishop's work is so understated that it took the appropriation of her techniques in the bolder style of Lowell to make most nonpoets recognize their implications for renewing the current language of poetry. Meanwhile, younger poets like John Ashbery and James Merrill, who would later emerge as powerful masters of understatement themselves, were still in the process of discovering an idiom and voice of their own. In that process they were quietly mining Bishop's work for all it was worth.

Both Ashbery and Merrill were particularly drawn to Bishop's eloquent, conversational lyricism, and, in their different ways, to her treatment of the mysterious latencies shadowing the details of common life. For Lowell's "Skunk Hour," the conversational treatment of idiom and the approach to the timing of a poem were just as important as the handling of detail and the treatment of quatrains. Both "The Armadillo" and "Skunk Hour" employ irregularly rhymed stanzas in an underplayed, conversational way, placing little stress on rhymed words. (Compare the heavily stressed, almost brutal rhymes of *Lord Weary's Castle*.) Moreover, both begin with what appear to be casual, almost neutral, observations that gradually acquire emotional and symbolic charge. Although the disturbed interjections of Lowell's middle stanzas add a piercing personal note ("My mind's not right") and the private significance of the imagery becomes overwhelmingly apparent in a way unlikely in Bishop, Lowell's closing stanzas are actually quieter than Bishop's in "The Armadillo." In fact, while each poem closes brilliantly, in her last stanza Bishop seems indignantly Low-

ellesque, while in his, Lowell out-Bishops Bishop with a telling
climax that is imagistic, symbolic, and mordantly, savagely understated.

In stressing the important specific debt Lowell owed to Bishop,
I have no desire to overstate it. Rather, I am attempting to dramatize how a method of understatement could have a vital, pervasive,
and long-standing impact upon the language of poetry. Lowell told
an interviewer, "The poets who most directly influenced me were
Allen Tate, Elizabeth Bishop and William Carlos Williams. An
unlikely combination! . . . but you can see that Bishop is a sort of
bridge between Tate's formalism and Williams's informal art."[27]
Bishop could offer Lowell specific ways to achieve a new carpentry,
to satisfy a need for formal control while maintaining an openness
to significant detail and an appearance of informality. Lowell had
learned lessons about tone and structure that he applied for the
rest of his life, just as Bishop learned things from Lowell's success
that would encourage a more autobiographical sort of poetry. What
Lowell had learned was something subtle that he felt himself always in danger of forgetting. The words of Octavio Paz are appos-
ite here. "We are drowning not in a sea but in a swamp of words.
We have forgotten that poetry is not in what words say but in what
is said between them, that which appears fleetingly in pauses and
silences. In the poetry workshops of universities there should be a
required course for young poets: learning to be silent. The enormous power of reticence—that is the great lesson of the poetry of
Elizabeth Bishop."[28] Whenever Lowell's autobiographical poetry is
at its most effective, there is always an element of reticence. From
Elizabeth Bishop, Lowell had learned the need to be silent.

The power of reticence could be no more directly illustrated in
Bishop's own work than in a poem like "Twelfth Morning; or What
you Will" (1964), in which the poem's underlying concerns are like
the quiet, pervasive background of a tapestry with a vivid foreground. Here it is a "thin gray mist" that gives those foreground
objects their strange accentuation, as one seeks, among the deso-
late dunescapes at Cabo Frio ("Cold Cape"), for something with
which to identify. The language moves from plain to lustrous and
back to plain.

> Like a first coat of whitewash when it's wet,
> the thin gray mist lets everything show through:

the black boy Balthazár; a fence, a horse,
    a foundered house,

—cement and rafters sticking from a dune.
(The Company passes off these white but shopworn
dunes as lawns.) "Shipwreck," we say; perhaps
    this is a housewreck.

The sea's off somewhere, doing nothing. Listen.
An expelled breath. And faint, faint, faint
(or are you hearing things), the sandpipers'
    heart-broken cries.

The fence, three-strand, barbed-wire, all pure rust,
three dotted lines, comes forward hopefully
across the lots; thinks better of it; turns
    a sort of corner . . .   (CP, 110)

Acerbic throwaway phrases trace the forlorn life of the place. The
sea ("off doing nothing") breathes quietly. The sandpipers are
heartbroken; "lawns" are shopworn. These observations do more
than just paint the scene; they paint the bleak mood of the observer, through a series of telltale personifications. The one personality that succeeds in remaining buoyant is Balthazár. Laboring
under a huge can of water, which becomes his emblem, surrounded by depressing circumstances, this boy is irrepressibly
alive!

            But the four-gallon can
    approaching on the head of Balthazár
    keeps flashing that the world's a pearl, *and I,*
        I am

    its highlight! You can hear the water now,
    inside, slap-slapping. Balthazár is singing.
    "Today's my Anniversary," he sings,
        "the Day of Kings."   (CP, 110–11)

The date, "Twelfth Morning"—the feast of the Epiphany—is significant. Like the star signifying Christ's birth that appeared to the
Wise Men on that day, Balthazár's can shines forth. Named after

one of the Three Kings, he is buoyed on his own journey, however, not by religious ecstasy, but by an ecstacy in his own ego—a frank delight in self. Bishop isolates this "highlight" in the scene, a point of consolation that emerges from the thin mist, speaking volumes. Is that thin mist itself an emblem of too-ready despair? Marie-Claire Blais remarked: "Much of Bishop's poetry is a result of the struggle for accommodation with what is intolerable in life. Some poets have turned this to struggle and hate, but she has arrived at a kind of pure nostalgia that is both past and present and at peace."[29]

Balthazár dramatizes the value of accommodation because he wears his poverty so lightly. He bears his slapping can as if it were a kingly crown, a gift for the newborn savior. The tense edges of Bishop's own accommodation—which contains, after all, an element of protest against the intolerable—are keenly felt in "The Riverman," a poem that offers Bishop's version of magical realism. Here is a remarkable interior monologue in which (to quote the poem's introductory note) "A man in a remote Amazonian village decides to become a *sacaca,* a witch doctor who works with water spirits" (*CP,* 105). This note acknowledges that many details of the poem are drawn from *Amazon Town* by Charles Wagley, an American who lived and worked in Brazil for many years as both an anthropologist and an administrator of educational and public-health programs. The source of "The Riverman" is worth discussing, because that source embodies an unconsciously condescending attitude toward the third world that is distinctly at variance with Bishop's own. Halfway through the poem, Bishop's riverman asks,

> Why shouldn't I be ambitious?
> I sincerely desire to be
> a serious *sacaca*
> like Fortunato Pombo,
> Or Lúcio, or even
> the great Joaquim Sacaca.   (*CP,* 107–8)

Compare this with a passage from *Amazon Town* to see how skillfully Bishop has lifted and transformed the material: "None of the shamans living in the Ita community, however, is a great pagé. The great ones, everyone in Ita agrees, lived about a generation ago. They were called *sacacas.* Such famous men as Joaquim Sacaca

. . . Fortunato Pombo . . . and Lúcio . . . were pagé *sacacas*.[30]
Bishop takes all of her names from the source, but her narrative,
adopting the point of view of the riverman himself, recreates his
awe in the face of his great forebears, his humility, his pride, his
defiance, his sense of responsibility. Wagley's tone is certainly hu-
mane, but he remains "objectively" remote, secure in North American assumptions of cultural superiority. He emphasizes the
practical value of understanding the native viewpoint if North
Americans are to succeed in benefiting the locals by, for example,
getting Western medicine accepted. Here is a characteristic passage from his book: "By knowing the folk beliefs of the people with
whom they are working . . . anyone bringing new ideas and methods into a folk society would be able to avoid many conflicts. . . .
New concepts may be explained in terms understandable to the
people, and many old customs and beliefs may be replaced with
greater ease."[31] Here there is no question of learning the old beliefs
to appreciate their mystery or beauty, nor is their any doubt that
they ought to be replaced. Bishop's approach could not be more
different; as a poet, she does not impose, she discovers. She attempts to enter the mind of the riverman, not to convert him, but
to learn his secrets. Ranging outside the European tradition, exploring the logic of an archaic culture, Bishop shows the riverman
to be a figure of imagination seeking humbly but defiantly to serve
his people, within a tradition wholly different from any Western
model.

There are no gaps in *time*. The riverman is a *contemporary* of the
poet's, and he has been touched by modern culture, but there is a
large gap in *consciousness*. He draws his metaphors from a curious
mixture of machine and moonlight, modern and wild:

> Hearing the dolphin ahead,
> I went down to the river
> and the moon was burning bright
> as the gasoline-lamp mantle
> with the flame turned up too high,
> just before it begins to scorch.   (CP, 105)

Clearly a man who has lived with gasoline lamps, he makes a later
reference to the light in the underwater realm of Luandinha as
"like at the cinema." His outlook offers a singular blend of moder-

nity and primitivism. He has experienced elements of modern technology, but a rude and vital mythology rules his imagination.

Realism blends with magic; one feels the presence of poverty. Awesome ritual is limited to mysterious objects that are cheap and obtainable:

> They gave me a mottled rattle
> and a pale-green coral twig
> and some special weeds like smoke.
> (They're under my canoe.)   (CP, 107)

The vivid, precise, and dreamlike aura that Bishop mastered early arises from the simple phrasing, the matter-of-fact tone, the accumulating detail, that the riverman uses to describe uncanny events.

> I waded into the river
> and suddenly a door
> in the water opened inward,
> groaning a little, with water
> bulging above the lintel. . . .

> They gave me a shell of *cachaça*
> and decorated cigars.
> The smoke rose like mist
> through the water, and our breaths
> didn't make any bubbles.
> We drank *cachaça* and smoked
> the green cheroots. The room
> filled with gray-green smoke
> and my head couldn't have been dizzier.   (CP, 105–6)

Supporting the mystery of these events is a curious, intentional flatness of tone. The riverman's magical initiation is very much like an ordinary drinking session. Attached to his region and time, the riverman explores the imagination as richly as his circumstances allow. But he never exaggerates.

His relationship to his society is at the heart of things. He is doing something earthy, sensuous, and illicit. Being called by "The Dolphin" to serve the sexy Luandinha erects a barrier between the man and his wife:

> I look yellow, my wife says,
> and she brews me stinking teas
> I throw out, behind her back.   (CP, 106)

Because he studies to transform earthly dross by a special intuition ("everything must be there / in that magic mud"—CP, 108), his intimate knowledge of "the deep, enchanted silt" will yield blessings for which he will be, like the artist whose role is always to dredge beauty out of the muck, both honored and abhorred. He hides from his fellow villagers and kinsmen, beginning to think and live like an outsider. But his intentions are beneficent.

> Godfathers and cousins,
> your canoes are over my head;
> I hear your voices talking.
> You can peer down and down
> or dredge the river bottom
> but never, never catch me.
> When the moon shines and the river
> lies across the earth
> and sucks it like a child,
> then I will go to work
> to get you health and money.   (CP, 109)

The image of the earth giving suck to the river, which has overtones reminiscent of the sea swinging above the earth's rocky breasts in "At the Fishhouses," suggests that in the conjunction of water with crude earth rests the ultimate maternal source of wisdom, comfort, and value.

The riverman's stealthy yet taunting posture, which brands him as society's enemy *and* friend, is historically in keeping with Wagley's observation that the pagés of the Amazon are officially banned by a society that continues to consult them on the sly.[32] More importantly, it reinforces the idea that the riverman is Bishop's brother in art, a kinship she acknowledges despite his alien setting and sensibility. As in Bishop's own work, the riverman's power to transform the ordinary, to make mud into magic, depends, first, on answering a strange call and, second, on serious study and devotion, reflected in imagery of "total immersion."

By 1960, when "The Riverman" was first published, Bishop had lived in Brazil nine years. She had gone beyond the "tourist" doubts of "Arrival at Santos" or "Questions of Travel," in that she no longer, in fact, questions the value of travel. "The Riverman" reveals an author who is now able to penetrate and comprehend the alien consciousness of a Brazilian native from a distant place and class. Her poems are no longer about the act of observation (as "Brazil, 1502" and "Questions of Travel" had been); instead they frankly observe. After *Questions of Travel* was published in 1965, she continued to produce poems that respond quite directly to the overwhelming sensuous and emotional messages that Brazil had to offer. Of these poems, brought together under the heading "New and Uncollected Work" in the 1969 *Complete Poems* along with three earlier pieces from the 1930s, perhaps the four remarkable prose poems of "Rainy Season; Sub-Tropics" (1967) and the astonishingly vivid "Under the Window: Ouro Prêto" (1966) are the best. Though, as a group, they do not quite match the standard set by *Questions of Travel,* they continue a process of immersion begun fifteen years earlier. Bishop had reached a new plateau. Brazil had begun to yield its ripe and varied secrets. Her version of its geography comprehended dialect, culture, history. Her subtle appreciation of how geography influences the actions of individuals is evident throughout "Brazil," but nowhere are the effects of geography more broadly felt than in the story of the criminal Micuçú, "The Burglar of Babylon."

Not every critic may like this poem as much as I do. Deliberately conceived in a popular vein in response to an event that riveted public attention in Rio, it harks back to the old-style broadside ballads that sang the exploits of heros and murderers. While the versification flirts with doggerel, as most lengthy ballads do, and while the poem does not appear to demand the intensive sort of reading that Bishop's best poems generally require, I find it an excellent poem of a sadly neglected kind, a kind that, through an easy narrative style that does not sacrifice opportunities for complexity and irony, makes the work of a serious poet available to a broader audience. One audience Bishop had in mind can be gleaned from the fact that the poem was later published in a volume of its own as a children's book, with woodcut illustrations by Ann Grifalconi, under the title *The Ballad of the Burglar of Babylon.* Bishop said, in a note to that edition, "The . . . story is taken, often word for word, from the daily papers, filled out by what I know of the place and the people."[33] Despite its intended accessibility to children, quite a bit of social observation and insight is packed in. In fact, it offers a more inclusive vision of Brazilian culture than any other single poem by Bishop. In particular, it looks at most of the major strata of Brazilian society: we note the tone of the shocked outsider speaking the poem's opening passage; the patriotic career army officer who in dying commits "his soul to God / And his sons to the governor"; the "auntie" of the killer and the cynical patrons of her drink shop; and Micuçú himself. Here at last, Bishop, who had studiously avoided mimicking Auden,[34] found an appropriate occasion to modify one of Auden's forms, his modernized ballad style. The off rhymes, running rhythms, and relaxed diction contribute to its balance of folk qualities against sophisticated modernity. However, unlike Auden, Bishop's purpose is not biting satire but pathos. As the narrative breezes from event to event, not only do we come to understand a complex tragedy (which is not just Micuçú's, for like the riverman, Micuçú is both an outlaw and a representative) but we absorb a great wealth of social fact, the tragedy's determinants. The ballad form serves well; its graceful, understated movement gathers weight without apparent effort, until one returns to the opening lines, which now epitomize a whole culture.

Thoroughly Brazilian in detail, the poem's structure reminds one of another folk art, the American gangster films of the thirties, in which a deadly outlaw emerges as the inevitable product of a flawed society.

> On the fair green hills of Rio
>> There grows a fearful stain:
> The poor who come to Rio
>> And can't go home again.   (CP, 112)

The poem deliberately opens with the kind of thumping rhythm and the tone of a popular broadside that is *not* what one expects from Bishop, but this is balanced against a more characteristic delicacy of imagery and thought, in the following stanzas:

> On the hills a million people,
>> A million sparrows, nest,
> Like a confused migration
>> That's had to light and rest.

The movement is from easy journalistic generalization to the surprising, compassionate precision of the Bishop simile. Even more confused than the sparrows, this human migration does not move on: "they cling and spread like lichen, / And the people come and come." On these fair green hills, pastoral values and human will are undermined, and people act instinctively, without conscious thought or goal, like birds or, worse, like fungus. Micuçú comes from this place, where even the names are fearful:

> There's the hill of Kerosene,
> And the hill of the Skeleton,
> The hill of Astonishment,
> And the hill of Babylon.

Alone among the undifferentiated flock, Micuçú emerges as possessing decisiveness and will. But these qualities cannot save him from destruction.

Micuçú is allowed some attributes of the outlaw as folk hero—he has killed uncounted numbers of people; he has "escaped three times / from the worst penitentiary"; he rivets the attention of an entire city; he can assume a patriarch's voice, calling a *mulata* "daughter" and a buzzard "my son"—because he stands outside or above society; he so terrifies a troop of soldiers that "one of them, in a panic, / Shot the officer in command" (*CP*, 114). He is also human; he loves the "auntie, / who raised him like a son" (*CP*, 113). His aura of glamor, however, is soon tarnished by the comment of one of the drinkshop customers after his death: "'He wasn't much of a burglar, / He got caught six times—or more'" (*CP*, 117). His uncertain heroism rests not so much on the romance of lawbreaking as, like Bogart's gangsterish heroism in *High Sierra*, on grim acceptance of his fate. He cannot remain quietly in jail, because unlike the protagonist of "In Prison," he yearns for freedom, and will pay the price for even a moment more of it. Like the narrator of that early story, however, he recognizes that "freedom is knowledge of necessity." He tells his auntie that,

> "The soldiers are coming,
> And I've got to disappear.

> "Ninety years they gave me.
> Who wants to live that long?

I'll settle for ninety hours,
    On the hills of Babylon.

"Don't tell anyone you saw me.
    I'll run as long as I can.
You were good to me, and I love you,
    But I'm a doomed man."   (*CP*, 113)

As "Questions of Travel" suggests, choices are "never wide and never free," but Micuçú achieves a certain dignity by accepting consequences and living them out.

The poem's perspective shifts rapidly in an effort to tell the whole story. One perspective is that of the excited city, its citizens absorbed in the manhunt, the rich people following the action with binoculars. (Bishop acknowledged that, in real life, she was one of them.) It switches to the customers in auntie's drinkshop, who swear and spit sympathetically; then to the nervous soldier who panics and kills his CO; then, remarkably, to the calm and trance-like clarity experienced by the burglar himself in his final two days, from the peep-peep of the peanut vendor's whistle on the beach far below, to the panting of the climbing soldier who "never got very near" (*CP*, 116) but who finally killed him. Unlike Bogart, who almost never gave in to fear, after Micuçú "missed for the last time," he panicked, an ordinary man rather than a hero after all, and, so he ran for shelter and "got it, behind the ear." He has made a mistake he will not survive. As consciousness leaves Micuçú, we remain inside his mind, finding there, not thought, but a lingering intensity of sensation.

He heard the babies crying
    Far, far away in his head,
And the mongrel's barking and barking.
    Then Micuçú was dead.

His last perceptions are symbolically of the elemental cries of the helpless or unpedigreed. He ends with awareness of need, as he began.

Micuçú, who has galvanized the attention of a whole culture, is a touchstone for that culture. After his death the focus shifts, first to the community as a whole, then to the chief sufferer of the tragedy.

> The police and the populace
>> Heaved a sigh of relief,
> But behind the counter his auntie
>> Wiped her eyes in grief.   (CP, 117)

Auntie, the survivor, cannot understand or accept what has come to pass.

> "We have always been respected
>> My shop is honest and clean.
> I loved him, but from a baby
>> Micuçú was always mean.
>
> "We have always been respected.
>> His sister has a job.
> Both of us gave him money.
>> Why did he have to rob?
>
> "I raised him to be honest,
>> Even here, in Babylon slum."

Auntie lacks Micuçú's fatalistic resolution. Her statements undercut the poem's initial, sweeping implications of social determinism, establishing a more complex and balanced viewpoint. If Micuçú's meanness was innate, perhaps it was not the product of that "fearful stain" after all. But the poem goes on to mention that "this morning the little soldiers / Are on Babylon hill again." They are after "another two"—the cycle of crime and retribution grinds onward. The tone of this finale is complex. We are quietly informed that "they say they aren't as dangerous / As the poor Micuçú." "Poor Micuçú" was a depraved killer, genuinely dangerous, but at the same time, he commands understanding. The final two stanzas bring the tale full circle, repeating the first and last stanzas of the prelude, emphasizing that a mean man will get meaner coming from such a place. Micuçú's tragedy stems from a combination of factors: innate human depravity, chance, and cultural determinants. But because of his knowledge of necessity, Micuçú lives his life, however brief or thwarted, on his own terms. He insists on freedom while facing doom. Clinging to a dangerous notoriety, a man may taste the brisk, thin air of freedom "on the hills of Babylon." But the waste is staggering and grinds on.

Bishop seems deeply drawn to this contemporary folktale's revelation of the persistent longing for joy and power buried in the human spirit. Both in her Key West poems and in "Brazil," she studied men and women pushed to extremes in quest of mere survival, finding evidence, in their actions, of joy and hope, or, if there is not room for hope or joy, then dignity and resignation in the face of necessity. As Lowell justly remarked, "What cuts so deep is that each poem is inspired by her own tone, a tone of large, grave tenderness and sorrowing amusement."[35] Bishop's Brazil was no longer just a theater for the tourist. She was now implicated in its unfolding human patterns.

«Elsewhere»
Nova Scotia and Private History

After Bishop arrived in Brazil in November of 1951, she turned out "Arrival at Santos" rather quickly. It appeared in the *New Yorker* in June of the following year. She then published no more poetry about Brazil for three years. She published no poetry at all in 1953 or 1954. From 1955 on, her production increased, and it was split almost equally between poems about Brazil and poems remembering her Nova Scotia childhood, a subject she had never treated in poetry before, although she had touched on that time in Nova Scotia as the background to a few stories such as "The Baptism" (1937) and "The Farmer's Children" (1948). It was with prose that Bishop chiefly occupied herself during her first years in Brazil. In 1953, she produced two autobiographical stories of childhood set in Great Village, Nova Scotia: "Gwendolyn" and the brilliant "In the Village." At the same time, she was at work on a translation of the Brazilian classic *Minho Vida de Menina,* a diary written just before the turn of the century by a young girl living in the mountain town of Diamantina. Published in 1957 under the title *The Diary of "Helena Morley"* (Bishop would have preferred to call it *Black Beans and Diamonds*), it is an extraordinary work, full of the poetry of everyday life. Bishop learned much, during the long task of translation, about the art of achieving "absolute naturalness of tone," the quality she most admired in Herbert, when adopting the voice of a child.[36] What she learned went directly into the autobiographical stories of 1953, and later into the post-1955 poems and stories about her childhood that would become an increasingly important aspect of her work.

Somehow the combined factors of the remoteness of Brazil, her early happiness there, and perhaps also the exotic and unforeseen details that she found ever before her eyes, served to turn her imagination back toward its roots, toward the homely exoticism of childhood. Virtually all of her Nova Scotia writing in prose and verse deals in some form or other with really painful loss, the loss of one's mother, the death of a friend, the death of a young cousin, and this is as we might expect, given her early history. Yet the prevailing qualities of this writing are perhaps unexpected, in light of the apparently grim subjects. Along with a pervasive nostalgia, one finds charm, simplicity, humor, gracefulness, and a kind of preternatural clarity that seems to embody what Bishop meant when she spoke of "our infant sight."

In the *Complete Poems: 1927–1979,* as in the 1969 "complete" poems, *Questions of Travel* is divided into two sections, "Brazil" and "Elsewhere." Elsewhere is most often Nova Scotia. When *Questions of Travel* was first published in 1965, these two sections were joined by the autobiographical story "In the Village." Since the book is more powerful and coherent with the story than without it, I will discuss "In the Village" as it first appeared in book form, as a part of the larger whole of *Questions of Travel.* The story is an extraordinary exploration of the child's most staggering loss of all, the loss of her mother to insanity when Bishop was a child of five.

To recapitulate the events behind the story: the death of her father when she was still a baby triggered insanity in her mother. Elizabeth was taken to live with her mother's parents and sister in Nova Scotia, while her mother was confined to a mental institution near Boston. "In the Village" describes with grave tenderness the return of her mother to her native village, after treatment had failed, in the vain hope that familiar scenes might restore her mental health. The fitting of a purple dress, the widow's first tentative step out of black, provoked a new and decisive bout of madness. Evidently her mother could not relinquish the right to mourn.

The narration alternates without comment between images of the world's piercing, consoling beauties and its devastating losses, and the imagery of both consolation and loss is so intense that, in the words of David Young, "the whole texture of the story shines with magic."[37] The events are seen through the eyes of the five-year-old girl, although the voice is a version of the adult self, and the images of consolation and loss that are the chief vehicles for advancing the action serve also as objective correlatives for emotions the child cannot yet understand, although one knows they will haunt her until she does. The most important of these, the mother's scream, is established with strange intensity at the beginning and reappears cyclically as a motif emblematic of shattering, enduring loss that threatens to color all one sees. "A scream, the echo of a scream, hangs over that Nova Scotia village. No one hears it; it hangs forever, a slight stain in those pure blue skies, skies that travelers compare to those of Switzerland, too dark, too blue, so that they seem to keep on darkening a little more around the horizon—or is it around the rim of the eyes?—the color of the cloud of bloom on the elm trees, the violet on the field of oats; something darkening over the woods and waters as well as the sky" (*CProse*, 251).

This is prose of stunning poetic intensity. Its visionary clarity, its startling turns of thought, show the hand of a master. The mind moves, as a child's might, from the scream's eternal persistence to the sky's pure, symbolic blue; stained and darkening, that sky is consolingly beautiful but almost too intense, and it is vulnerable to the spreading effect of the scream. The narrator has an adult's awareness of the passage of time, yet the eye moves and sees with childlike simplicity and freshness. The adult voice never intrudes to explain for the child. The decisive event, the final mental collapse of Bishop's mother, is related with surprising indirectness. It hovers in the background, while the foreground is crammed with details of the child's mostly pleasant days in the village. The child is an observer, but even that role is limited by the fact that adults frequently send her on errands to shield her from what is happening. But these diversions are a thin mist at best, and as in "Twelfth Morning," "everything shows through." The child cannot control events (even her adult relations cannot), but she must endure their terrible consequences. "The scream hangs like that, unheard, in memory—in the past, in the present, and those years between. It was not even loud to begin with, perhaps. It just came there to live, forever—not loud, just alive forever. Its pitch would be the pitch of my village. Flick the lightning rod on top of the church steeple with your fingernail and you will hear it" (*CProse,* 251). The scream is alive forever because its consequences live forever. Lost or broken treasures provide further analogues for the mother's collapse, such as the costly household goods shipped north from Boston, and the child's lost, trivial, remembered prizes. When the child and grandmother unpack the mother's things, mother is conspicuously absent. Among "painfully desirable" cups from two China barrels, we find "more broken china. My grandmother says it breaks her heart. 'Why couldn't they have got it packed better? Heaven knows what it cost'" (*CProse,* 256). The child absconds with a sharply pointed ivory stick from "a case of little ivory embroidery tools. . . . To keep it forever, I bury it under the bleeding heart by the crab apple tree, but it is never found again" (*CProse,* 257). The desire to preserve "forever" leads to loss, loss under the "bleeding heart." When the child is given a five-cent piece by the painfully poor but sympathetic dressmaker who has witnessed the mother's scream, "I put my five cent piece in my mouth for greater safety on the way home, and swallow it. Months later, as far as I know, it is still in me, transmitting all its precious metal into my growing teeth and hair" (*CProse,* 259). The desire for absolute safety, for eternal possession, leads to further loss but also to precious, if painful, physical (and perhaps psychic) transmutations.

Set against these correlatives for searing loss is a correlative for absolute beauty, the *"clang?"* of Nate the blacksmith's hammer striking the anvil.

> Clang.
> *Clang.*
>   Oh, beautiful sounds, from the blacksmith's shop at the end of the garden! Its gray roof, with patches of moss, could be seen above the lilac bushes. Nate was there—Nate. . . .
> *Clang.*
> The pure note: pure and angelic.
> The dress was all wrong. She screamed.
> The child vanishes.   (*CProse,* 252–53)

The child's incomplete knowledge of the circumstances, her mistaken sense that the dress being all wrong was the real source of the scream, is preserved. The transient purity of the blacksmith's clang, symbolic of the consoling power of art, stands against the eternal sound of the mother's scream. Much that typifies Bishop's work in general is implicit in this passage—the honest intimations of bewildered pain, the longing for absolute purity, and even (one might say) the tendency of the observer to vanish, leaving us only with complex and living observations. But the observer never really vanishes. One can always divine the observer's response from the way objects are characterized. The rest of the story provides lucid details that partially console the afflicted child, whose need and pain shape the observation in unstated ways.

Charles Tomlinson proposed that "we would like also to enter the more complicated moral universe of the mother, a world of alienation such as Miss Bishop courageously explores in 'The Man-Moth.'" Yet such a treatment here would contradict Bishop's intention, and implies that the complexity of the child's own moral universe has not been recognized. Tomlinson correctly observes, "Throughout the story a kind of psychological imperative operates in keeping the pain at a distance."[38] However, this is not (as he suggests) a weakness; it is part of the essential character of the story and permits Bishop to depict with unsentimental psychological precision the way a five-year-old child deals with overwhelming and bewildering emotion. She keeps it at a distance. The same process is delineated in the moving "First Death in Nova Scotia" (1962) in which the child—there slightly younger, since the mother is present—is shown attempting to come to terms with the death of her little cousin Arthur. She projects herself emotionally into several objects that are in the cold room containing the coffin, objects that the child identifies with the cousin, in an attempt to bring him alive through them. To face the reality of death is simply too much for her, and that certifies how intense the pain really is. It *must* be kept at a distance. The detached tone does not deny emotion. Instead, it allows it to emerge more truly and poignantly. In "In the Village," the child tries to push the mental collapse of her almost unknown mother into the background. Had one seen into the mother's mind, the tense and fragile integrity of the child's perspective would be violated. The sound of the scream recurs hauntingly throughout the story, and clearly echoes forever in the writer's life. It is not "cancelled" (as Tomlinson insists) by the blacksmith's hammer, but is merely driven into deeper recesses, "not loud, just alive for ever." Pain, kept at a distance, is all the keener and more persistent for that.

> Clang.
> *Clang.*
> Nate is shaping a horseshoe.
> Oh, beautiful pure sound!
> It turns everything else to silence. . . .
> It sounds like a bell buoy out at sea.
>> It is the elements speaking: earth, air, fire, water.
>> All those other things—clothes, crumbling postcards, broken china; things damaged and lost, sickened or destroyed; even the frail almost-lost scream—are they too frail for us to hear their voices long, too mortal?
> Nate!
> Oh, beautiful sound, strike again!   (*CProse*, 274)

The scream seems to fade, to be "almost lost." But among all those correlatives for pain that it recalls, "things damaged and lost, sickened or destroyed," this story's very existence shows that the "frail almost-lost scream" still vibrates in memory as it lives in the sky. The pure note of art consoles but does not cancel. Art is short; pain is long. But perhaps that consolation is enough to keep one going.

Throughout "In the Village" the familiar theme is sounded: The longing to escape disturbing realities into a sphere of lucid, permanent beauties. The child learns, however, that real loss cannot truly be escaped. The packages, faithfully assembled by her grandmother, that the girl brings weekly to the post office, serve as keen, periodic reminders of a tie that might have brought happiness instead of pain. The complex and charming life of the village goes on and offers compensations, and one sees it as she passes to the post office, but the reality of loss goes on too. Read empathetically, this story, with its delicate balance of loss and consolation, of avoidance and quiet courage, provides a map of Elizabeth Bishop's private world.

Jan B. Gordon comments regarding Bishop's handling of the narrative: "There is a certain surface tension always present in Elizabeth Bishop's art that is at least partially the result of the loss of *privilege* in every sense of the word: the narrator's sense of an ad-

vantage to perspective; an access to secrets, unknown to the protagonists in her poems; or even the subtlety of an untrustworthy
vision which might confer aesthetic advantage by granting the
reader the right to acknowledge a false subjectivity."[39] For Gordon,
this renunciation of privilege goes too far, and Bishop loses too
much. Although privileged narratives like "The Riverman" or
"The Burglar of Babylon" are, in fact, by no means uncommon in
her writing, Bishop's works often do turn on the renunciation of
privilege, upon presenting the surface of the world from a particular, deliberately limited, point of view. If, as I have suggested, the
tension in Bishop's work most often derives from dramatizing the
mind in action, then, by renouncing narrative privilege, Bishop
can here reveal the wonder and frustration of a child's experience.
The reader is made to *feel* the limits of the child's understanding.
The story's particulars deftly define a social order, complete with
assumptions about, say, how men and women should act about a
fire: the women hysterical; the men stoic, silent, and able. The
mother's madness is perhaps simply an intensified version of this
acceptable female helplessness. The child unconsciously absorbs
all this. But the adult reader can see the effect it will have, an
effect as complex as the experience itself, since the tragedy is
woven inextricably with consolations: the artificer's beautiful
"*Clang,*" the crude and unshakable vitality of the family cow.

The poems of Bishop's "Elsewhere" section are more personal
than any she had written so far. Like "In the Village" they explore
images of loss and suffering. "Manners" sketches the demise of a
social order with the same understated grace with which "First
Death in Nova Scotia" reveals the child's first experience of death;
"Visits to St. Elizabeths" sees Ezra Pound's madness from the
ironic perspective of a children's rhyme. The latter poem reveals as
clearly as any she wrote her power to explore questions of mature responsibility from a child's perspective. Pound's weaknesses and
failures, his childish egotism, are delineated with the same un-
swerving accuracy as his courage and triumphs. The pattern and
rhythms of "This is the House that Jack Built" achieve in her
hands a relentless logic that, while it keeps all Pound achieved and
perpetrated in balance, drives straight at the climactic word
wretched, the one unflinching word that, after the crimes and after
the glory, sums Pound up.

Bishop's focus on personal loss, on the private toll of existence, is a vein deeply mined in her final book, *Geography III*. In *Questions of Travel* Bishop decisively expanded her scope, showing a subtle command of both public and private history. Although the lure of enclosure and solitude remained, although the hiding blanket of "high fog" beckons and comforts, solitude now becomes a source of strength, a temporary refuge. Bishop developed a sustaining faith—a faith in the revelatory power of transient fact, in what she modestly called a "perfectly useless concentration."[40] By the right attention to the exterior, one can drive to the interior.

« The Art of Losing»

GEOGRAPHY III

The Necessity of Loss

Geography III (1976), Elizabeth Bishop's last book, marks the final stage in her artistic development. The poems offer considerations of three related themes: (1) the necessity of loss; (2) the enigmas of travel; and (3) the rewards and liabilities of enclosure—of life lived on islands, in small worlds, and quiet rooms. Coming back to these central concerns one last time, with a new decisiveness, Bishop created a fitting capstone for her career. She had begun writing from her knowledge of isolation and of the terrifying risks of love. In her early phase, she created fables about beings who chose imprisonment and paid its price. Their emphasis is on the *choice* of isolation, on deliberate flight to islands of Imagination. The author's anxieties are objectified through her characters, but she remains detached. Later, in poems like "The Fish" and "Roosters," she developed a voice that might be called the impersonal I. One comprehends the fish as fully as one can, then lets it go. The fish emblematizes the impossibility of trying to hold on to something beautiful and elusive—it remains alive only as long as it is allowed to swim in another element. Her way of overcoming isolation in these poems was to engage in a "self-forgetful, perfectly useless concentration,"[1] because it allows one to possess, for a moment at least, through the appropriating power of imagination.

The poems and stories about childhood that grew out of her stay in Brazil demanded a new perspective and created a new voice, the personal I. The poet emerges as a distinct individual with a private history. The poetry of Bishop's later phase is personal, even intimate, without being confessional. The poems reveal few circumstances of the poet's adult life. Never does she present detailed biographical revelations that extend beyond the age of ten. Lowell has shown that even the poetry of early childhood can have a confessional edge, but the tone of Bishop's childhood writing is never confessional; instead, it is elegaic. The drift of the poems of *Geography III*, taken together, is toward a reconsideration of life, one's own life, not in terms of that life's particular circumstances and decisions (as in Lowell), but in terms of its chosen way of thinking and seeing, in terms of a whole bundle of latent assumptions, commitments, and predilections that bind the person and the artist. On this level, the questioning cuts close indeed. Private and public history merge in poems that quietly look at the past. Harold Bloom observed of *Geography III:* "Where the language of personal loss was once barely suggested by Bishop, it now begins to usurp the meditative voice. An oblique power has been displaced by a more direct one, by a controlled pathos all the more deeply moving for having been so long and so nobly 'postponed.'"[2] But while Bishop's later poetry is surely more direct, the meditative voice is never usurped, for these poems are in fact meditations not just on personal loss but on the universality of loss. As her work became more personal, it became less hermetic, more in touch with the common stock of human experience.

Mark Strand called her a "survivor" (*CP*, dust jacket), but her approach to survival now implies a greater acceptance of risk. A master of the art of renunciation, she had, in her earlier work, refused to possess in order to escape the necessity of loss. But now, to use her own phrase from "One Art," she has mastered "the art of losing," a needed corollary to the art of having, since "so many things seem filled with the intent / to be lost." That poem begins with the pat assurance of a school-room maxim, a tone she had mastered long ago in "Casabianca."

> The art of losing isn't hard to master;
> so many things seem filled with the intent
> to be lost that their loss is no disaster.   (*CP*, 178)

Under the veneer of assurance is an irony, reflected in the pert rhymes, directed at oneself for desiring permanence or, failing permanence, for wanting an art that masters the impermanent.

Lose something every day. Accept the fluster
of lost door keys, the hour badly spent.
The art of losing isn't hard to master.

Then practice losing farther, losing faster:
places, and names, and where it was you meant
to travel. None of these will bring disaster.

I lost my mother's watch. And look! my last, or
next-to-last, of three loved houses went.
The art of losing isn't hard to master.

This is possibly the most offhand-seeming, most conversational villanelle ever written, but as the voice grows more harried, the losses catalogued become not just more serious but more personal. The casual catalogue grows increasingly self-referential. For example, the phrase "where it was you meant / to travel," although distanced slightly by the second person, relies on the reader knowing that Bishop made travel the business of her life, and the "three loved houses," one in Key West and two in Brazil, are very much her own.

Bishop deploys the villanelle's demand for repetition with powerful ironic effect, since the form itself compels her to defend the ease of mastering loss even as the scale of losses mounts.

I lost two cities, lovely ones. And, vaster
some realms I owned, two rivers, a continent.
I miss them, but it wasn't a disaster.

Ownership has become not just a matter of the literal or legal but of the symbolic and emotional. If the loss of these vast or lovely places wasn't a disaster, it was something just barely short of one. The *real* disaster is saved for the last.

—Even losing you (the joking voice, a gesture
I love) I shan't have lied. It's evident
the art of losing's not too hard to master
though it may look like (*Write* it!) like disaster.

Bare emotion and form as a means to emotion merge stunningly in the final line. Bishop relies on a reader aware of her reputation for reticence. Her desperate "(*Write* it!)" implies that she must *force* herself to use the word *disaster* in a personal context, even though it is hedged by transparent disclaimers and demanded by the villanelle's form. This archaic French pattern serves to release something almost too private to utter; perhaps she has chosen it as a way to compel the poem to close on one tortured, almost self-pitying word—*disaster.*

Here she confesses to ownership—as if for the first time. In "Questions of Travel" Bishop was at the start a mere tourist. But now Brazil is a possession; unlike the fish, it is something she has not renounced, although it too is lost. "I lost two cities, lovely ones. And, vaster / some realms I owned, two rivers, a continent." Her first poem about possession had claimed, "We'd rather have the iceberg than the ship," apparently preferring, but at last renouncing, an imaginary thing of beauty. But now she lays claim to losses in the real world: "Even losing you . . ." The person she has lost—no doubt her friend Lota Soares, who died in 1967 (several years after that, Bishop finally left Brazil for good)—drives home the finality of loss. She has faced the necessity of losing and through that has won the freedom to possess. As the protagonist of "In Prison" had insisted forty years earlier, "Freedom is knowledge of necessity" (*CProse*, 191). In Bishop's work everything worth having carries a price, and here the price is the pain of loss, which was known from the start to be inevitable. One recalls the arid vision of inevitable loss that concludes "Song for the Rainy Season" (*CP*, 101), a rare poem in which she permitted herself to celebrate the perilous joys of transient affection. Bishop's style evolved, it appears, out of personal need, a need to embrace not only the abstract beauty of "map-maker's colors" but things of flesh and blood. Lloyd Schwartz has insightfully suggested: "The real audience at this lecture on the bearability of loss, it turns out, is the expert herself—she has been trying to convince herself that any loss can be endured. And finally, she is forced to admit that she was right; she really may not have believed it, or wanted to believe it, before. Apparently any loss, no matter how great—even this loss—can be lived through." One returns to Randall Jarrell's brilliant earlier comment: "Instead of crying with justice, 'This is a world in which no one can get along,' Miss Bishop's poems show that is barely but perfectly possible—has been, that is, for her."[3] Jarrell's insight is still true, but the price of "getting along" has risen steeply. Along with a greater acceptance of risk has come a greater willingness to share the common rewards and penalties of human life. Although she had always confronted loss as the price of possession, she now demonstrates the urgent need to keep paying it—showing an acceptance of a world that is not "serious, engravable," as "Over 2,000 Illustrations" had wished, but absurd and mutable and precious. The painful art of losing requires one to meet the challenge of love.

The hero of "In Prison" spoke with excitement of his coming incarceration, which would serve to enhance pleasure through enclosure and concentration. In "Crusoe in England" she presents a figure reminiscing about an unwilling incarceration. On Crusoe, the effect of concentration is to bring him face-to-face with emptiness. The poem is a summing up, a reconsideration of questions that had haunted her work from the start. It is also an allegorical reconsideration of her own life. Crusoe's kinship to the solitary figures of her early fables is profound, but for all his social isolation he knows the pleasures and compensations of the sensuous world with an immediacy they could not share. Here is, not Defoe's Puritan allegory on the value of piety and industry, nor the romantic assertion of triumph over solitude made of the novel by later readers, but an entirely new vision of a popular and durable myth. (As her Crusoe remarks, "None of the books has ever got it right"—CP, 162.) His main threats are, not physical want or hostile islanders, but boredom, sensory deprivation, and loneliness—what might be called the symbolist preoccupations. What Bishop explores is the ambiguity of identity, the ambiguity of possession, and his life emerges as an emblem of contemporary displacement. Crusoe "owns" his island, but he is deprived of all value. His means of survival—spiritually as well as physically—is to drain what sustenance he can from a barren place. For he is its Crusoe in extremis, with no beached ship, as in Defoe, providentially serving up its hoard of food, tools, and treasure. What he does possess are, characteristically for Bishop, objects that most would scorn or overlook.

> Well, I had fifty-two
> miserable, small volcanoes I could climb
> with a few slithery strides—
> volcanoes dead as ash heaps.

As in "One Art," Crusoe speaks of these explicitly in terms of ownership.

> The turtles lumbered by, high-domed,
> hissing like teakettles.
> (And I'd have given years, or taken a few,
> for any sort of kettle, of course.)
> The folds of lava, running out to sea,
> would hiss. I'd turn. And then they'd prove
> to be more turtles.
> The beaches were all lava, variegated,
> black, red, and white, and gray;
> the marbled colors made a fine display.
> And I had waterspouts. Oh,
> half a dozen at a time.   (CP, 163)

The island is both a realistic place and a hallucinatory vision that blends frustration and false promises with genuine, if curious, beauty. Bearing all its marvels, the language flows with a stunning colloquialism, mirroring the twists, turns, and sudden stops of cultivated speech. Crusoe owns things because no one would care to dispute his claim, but things he longed to possess, things as commonplace as a kettle, were lost. "His" waterspouts are "beautiful, yes, but not much company." Lovely things are empty when one cannot share them—a significant motto for a traveler's life.

With self-pity as his only companion—

> I told myself
> "Pity should begin at home." So the more
> pity I felt, the more I felt at home

—he lists the things that got him through his long sojourn by relieving the ennui of unwilling self-absorption. Bishop had fended off self-pity throughout her career, but here it is accepted as a familiar friend, another humanizing touch. But there is never enough variety. The sun is, significantly, as singular and barren as the man who watches it.

> The sun set in the sea; the same odd sun
> rose from the sea,
> and there was one of it and one of me.
> The island had one kind of everything.   (CP, 163)

For this sophisticated Crusoe of sad wit, who can speak of a vol-
cano as "*Mont d'Espoir* or *Mount Despair* / (I'd time enough to play
with names)" (*CP*, 165), the island swims in a symbolic poverty of
detail:

> one tree snail, a bright violet-blue
> with a thin shell, crept over everything,
> over the one variety of tree,
> a sooty scrub affair.   (*CP*, 163–64)

Where beauty exists, it is discovered; but nowhere save on this
emblematical island has Bishop found a landscape so scanty of correspondences. Is this landscape a vision of Bishop's pre-Brazilian
emotional life? Crusoe remains the reluctant solipsist; his survival
requires a perpetual flight from the self, from the "miserable philosophy" that he counts as "the smallest of my island industries"
(*CP*, 164). He flees through his home brew, through his weird
sounding flute, through dyeing "a baby goat bright red" (*CP*, 165),
through wishing to know more facts. None of these flights suffices
for long. Worst of all is the flight into dreams; the profoundest and
most frightening of his nightmares involves a proliferation of his
possessions:

> infinities
> of islands, islands spawning islands,
> like frogs' eggs turning into polliwogs
> of islands, knowing that I had to live
> on each and every one eventually,
> for ages, registering their flora,
> their fauna, their geography.

Bishop implicitly invites us to compare Crusoe's nightmare with a
nightmare version of her life of observations: a career of infinite
but barren travel, in which the only form of reproduction is the
mechanical creation of more insanely detailed but barren places to
travel to. It is the mind's own monstrosities that most terrify.

What relieves all this is the arrival of Friday, some "company."

> Just when I thought I couldn't stand it
> another minute longer, Friday came.
> (Accounts of that have everything all wrong.)
> Friday was nice.

> Friday was nice, and we were friends.
> If only he had been a woman!
> I wanted to propagate my kind,
> and so did he, I think, poor boy.

Friday makes things bearable, even if procreation is impossible. The analogy with Lota is transparent. Crusoe's terse "Friday was nice" suggests a range of emotion hiding behind the blandest of phrases. The pungent sexual impact of the scene is meant to disturb. Images of frustrated or meaningless propagation have cycled through the poem, and they reach their culmination here.

After they are taken off the island, Crusoe hankers after those years of lost intensity, when each least object vibrated with significance because there was so little else. When the poem began, Crusoe was back in England (just as Bishop was back in Boston), scanning the papers for news of his lost island. Ironically, now only the island, his lost possession, has meaning.

> The knife there on the shelf—
> it reeked of meaning, like a crucifix.
> It lived. How many years did I
> beg it, implore it, not to break?
> I know each nick and scratch by heart,
> the bluish blade, the broken tip,
> the lines of wood-grain on the handle . . .
> Now it won't look at me at all.   (CP, 166)

That intense correspondence with a few necessities, grown emblematical through long use and association, makes a new life hard to construct. Friday's death to measles, a childhood disease of civilization, and the implicit guilt of exposing him to that, are the ironic losses that crown a period of strangely accidental, ambiguous possession, possession one might rather have done without but that now one cannot live without.

In "The Fish," Bishop had dramatized the immediate moment. The poems of *Geography III* ponder the past—a past that like all valuable possessions, is emotionally complex, and in danger of being lost. For Crusoe, the past holds both pleasure and pain, but it cannot be excluded from any reckoning of the present. Bishop wrote to Anne Stevenson in 1964: "Because of my era, sex, situation, education I have written, so far, what I feel is a rather 'precious' kind of poetry, although I am very much opposed to the precious."[4] Bishop's earlier work may or may not be "precious" (I don't think the term applies to more than a small part of her writing), but *Geography III* achieves a note of striking authority—not just the authority of observation but that of participation. Perhaps only memory, the historian's art, can keep the knife speaking. But the blade of memory cuts two ways.

Another poem that makes discrete but telling use of memory, "Five Flights Up," is set at dawn—always, for her, a moment of decision. Here, the choice is whether to give up or to keep trying. The transition into day introduces a fresh world, (apparently) washed clean of memory. Waiting for the light, the observer, set apart in a high room, listens as neighboring animals greet the day.

> Still dark.
> The unknown bird sits on his usual branch.
> The little dog next door barks in his sleep
> inquiringly, just once.
> Perhaps in his sleep, too, the bird inquires
> once or twice, quavering.   (CP, 181)

The poem personifies animals very carefully. The bird's and dog's questions ("—if that is what they are—") are answered "directly, simply, / by day itself." The bird yawns, like a person. The master treats his dog like a person. He shouts "You ought to be ashamed!" But the dog "bounces cheerfully up and down; / . . . Obviously he has no sense of shame." The problem is that the observer *does*. While for bird and dog

> everything is answered,
> all taken care of,
> no need to ask again

for people, consciousness can be more dangerous. Although none of this is stated explicitly, the poem ends with a stunning and decisive shift of ground from the simple, direct activity outside the window to the trouble inside.

> —Yesterday brought to today so lightly!
> (A yesterday I find almost impossible to lift.)

The movement inward, the sudden confession of being at odds with life, is a powerful new note. The past is a shameful burden that can crush despite dawn's lightness. Here there are no miracles for breakfast. However, the will to lift yesterday characteristically remains; the word *almost* bears much of the weight, a testimony to endurance and perhaps also to curiosity about the unfolding dawnscape and what lies beyond it. Here again life seems "just barely" possible.

The prevalence of dawnscapes in Bishop's poetry reflects her fascination with this mysterious moment of transition into conscious life. Of course, half-light and twilight and dawn were points of particular appeal to symbolist poets, but Bishop's use of these settings is different. While for some poets these are times of dreaminess, of calm and release, of ambiguous intimations of death, by contrast, Bishop's poems confront the need for decision: a decision whether to go on with it all. (One recalls in this context "Roosters," "Love Lies Sleeping," and "Anaphora.") Although the sun biases the case by gilding the world with beautiful light, that light is bright enough to illuminate fundamental losses held in memory. Bishop's dawn poems reflect her powers of reconciliation. They accept necessity: the transition to day must be endured.

Enigmas of Travel

In Bishop's last work, travel becomes less and less literal, more and more enigmatic and symbolic. The now familiar oppositions between vicarious and real travel, between the fictive and the historical, reappear in newly formulated terms. This is particularly true of that mystical exploration "In the Waiting Room" (1971). Here is a child Pascal would have approved of; but though she is *"just sitting quietly in [a] room"* (CP, 94), she travels vastly and strangely, and the roots of a poetic vocation are uncovered. A young girl, surrounded by adults in a dentist's waiting room, sits alone waiting for her aunt. No one is paying attention. She has no function to serve. The girl discovers paradoxically not only her solitude but her identity with the larger world outside. She gains awareness of real alternative worlds that are strange, alluring, frightening—but just as valid as one's own. Reading the *National Geographic* (a vicarious form of travel), she discovers unsettling actualities that provoke an experience mysteriously com-

bining knowledge of possession and identity with intimations of
loss, displacement, and personal obliteration.

> A dead man slung on a pole
> —"Long Pig," the caption said.
> Babies with pointed heads
> wound round and round with string;
> black, naked women with necks
> wound round and round with wire
> like the necks of light bulbs.
> Their breasts were horrifying.
> I read it right straight through.
> I was too shy to stop.   (CP, 159)

The *National Geographic*'s colonialist perspective, a perspective the
child sometimes sees through, betrays itself through that journal's
peculiar failure to see "a dead man slung on a pole" as human. But
the child displays a cultural value she has *already* imbibed when
she says, "Their breasts were horrifying." Since the speaker is a
girl, her statement betrays fear not simply of sexuality in general
but of her own sexuality. The Northern world of the dentist's waiting room, a place where we carry out an unpleasant duty to ourselves, is overdressed, stuffy, and careful, a place of "arctics and
overcoats." The girl is made uncomfortably aware of a common
humanity cutting across racial and cultural boundaries. Her comparison of the women's necks to something familiar but wrong—
light bulbs—heightens the terror, of course, by beginning to make
another culture's more extravagant gestures familiar enough to
seem meaningful. The experience is frightening, but it is not
shunned. The line "I was too shy to stop" reveals, in its wry, precise way, the child's profound respect, not simply for the authority
of pictures and the printed word, but also for the diversities of
geography. This moment refers both to the mapmaker *and* the historian. Her immersion in remote experience is penetrated by a cry
from *this* world,

> an *oh!* of pain
> —Aunt Consuelo's voice—
> not very loud or long.   (CP, 160)

The interpenetration of close and distant worlds calls forth a mystical state in which identity is both gained and surrendered.

What took me
completely by surprise
was that it was *me:*
my voice, in my mouth.
Without thinking at all
I was my foolish aunt,
I—we—were falling, falling,
our eyes glued to the cover
of the *National Geographic,*
February, 1918.

By a reflex, by a response that comes "Without thinking at all," the girl suddenly grows aware of her human identity and through that loses her childlike innocence of self, her innocence of the fact that she is a separate, lonely being. Paradoxically, this recognition begets a sense of connectedness—even identity—with the rest of mankind. All are alone, all falling. Her eyes cling to small certainties like the date of her magazine to counteract the unsteadying effect.

I said to myself: three days
and you'll be seven years old.
I was saying it to stop
the sensation of falling off
the round, turning world
into cold, blue-black space.

Bishop's child-persona here takes another step toward self-awareness. The whole effort of the observant but young child in "In the Village" was to block out awareness of what she was losing, as she watches her mother's sanity give way. Here, the slightly older child begins to confront the planet's threatening but irresistible diversity. The *National Geographic* symbolizes that planet's awesome breadth and the insignificance of herself or any other separate person. But even more, it betrays the emptiness of what we call real and the insubstantiality of the boundaries upon which we smugly rely—the boundaries between selves; the boundaries between cultures.

But I felt: you are an *I,*
you are an *Elizabeth,*

> you are one of *them*.
> *Why* should you be one, too?

Subject creates object. Her thoughts unfold with logical inevitability. As soon as one becomes an *I*, one becomes an *Elizabeth*, a social being burdened with a name and not an autonomous soul. To be an Elizabeth makes her one of *them:* the adults sitting dully in the waiting room, or the distant tribesmen with their horrifying dress. *Both* seem strangely foreign, yet the child must study them, "to see what it was I was." She has enjoyed no moment of pure, unalloyed being. Without having asked, one is immediately usurped, made part of a larger whole, a North & South.

> I knew that nothing stranger
> had ever happened, that nothing
> stranger could ever happen.

The *them* that she is part of extends beyond the adults clustered in the waiting room, then circles back into herself.

> Why should I be my aunt,
> or me, or anyone?
> What similarities—
> boots, hands, the family voice
> I felt in my throat, or even
> the *National Geographic*
> and those awful hanging breasts—
> held us together
> or made us all just one?   (CP, 161)

These questions, unanswerable, grope toward the elusive substance of identity, the blank strangeness of being. The child goes on asking fundamental, unanswerable questions: "How had I come to be here, / like them . . . ?" The bright, stuffy waiting room, a microcosm of polite, cluttered adult society, grows insubstantial,

> Sliding
> beneath a big black wave,
> another, and another.

Finally the rhythm of vertigo simply and abruptly stops. One returns to the waiting room, more or less as it was.

> Then I was back in it.
> The War was on. Outside,
> in Worcester, Massachusetts,
> were night and slush and cold,
> and it was still the fifth
> of February, 1918.

The suggestiveness of these lines deserves comment. "The War was on" seems to expand from a factual acknowledgment of World War I to an implicit generalization about the human condition, and this is supported by reference to "night and slush and cold," to the chill, dark muddle that the world so often seems. So while the external facts remain unchanged, and one can even repeat them with a certain comfort, the universe has been utterly transformed. This poem has the quality of a memoir of a formative experience, perhaps *the* formative experience, leading to an unconscious acceptance of the responsibility of a poetic vocation. (The parallel I have in mind is Whitman's "Out of the Cradle. . . .") The experience in the waiting room is a telling piece of spiritual autobiography: facets of the child's recognition reach toward every aspect of the mature poet's work. At the same time, the experience is universal in its recognition of the mysteries of identity, the weight of history, and the obstacles to human understanding.

Small Worlds and Quiet Rooms

Bishop's later poems are just as inclined to explore enclosures or objects within frames as her earlier work had been, but there are important developments. In the earlier work, enclosures and frames dangerously limit as they protect, and the chance of escape is only hinted at. They threaten to cut one off, to enforce a purely vicarious life. They inspire a sterile kind of imagination. In her later work, enclosures and frames tend to open dramatically, both outward and inward, as "In the Waiting Room" and "Crusoe" did. These small worlds and quiet rooms hold an extraordinary intensity within. When the framed object is a small painting that has been in the family for years, it becomes the occasion for a keen look at the value of art and the past, at what even a tiny framed "world" can contain.

"Poem" (1972) considers another work by the painter of "Large Bad Picture," her great-uncle George Hutchinson. Unlike the bad picture, which was large and pretentious, this one is slight and unassuming. Unlike the technically inept bad picture, this one shows an impressionist's deft *suggestion* of detail. (In fact, we learn, the painter was misrepresented in the earlier poem. Instead of acquiescing to lack of talent and becoming "a schoolteacher," he went to England and achieved membership in the Royal Academy.) What remains constant from the earlier poem to the later is the underlying dramatic movement.

"Poem" begins by dryly noting the external qualities of the painting: its tininess and obsolescence ("About the size of an old-style dollar bill"), its muted colors, its failure to "earn . . . any money in its life." This painting seems a trifling thing.

> Useless and free, it has spent seventy years
> as a minor family relic
> handed along collaterally to owners
> who looked at it sometimes, or didn't bother to.(*CP,* 176)

She presents its dashing, painterly, but conventional technique, sometimes with admiration, sometimes with small amusement, all the while deftly pulling in the picture's features.

> Elm trees, low hills, a thin church steeple
> —that gray-blue wisp—or is it? In the foreground
> a water meadow with some tiny cows,
> two brushstrokes each, but confidently cows;
> two miniscule white geese in the blue water,
> back-to-back, feeding, and a slanting stick.
> Up closer, a wild iris, white and yellow,
> fresh-squiggled from the tube.

The casual, cataloguing quality of the speech vividly suggests an observer's first really attentive encounter with a familiar object. She remains emotionally distanced, even as the painting's tininess demands her concentration, wondering wryly whether that "specklike bird" isn't really a "flyspeck looking like a bird."

At first, she had recognized the site only as someplace in Nova Scotia, where both she and her relative grew up. She dismisses the locale as fitting the genre Impressionist landscape—just as Santos had been dismissed as fitting the genre "foreign port." But then, as in "Large Bad Picture," the painting suddenly gains a new dimension.

> Heavens, I recognize the place, I know it!
> It's behind—I can almost remember the farmer's name.

This recognition shocks deeply submerged memories to the surface. The place is then slowly repossessed. Such investment does not dim one's shrewd scrutiny of the painter's technique, but it allows one to participate in the painting actively, bringing ambiguous detail (such as the steeple) or ignored detail (such as a certain spot of white) into focus.

> His barn backed on that meadow. There it is,
> titanium white, one dab. The hint of steeple,
> filaments of brush-hairs, barely there,
> must be the Presbyterian church.

The observer completes the landscape. And, of course, her response is the real subject of the poem. A shared memory transforms a work of art, making its contemplation not merely a cool aesthetic exercise but an emotional reply. The painter and the poet unite as their two sightings converge—the recognition and recreation is a collaboration in which each plays a part. Short, abrupt phrases capture the effect of thinking aloud, feeling one's way, at a pace that suggests growing entrancement.

> I never knew him. We both knew this place,
> apparently, this literal small backwater,
> looked at it long enough to memorize it,
> our years apart. How strange. And it's still loved,
> or its memory is (it must have changed a lot.)   (CP, 177)

One loves, not the place itself or the painting, but the place as it was, as it remained in the painting and locked in one's memory—the continuity to the past, the slowness to change that hung about a former time, which this casual sketch, "done in an hour, 'in one breath'" recaptures.

Because of its power to recreate a world, this tiny, apparently insignificant study becomes, in a sense, life itself—that is, it brings one as close to this *piece* of life as one will ever get again.

> Our visions coincided—"visions" is
> too serious a word—our looks, two looks:

art "copying from life" and life itself,
life and the memory of it so compressed
they've turned into each other. Which is which?

Bishop casually compresses a complex view of art into a few lines.
She notes that "'visions' is too serious a word" partly out of mod-
esty, no doubt—but she also sets her "look" apart from the visionary, romantic way of seeing that has become a habit of mind and
speech. Here is no "vision"—something transformed by imagination—but something that really happened. Imagination plays a
role, of course, in the recreation of this scene, but in no sense does
Bishop claim prophetic insight. What she does claim is that the
scene summoned up is as close to remembered "life" as one can
come—which is not a modest claim at all.

Life and the memory of it cramped,
dim, on a piece of Bristol board,
dim, but how live, how touching in detail
—the little that we get for free,
the little of our earthly trust. Not much.

Not much, but perhaps enough. The understatement here is devastating. Bishop's whole career was devoted to "the little that we
get for free." Her eye for overlooked detail had created a poetic
world as immutable as language but melancholy in its transience.
Like her great-uncle the painter, she had captured things that
really happened on their way to becoming changed or lost.

"Memory is a kind / of accomplishment," said Williams.[5] The
painting, a "minor family relic," accomplishes a link in the gener-
ations even as it symbolizes change. By the close, one has forgotten
to notice the painterly technique, the strokes and squiggles and
dabs, and the picture lives, freshly and with emblematic force. It
has come to seem not merely "about the size of an old-style dollar
bill" but

About the size of our abidance
along with theirs: the munching cows,
the iris, crisp and shivering, the water
still standing from spring freshets,
the yet-to-be-dismantled elms, the geese.

This is one of the finest closings Bishop ever wrote. Bishop joins
with her ancestor in recreating a place that neither could render

alone, a scene with a past and a future that it would have been a shame to miss. Composed in quietly stunning language—listen to the way "the iris, crisp and shivering" sits delicately on the tip of the tongue and how, by appropriate contrast, "the munching cows" works the back of the jaw—the moment resonates with loss and gain. Elms, dismantled branch by branch after Dutch elm disease, still live in this painting and in memory. The possessions of memory cannot overrule the destruction of time, but a lost world still lives *there*, "dim, on a piece of Bristol board." Bishop's poetry explores the "size of our abidance"—the scope of achievement within the limits of this world.

The link between memory and art is essential. Neither memory nor art can transform the world, but each keeps realities alive in the face of loss. Perhaps more important, art bridges isolation or detachment, as her own detachment dissolves before the image created by her great-uncle. Whether in words or on canvas, art preserves what really happened with such vigor that it seems to happen again. Here is not merely art "copying from life" but something almost indistinguishable, for the moment, from "life itself." Like life itself, memory is ambiguous: it can be a burden, making "yesterday . . . almost impossible to lift," as in "Five Flights Up" (*CP,* 181). It can also offer solace. To turn toward memory and history is to accept the common human lot.

The surreal glimpses always present in her work become more than just glimpses in *Geography III.* For example, "Objects & Apparitions," the tribute to collage-in-a-box artist Joseph Cornell that Bishop translated from the Spanish of Octavio Paz (it was included in the first edition of *Geography III,* the only translation she ever included in a book of original poems), shows continued alertness to the way art can renew the ordinary, opposing the destruction of time.

> Minimal, incoherent fragments:
> the opposite of History, creator of ruins,
> out of your ruins you have made creations.   (*CP,* 275)

In *Geography III* Bishop made creations out of her own ruins. Joseph Cornell would appreciate the transforming power of context displayed by Bishop's quotation of fragments from the nineteenth-century primer *First Lessons in Geography,* which serve as an epigraph to the volume. The simplistic questions from the old geography text, with their sound of catechism, are transformed, becoming open-ended and enigmatic, a poignant *trouvée,* an oddly mysterious found object that speaks to our spiritual displacement. The old faith in Geographic certainties being lost, these questions seek objects that are not there but should be there. As in the boxes of Cornell:

> The apparitions are manifest,
> their bodies weigh less than light,
> lasting as long as this phrase lasts.

Bishop's translations can be suggestive because the poems she chooses to translate are, almost inevitably, more explicit in their declarations of intention and value than Bishop ever cares to be. They often state principles to which she would have assented. Her own poetry is, like Cornell's boxes, a:

> Theatre of the spirits:
> objects putting the laws
> of identity through hoops.

For Bishop, a painting like the one described in "Poem" is a theater of the spirits. So is the writing desk in "12 O'Clock News" (1973). In a certain mood, a writer's desk drifts toward the geography of a strange and destitute planet. One implicit purpose of "12 O'Clock News" (*CP,* 174) is to satirize the smugness and condescension of North American observers toward Brazil. But there is also a personal reference to the loneliness and frustration of the writer's life. The workplace takes on a life of its own as a barren moonlit battleground. The bizarre and lonely life of the workplace reflects the time and intensity the writer pumps into it. The gooseneck lamp a dead moon? The typewriter an elaborately terraced escarpment? A pile of manuscripts a landslide exposing soil "of poor quality"? These tongue-in-cheek transformations turn the speaker, a condescending newscaster, into a gigantic modern-day Gulliver, while the tiny "indigenes" of the strange landscape are Lilliputians: the typewriter eraser is a "unicyclist-courier . . . with . . . thick, bristling black hair" (*CP,* 175). The poem ironically suggests how condescension (for her the greatest of sins) warps the world into a comforting place where others can be discounted as foolish and inferior. On another level, she hints at the anxiety and dislocation

a writer feels when faced with a pile of manuscripts "of poor quality" (*CP,* 174).

Although the poems discussed so far begin within a frame, then
penetrate outward (and deeper inward), in some, the enclosure can
be an imagined haven that one contemplates in the course of
travel. Such a case is "The End of March" (1975), which Harold
Bloom calls "another great poem of the American shoreline to go
with Emerson's *Seashore,* Whitman's *Out of the Cradle . . .* and *As
I Ebb'd . . .* , Steven's *The Idea of Order at Key West,* and Crane's
Voyages I." [6] The poem holds its own amidst this heady company by
relying on cool understatement, a conversational tone, and a sense
of immense power in reserve. The opposition between one's yearning for enclosure and peace and the exposure of the windy beach
at Duxbury, Massachusetts, is enacted on a forbidding March day.

> It was cold and windy, scarcely the day
> to take a walk on that long beach.
> Everything was withdrawn as far as possible,
> indrawn: the tide far out, the ocean shrunken,
> seabirds in ones or twos.   (*CP,* 179)

The way is strewn with puzzles, which suggest that this indrawn
place, where correspondences are in retreat, was recently the site
of some enigmatic activity or meaning.

> Along the wet sand, in rubber boots, we followed
> the track of big dog-prints (so big
> they were more like lion prints). Then we came on
> lengths and lengths, endless, of wet white string,
> looping up to the tide-line, down to the water,
> over and over. Finally, they did end:
> a thick white snarl, man-size, awash,
> rising on every wave, a sodden ghost,
> falling back, sodden, giving up the ghost. . . .
> A kite string?—But no kite.

Intriguing, but what do they amount to? As in so many other large-
scale poems, Bishop lays out details like paints on a palette, to be
blended and shaped later.

Set against this shrunken, puzzling world is the object of the
journey: a place not unlike a hermit's cell in which to be indrawn
but comfortable.

> I wanted to get as far as my proto-dream-house,
> my crypto-dream-house, that crooked box
> set up on pilings, shingled green.

It reminds one of Edwin Boomer's shoreward house "not for living in, for thinking in" (*CProse,* 172) and of "The Monument":

> "piled up boxes,
> outlined with shoddy fret-work, half-fallen off,
> cracked and unpainted. It looks old."   (*CP,* 24)

Like the monument, this house is an ambiguous, decaying shrine. Bishop recreates it in brilliant, funny, deprecating language: "a sort of artichoke of a house, but greener / (boiled with bicarbonate of soda?)" (*CP,* 179). This rundown, disheveled place, despite (or perhaps because of) its many dubious details, lures one on. Like Edwin Boomer's little house it promises to isolate, protect, and concentrate the imagination. Its emptiness is its allure.

> I'd like to retire there and do *nothing*
> or nothing much, forever, in two bare rooms:
> look through binoculars, read boring books,
> old, long, long books, and write down useless notes,
> talk to myself, and, foggy days,
> watch the droplets slipping, heavy with light.
> At night, a *grog à l'américaine.*   (*CP,* 179–80)

Of course, the urge to "retire" and "do *nothing*" is something each of us feels from time to time, on March days of the soul when everything "is withdrawn as far as possible, / indrawn" (*CP,* 179). But escape through concentration in the self, for all its dangers, also has value, and that value emerges implicitly as the poem opens upon its final recognition.

In Bishop's offhand way, she has made this house the object of a quest, and the quest is not fulfilled. Indeed, a thought of what would make the house perfect reminds her of why it won't work out:

> A light to read by—perfect! But—impossible.
> And that day the wind was much too cold
> even to get that far,
> and of course the house was boarded up.   (*CP,* 180)

Of course, the "perfect" always is "impossible." Turning away from the house is the poem's decisive action, and it leads toward a passage of extraordinary beauty. The house has been imaginatively created, then renounced, in the face of forbidding realities. Is the brief but dazzling vision that follows nature's reward for that renunciation?

> On the way back our faces froze on the other side.
> The sun came out for just a minute.
> For just a minute, set in their bezels of sand,
> the drab, damp, scattered stones
> were multi-colored,
> and all those high enough threw out long shadows,
> individual shadows, then pulled them in again.

The elements laid on the palette at last come together as a vivid canvas. The surprising word *bezels* is perfect. Bishop emphasizes the transience of this revelation, but transience only enhances its appeal. The "individual shadows" lend the transformed stones will and personality, to which the imagination gladly consents.

> They could have been teasing the lion sun,
> except that now he walked behind them
> —a sun who'd walked the beach the last low tide,
> making those big, majestic paw-prints,
> who perhaps had batted a kite out of the sky to play with.

Harold Bloom has concluded: "The trope of the lion-sun, magnificent in itself, and charming in its solution of the earlier emblems of the puzzle, affects us so strongly because the poem, and so much of Bishop's poetry, gives us the necessity of redressing an achieved *poverty,* in Emerson's sense (which is also Stevens') of *imaginative need.*"[7] Imaginative need is answered by a mind refreshed by a quest for an enigmatic life of enclosure. The parallel to Emerson and Stevens is apt, but here they are dramatized and demystified. The renunciation of the quest to reach the dream house makes possible the expansive vision (here one may use the term) with which the poem ends. "The lion sun . . . / —a sun who'd walked the beach the last low tide" has a surreal energy that grows out of the circumstances of everyday life. Evidently, the surrealism of everyday life sometimes needs help from imaginary "*grog à l'américaine.*"

«The Moose»

Perhaps no poem in *Geography III* more fully embodies all the strengths of Bishop's late period than "The Moose."
"The Moose" was twenty years in the writing, before it was finally
published in 1972. It is her longest poem, and it beautifully combines the qualities of inwardness and adventure. Begun during her
first years in Brazil, when she was writing the first autobiographical stories of her childhood, its composition spans her later phase.
The bus ride it embarks on, away from Nova Scotia, toward Boston, her two Northern homes, emblematizes what she had called
in an interview "This strange life of travel." The poem is a long
good-bye. The first word, *From*, sets us in motion away from provinces that are also home. The first six stanzas are one long sentence, and this sentence serves to characterize the region from
which the bus departs. Drab and provincial, tied to the daily monotony of "fish and bread and tea," it contains its share of familiar
marvels. For example, it edges the Bay of Fundy, one of nature's
most remarkable creations:

> home of the long tides
> where the bay leaves the sea
> twice a day and takes
> the herrings long rides,
>
> where if the river
> enters or retreats
> in a wall of brown foam
> depends on if it meets
> the bay coming in,
> the bay not at home.   (CP, 169)

The bay is *home* to the long tides; it is personified as a domesticated
creature: "the bay coming in, / the bay not at home." This extraordinary natural fact, the evacuation of the bay of Fundy with each
low tide, followed, at high tide, by the return of the bay, which
causes a reverse waterfall in the St. John River, is treated as an
ordinary, habitual event, but the language also keeps it startling.
Passing familiar marvels, the bus embarks on a pilgrimage that
modulates into the unknown.

There are surprising, even lurid harmonies. The same red sun that in setting

> veins the flats'
> lavender, rich mud
> in burning rivulets

links them to the red roads. The neat churches express an unusual accord with nature, their white clapboard sides bleached and ridged like the clamshells that line Fundy's beaches. Riding away, one is separated from these surprising harmonies, but, in the act of parting, one takes note of and reaffirms them.

Bishop's finest poems almost always give the appearance of digressing or wandering while they accumulate elements that gradually acquire symbolic weight. Only in the fifth stanza, after the home setting is established, does the dramatic situation of the speaker begin to emerge. There the inclusive initial sentence finds its subject and predicate after a very long prepositional phrase: "From narrow provinces . . ./ . . . a *bus journeys* west" (my italics). The observer is in transit; enclosure in the bus dramatizes a characteristic and comfortable poetic posture that opens on a realm that is homely but increasingly dreamlike.

> the windshield flashing pink,
> pink glancing off of metal,
> brushing the dented flank
> of blue, beat-up enamel;
>
> down hollows, up rises,
> and waits, patient, while
> a lone traveller gives
> kisses and embraces
> to seven relatives
> and a collie supervises.   (CP, 169–70)

The bus is faithful, "patient," adapted to human ways. Its idling motor presides over a good-humored reaffirmation of family affection that marks the continuing departure from home. The opening's general image of the pastoral Maritime Provinces gives way to a specific bus trip (or pilgrimage), made in a dented vehicle that fully harmonizes with the setting. The bus is a human link in a poor country. It will come to seem a vessel of our common destiny.

The dreamlike creeps forward as home begins to fall behind. Fog encloses the bus, isolating it and surrealistically transforming the place from which it takes farewell. Meanwhile, the pace accelerates. The six-stanza-long opening sentence balances unequally against the clipped sentence: "The bus starts." Now that one is moving faster, close study of the roadside gives way to intriguing glimpses. The towns mentioned as she passes are next on the way from her Nova Scotia home. The rhyming is casually effective.

> One stop at Bass River.
> Then the Economies—
> Lower, Middle, Upper;
> Five Islands, Five Houses,
> where a woman shakes a tablecloth
> out after supper.
>
> A pale flickering. Gone.   (CP, 170)

We slip past, touched by fleeting sensations.

> The Tantramar marshes
> and the smell of salt hay.
> An iron bridge trembles
> and a loose plank rattles
> but doesn't give way.

These glimpses hint at a larger world, which, from one's perspective inside the bus, one cannot actually see: a smell, a sound, a quiver of insecurity.

Out of this fogbound mystery emerge two rubber boots that belong to a woman who boards the bus. Her look, her remark, and her bright tone support the consistent mood, embodying openness to common experience.

> A woman climbs in
> with two market bags,
> brisk, freckled, elderly.
> "A grand night. Yes, sir,
> all the way to Boston."
> She regards us amicably.   (CP, 171)

Here the wording might be prose, and throughout it is of remarkable plainness, rising effortlessly to eloquence only when eloquence is needed. For the old woman, even this foggy night is grand. Fog makes the familiar world seem alien and dislocated. The light and mist caught in New Brunswick pines "like lamb's wool" has the intimate discomfort of wool on flesh: "hairy, scratchy, splintery."

At last we reach the first of the poem's two decisive passages; it moves into a profound dream state as the passengers drift off to sleep, a state long prepared by evocations of home and fog. The domestic element lives in the conversation that is overheard, the homey speech of "Grandparents' voices."

> The passengers lie back.
> Snores. Some long sighs.
> A dreamy divagation
> begins in the night,
> a gentle, auditory,
> slow hallucination. . . .
>
> In the creakings and noises,
> an old conversation
> —not concerning us,
> but recognizable, somewhere,
> back in the bus:
> Grandparents' voices.

Their talk has the air of twice-told tales. It is not a philosophical discussion but a review of the facts. But it works like a slow, meditative hallucination, abstracting like the fog, rendering what shows through with emblematic intensity:

> uninterruptedly
> talking, in Eternity:
> names being mentioned,
> things cleared up finally;
> what he said, what she said,
> who got pensioned;
>
> deaths, deaths and sicknesses;
> the year he remarried;
> the year (something) happened.
> She died in childbirth.

> That was the son lost
> when the schooner foundered.   (CP, 171–72)

These lines marvelously recapture the experience of chance conversations overheard. One shares in the intimate talk of the
marriage bed, but since one doesn't know the people, the "recognizable" experience they discuss begins to stand for all human experience, set in the context of "Eternity." Overhearing, one notices
that this "clearing up" becomes more and more a tally of disasters:
a list of the different ways human dreams can be shattered, an
authoritative catalogue of loss. Even more significant than the list
is the response to it. The voices go on:

> He took to drink. Yes.
> She went to the bad.
> When Amos began to pray
> even in the store and
> finally the family had
> to put him away.

> "Yes . . ." that peculiar
> affirmative. "Yes . . ."
> A sharp, indrawn breath,
> half groan, half acceptance,
> that means "Life's like that.
> We know *it* (also death)."   (CP, 172)

Bishop's "Grandparents' voices" seem to affirm life as a whole, including its necessary sorrows, including even death. Their "peculiar affirmative," on the face of it a mere acknowledgement that
something happened, is repeated quietly, with no exhilaration,
certainly, but rather with resignation—"half groan, half acceptance." Even in this "Yes" one is not aspiring to transcendence. One
works with what is given.

The grandparents' voices almost certainly have their source in
the voices of the grandparents that raised her in Great Village.
This would account for the dreamy homeward drift that runs
counter to the fact of tedious departure. Amos, whose excessively
demonstrative devotion to God forms the climax of this catalogue,
parallels Bishop's mother Gertrude's excessive grief over her husband's death. Gertrude Bishop had to be put away by her reluctant

parents, while the young Elizabeth looked on. Bishop may have remembered or imagined overhearing such conversations as a child and grafted that hearth-and-bed knowledge onto the experience of the journey.

> Talking the way they talked
> in the old featherbed,
> peacefully, on and on,
> dim lamplight in the hall,
> down in the kitchen, the dog
> tucked in her shawl.

In leaving home, one finds it. Losses, the poem seems to say, one's own and the losses of those one loves, are among the necessities of human existence. To see that, and as far as possible to accept it, may be the only kind of freedom one can know. Once these facts are faced again, once these things are "cleared up finally," one is free to accept the offered balm of rest.

> Now, it's all right now
> even to fall asleep
> just as on all those nights.
> —Suddenly the bus driver
> stops with a jolt,
> turns off his lights.

Then the repose so briefly achieved is jolted by a surprising confrontation. The driver turns off his lights because of what he sees ahead. And what he sees emerges as possible support for the acceptance in the grandparents' voices.

> A moose has come out of
> the impenetrable wood
> and stands there, looms, rather,
> in the middle of the road.
> It approaches; it sniffs at
> the bus's hot hood.

The moose observes the phenomenon of the bus as the people observe the moose. In "The Fish," the creature from another element seems indifferent to humanity. Here the moose is herself curious. In their curiosity, the moose and the people on the bus are strangely equal.

Even this moose, a creature from the "impenetrable wood," reminds one, like the fish, of the homey, the familiar.

> Towering, anterless,
> high as a church,
> homely as a house
> (or, safe as houses).
> A man's voice assures us
> "Perfectly harmless. . . ."
>
> Some of the passengers
> exclaim in whispers,
> childishly, softly,
> "Sure are big creatures."
> "It's awful plain."
> "Look! It's a she!"
>
> Taking her time,
> she looks the bus over,
> grand, otherwordly.
> Why, why do we feel
> (we all feel) this sweet
> sensation of joy?   (CP, 173)

The universal feeling of joy shared by all the passengers contrasts with the atmosphere of universal sorrow and resignation established earlier. Just as sadness is universal, so is joy. Biologist Lewis Thomas suggests that people are programmed to respond in an affectionate way to certain kinds of animal activity. Thomas said, "The behavior released in us by such confrontations, is, essentially, a surprised affection. It is compulsory behavior and we can avoid it only by straining with the full power of our conscious minds."[8] Here is a biological form of necessity. The passengers on the bus are brought together. They enjoy the moose for what it is. They find in it a benign reflection of themselves. And then the time of contemplation passes and the demands of commerce resume. The bus driver simply turns the engine on again.

> "Curious creatures,"
> says our quiet driver,
> rolling his r's.

"Look at that, would you."
Then he shifts gears.
For a moment longer,

by craning backward,
the moose can be seen
on the moonlit macadam;
then there's a dim
smell of moose, an acrid
smell of gasoline.

The people who crane their necks are loath to lose sight of this animal, yet they silently consent to the resumption of the journey. The moose has swiftly become the kind of possession that *Geography III* keeps returning to, one held in memory. The moose seems intended to emblematize the homely beauties that partly reconcile one to life. She is one thing in a threatening world that is "high as a church" and "safe as houses." From an alien environment, not remotely human, she still communicates in her own way.

In the end, one loses sight of the moose and clings to a still more transient possession: smell. The "dim / smell of moose" is cut by the "acrid / smell of gasoline." That whiff of petroleum returns one to mundane facts. This symbolic glimpse of moose has depended on the dented, smelly bus. One abruptly returns from an elevated moment of meditative understanding to an awareness of the ordinary facts that occasioned it. The flat setting asserts itself over a transcendent moment, which remains only as a transient glimmer. Which is more real?

«New, tender, quick»

In "The Moose" Bishop found a narrative that could bring to life much of what she had been saying throughout her career. The "dreamy divagation" is as close as she ever came to stating the convictions that underlie her work. She wrote to Anne Stevenson: "My outlook is pessimistic. I think we are still barbarians, barbarians who commit a hundred indecencies and cruelties every day of our lives, as just possibly future ages may be able to see. But I think we should be gay in spite of it, sometimes even giddy—to make life endurable and keep ourselves 'new, tender, quick.'"⁹ Bishop's remark reminds one of her closeness to George Herbert. She is quoting "Love Unknown," on which she had based "The Weed" thirty years earlier. In Herbert's poem, God imposes a discipline of suffering in order to make a man "new, tender, quick." Throughout her life, Bishop remained on intimate terms with Herbert's poetry. Like Herbert, she suggests that only a lively but disciplined spirit can see aright. Bishop suggests that one must discipline the ego to a recognition of its need for devotion to the world, even if the world disappoints or dismays. This is the only way "to make life endurable," and it makes even gaiety possible. All possessions, her work suggests, are ambiguous. We may even be barbarous possessors. Possession implies the certainty of loss and suffering. But despite some yesterdays that she found "almost impossible to lift" (CP, 181), Bishop reveals a discriminating relish for that most ambiguous of possessions: life.

The paradox of Bishop's career is that its importance rests on her devotion to the humble and overlooked, the seemingly unimportant. Her imaginative attention to things that don't appear to matter keeps her own eye "new, tender, quick" and gives her work its special freshness. The vitality and cogency of her language confirm that the things she observes *do* matter and, often, that they contain a surprising beauty, even a surprising power to reconcile or console. The coherence of her work is implied by her consistent choice of subjects, which includes minor art objects, the poor, and tropical countries dominated politically and economically by North America. Amongst the discarded and ignored, she finds examples of integrity, dignity, courage, humor, and grace. In the grip of an unstated pessimism, her work nonetheless quietly seeks the affirmative, in that it everywhere implies that careful observations are worth making, that there are any number of things worth sticking around to see.

Bishop's work is sometimes acknowledged as masterly by those who, at the same time, perceive her as standing outside the mainstream of contemporary poetry. For example, Robert Mazzacco calls her "that cat curiosity did not kill. Also the cat who walks alone."¹⁰ Bishop really *is* a singular poet. No one who loves her work would want it any other way. But this should not keep readers from acknowledging that she is also a central poet or from appreciating why so many younger poets have made a point of doing her homage. Claims for her centrality rest most heavily, of course, on the sheer quality of what she has done, but it is also important to see that her work shares and responds freshly to the vital concerns of her contemporaries. If Karl Malkoff is right that "the defining characteristic of contemporary American poetry is its abandonment of the ego—the conscious self—as the inevitable perspective from which reality must be viewed,"[11] then Bishop's work is important in offering a viable alternative to the approaches that Malkoff's book, *Escape from the Self,* studies, those of the confessional and Black Mountain poets. For Bishop, escape from the self is convincingly achieved through the old-fashioned means of self-forgetfulness. As she said, employing phrases that I have often quoted: "What one seems to want in art, in experiencing it, is the same thing that is necessary for its creation, a self-forgetful, perfectly useless concentration. (In this sense it is always 'escape. . . .')."[12] An observing self can always be found in Bishop's writing, but its presence is made known with such subtle understatement that it is almost not felt. In confessional verse the self is borne like an albatross, and its escape is often the explicit, even desperate, issue of the poem. In Bishop's poems, most often the escape is already achieved (through that "perfectly useless" concentration) and the observation is moving on. Only in the earliest and latest poetry is the self implicitly or explicitly acknowledged. These poems help us to see how difficult and successful the achievement actually was.

A poet like Bishop inevitably raises certain questions. Anne Stevenson called her "finer than Lowell, though of course more limited."[13] The word *escape,* so important in the above letter to Stevenson, can be taken either negatively or positively, when one considers Bishop's "limits." Are Bishop's humble subjects and pastoral or dreamy divagations, even her elegance and technical control, part of an escape from the anxiety of modern experience? Bishop's poetry considers the temptation of escape, but it is not escapist, any more than George Herbert's is. Her poems resemble religious meditation in that they are neither a turning inward nor a turning away but a turning toward. But at heart Bishop is resolutely secular. What she turns toward is neither the mystical nor the eternal. It is the here and now, and it is the significant past. These she sees with that rarest of faculties, "infant sight."

NOTES

BIBLIOGRAPHY

INDEX

Introduction

1 Bishop to Robert Lowell, 14 February 1948, Houghton Library, Harvard University.

2 Mark Strand, dust jacket of Elizabeth Bishop, *The Complete Poems: 1927–1979*.

3 See, for example, Harold Bloom, "*Geography III* by Elizabeth Bishop."

4 Randall Jarrell, *Poetry and the Age*, pp. 234–35; Robert Lowell, "Thomas, Bishop, and Williams," pp. 497–99.

5 David Kalstone, *Five Temperaments*, p. 12.

6 Anne Stevenson, *Elizabeth Bishop*, p. 31. Jerome Mazzaro, "Elizabeth Bishop's Poems," p. 100.

7 Kalstone, *Five Temperaments*, p. 13.

8 M. L. Rosenthal, *The Modern Poets*, p. 235.

9 Donald Sheehan, "The Silver Sensibility: Five Recent Books of American Poetry," p. 106.

10 Robert Mazzacco, "A Poet of Landscape," p. 5.

11 James G. Southworth, "The Poetry of Elizabeth Bishop," p. 213; Peggy Rizza, "Another Side of This Life: Women as Poets," in *American Poetry since 1960: Some Critical Perspectives*, ed. Robert B. Shaw (Chester Springs, Pa.: Dufour Editions, 1974), p. 170.

12 Mazzaro, "Elizabeth Bishop's Poems," p. 100.

13 Elizabeth Bishop, *The Complete Poems: 1927–1979*, p. 42. Hereafter all quotations from this book will be cited in the text as *CP*, followed by the page number. Quotations from *The Collected Prose* will be cited as *CProse*.

14 For example, in 1960 M. L. Rosenthal said that although Bishop had done "exquisite and highly suggestive work [she has] touched the imagination of [her] generation very little" because she "remind[s] us only of what we have already been taught to value: elegance, grace, precision, quiet intensity of phrasing" (*The Modern Poets*, p. 235).

15 Willard Spiegelman, "Landscape and Knowledge in the Poetry of Elizabeth

Bishop," p. 203. Wallace Stevens, "Of Modern Poetry," *Collected Poems* (New York: Knopf, 1954), p. 240.

16 Spiegelman, "Landscape and Knowledge," and Bloom, "*Geography III* by Elizabeth Bishop."

17 Octavio Paz, *Children of the Mire: Modern Poetry from Romanticism to the Avante-Garde* (Cambridge: Harvard Univ. Press, 1974).

18 M. W. Croll, "The Baroque Style in Prose," in *Studies in English Philology,* ed. Kemp Malone and Martin B. Ruud (Minneapolis: Univ. of Minnesota Press, 1929), pp. 437–43, quoted in Elizabeth Bishop "Gerard Manley Hopkins: Notes on Timing in his Poetry," p. 7.

19 Typical of the critics' tendency to neglect the baroque affinity in favor of the romantic is a remark in Penelope Laurans's otherwise excellent article on Bishop's prosody. Laurans concludes that "The sense of the mind actively encountering reality, giving off the impression of involved, immediate discovery, is one of Bishop's links to the Romantics." The odd and telling misreading here is that Laurans bases her conclusion on a quotation from an interview in which Bishop explicitly states the importance for her of baroque prose, which, according to Bishop "attempted to dramatize the mind in action rather than in repose" (Ashley Brown, "An Interview with Elizabeth Bishop," p.14). Bishop was emphasizing her affinity to the baroque movement as she understood it by specifically *contrasting* it with the romantic tendency to recollect emotion in tranquility. Until this affinity with the baroque is better understood, misjudgments will continue to be made, even by intelligent critics. See Laurans, "'Old Correspondences': Prosodic Transformations in Elizabeth Bishop," p. 75.

20 Lloyd Schwartz and Sybil P. Estess, eds., *Elizabeth Bishop and Her Art.* Hereafter cited as *EBHA.*

Fables of Enclosure
NORTH & SOUTH I

1 Basil Bunting quoted in James Laughlin, "Rambling Around Pound's Propertius," *Field* 33 (Fall 1985): 30.

2 All dates following titles of poems and stories in the text indicate years of first magazine publication. Since Bishop's books usually took about a decade to come together, significant development could and did occur within a given volume. This is particularly true of *North & South.* The date of first magazine publication is usually an accurate indicator of the date of completion of Bishop's poems, if not of their initial conception. Though she occasionally took several years to finish a poem, the evidence of her letters to friends, which often include soon-to-be-published poems, suggests that she published poems almost immediately once she felt they were finished. For documentation of publication dates see Candace MacMahon, *Elizabeth Bishop: A Bibliography.*

3 Bishop's review of William Jay Smith's translation of Laforgue clarifies his importance for her and repays study. She especially values Laforgue's com-

plex, unrhetorical tone, quoting with approval his remark that "I find it stupid to speak in a booming voice and adopt a platform manner" and she laments that, inevitably, in translation, "the quickness, the surprise, the new sub-acid flavor, have disappeared." "The Manipulation of Mirrors," p. 24 (*EBHA*, p. 283).

4   Jarrell, *Poetry and the Age*, p. 235.

5   Bishop, "On Being Alone," p. 18.

6   Bishop to Marianne Moore, 31 January 1938, Rosenbach Museum & Library, Philadelphia.

7   Brown, "Interview," p. 13.

8   Lowell, "Thomas, Bishop, and Williams," p. 497, and Stevenson, *Elizabeth Bishop*, p. 80.

9   This story is best told in Robert Giroux's Introduction to *The Collected Prose*, pp. ix–xii, and in Bishop's story "The Country Mouse" (*CProse*, 13–33).

10 For more information see Stevenson, *Elizabeth Bishop*, pp. 17–50, and Robert Giroux's Introduction to *The Collected Prose*.

11 Alexandra Johnson, "Geography of the Imagination" (interview), p. 24.

12 For a sound discussion of this correspondence see Lynn Keller, "Words Worth a Thousand Postcards: The Bishop / Moore Correspondence."

13 David Lehman, "'In Prison': A Paradox Regained," p. 64.

14 Ibid., p. 71.

15 Bishop, "On Being Alone," p. 18.

16 Lowell, "Thomas, Bishop, and Williams," p. 497.

17 Brown, "Interview," p. 10.

18 Ibid.

19 She said "I don't like modern religiosity in general; it always seems to lead to a tone of moral superiority. . . . As for religious poetry and this general subject, well, times have changed since Herbert's day. I'm not religious but I read Herbert and Hopkins with the greatest pleasure" (Brown, "Interview," pp. 10–11). She observed in the same interview that Marianne Moore "has no particular 'myth,' but a remarkable set of beliefs appears over and over again, a sort of backbone of faith" (p. 11). The same might be said of Elizabeth Bishop.

20 G. S. Fraser, "Some Younger American Poets: Art and Reality," p. 461.

21 Kalstone, *Five Temperaments*, p. 26.

22 Brown, "Interview," p. 9.

23 Johnson, "Geography of the Imagination" (interview), pp. 24–25.

24 Honig, "Poetry Chronicle," p. 116. Compare also the many titles that identify Bishop as a mapmaker, that is, a charter of delicate, abstract worlds: for example, Jan B. Gordon's "Days and Distances: The Cartographic Imagination of Elizabeth Bishop," or Sybil P. Estess', "Elizabeth Bishop: The Delicate Art of Map Making."

25 Bishop to Marianne Moore, 13 April 1935, Rosenbach Museum.

26 Brown, "Interview," p. 13.

27 Richard Mullen, "Elizabeth Bishop's Surrealist Inheritance," p. 64.

28 Anne Stevenson, "Letters From Elizabeth Bishop," p. 261 (first published in Stevenson, *Elizabeth Bishop*, p. 66).

29 Brown, "Interview," p. 13.
30 Ibid.

Images of Florida
NORTH & SOUTH II

1   Bishop to Anne Stevenson, "Letters from Elizabeth Bishop," p. 261.
2   Bishop to Marianne Moore, 5 January 1937, Rosenbach Museum.
3   Bishop to Moore, 21 August 1935, Rosenbach Museum.
4   Brown, "Interview," p. 16.
5   Marianne Moore, "A Modest Expert: *North & South,*" p. 354 (also *EBHA,* p. 179).
6   Leo Marx, *The Machine and the Garden* (New York: Oxford Univ. Press, 1967). Donald Sheehan in "The Silver Sensibility" (1971, p. 106) was the first to recognize Bishop's alliance to pastoral.
7   Lowell, "Thomas, Bishop, and Williams," pp. 497–99; Jarrell, *Poetry and the Age,* pp. 234–35 (reprinted in *EBHA,* pp. 186–89 [Lowell] and 180–81 [Jarrell]).
8   John Ashbery, "*The Complete Poems.*"
9   Honig, "Poetry Chronicle, pp. 115–17, and Oscar Williams, "North but South," *New Republic,* 21 October 1946, p. 525 (also *EBHA,* pp. 184–85). Honig's article is a review of *Poems,* which contains *North & South* in its entirety.
10 Jarrell was the first of many to note this echo, saying that after reading the first and last lines of "Florida," "you don't need to be told that the poetry of Marianne Moore was, in the beginning, an appropriately selected foundation for Miss Bishop's work" (*Poetry and the Age,* p. 234).
11 Samuel Taylor Coleridge, *Shakespearean Criticism,* 2d ed., ed. Thomas Middleton Raysor, vol. 2 (New York: E. P. Dutton, 1960), Lecture IX, pp. 134–35.
12 Wallace Stevens, "O Florida, Venereal Soil," *Collected Poems* (New York: Knopf, 1954), pp. 47–48.
13 Kalstone, *Five Temperaments,* p. 22.
14 Ibid., p. 14.
15 Bishop to Moore, 31 January 1938, Rosenbach Museum.
16 Nemerov, review of *Poems,* pp. 179–80.
17 Lowell, "Thomas, Bishop, and Williams," p. 498 (*EBHA,* p. 234), and Jarrell, *Poetry and the Age,* p. 235 (*EBHA,* p. 181).
18 Johnson, "Geography" (interview), p. 24.
19 Moore, "A Modest Expert," p. 354 (*EBHA,* p. 179).
20 Richard Moore, "Elizabeth Bishop: 'The Fish,'" p. 254.
21 Robert Lowell to Bishop, 20 April 1958, Vassar College Library.
22 Dave Smith and David Bottoms, eds., *The Morrow Anthology of Younger American Poets* (New York: Morrow, 1985), p. 19.
23 Bishop, "As We Like It," p. 135.

24 John Ruskin, *The Literary Criticism of John Ruskin,* ed. Harold Bloom (New York: Norton, 1972), p. 65.

25 Bishop, "As We Like It," p. 137.

26 Ibid., p. 138.

27 Ibid.

28 Bishop to Marianne Moore, 5 May 1938, Rosenbach Museum.

29 Bishop, "Gerard Manley Hopkins: Notes on Timing in His Poetry," p. 7.

30 Ibid., quoting from Croll, "The Baroque Style in Prose."

31 Brown, "Interview," p. 14.

32 Johnson, "Geography" (interview), p. 24.

33 Marianne Moore, "Critics and Connoisseurs," *Collected Poems* (New York: Macmillan, 1951), p. 42.

34 Croll, "The Baroque Style in Prose," p. 442.

35 Ashbery, *"The Complete Poems"* (review), *EBHA,* pp. 201–2.

36 Ezra Pound, *Literary Essays,* ed. T. S. Eliot (New York: New Directions, 1968), p. 4.

37 Rosenthal, *The Modern Poets,* p. 253–55.

38 Bishop to Moore, 17 October 1940, Rosenbach Museum.

39 W. B. Yeats, "Lapis Lazuli," *Collected Poems* (New York: Macmillan, 1956), p. 293.

40 Brown, "Interview," p. 16.

41 Bishop's letters mention studying what we may assume is his house. See particularly her letter to Moore, 31 January 1938, Rosenbach Museum.

42 Bishop to Moore, 20 March 1939, Rosenbach Museum.

43 Brown, "Interview," p. 16.

44 Johnson, "Geography" (interview), p. 25.

45 Bishop to Moore, 5 May 1938, Rosenbach Museum.

46 Brown, "Interview," p. 12.

47 W. H. Auden, "Musée des Beaux Arts," *Collected Poems,* ed. Edward Mendelson (New York: Random House, 1976), p. 146; Randall Jarrell, "The Old and New Masters," *The Complete Poems* (New York: Farrar, Straus and Giroux, 1969), p. 332.

48 Howard Nemerov, review of *Poems,* p. 180.

49 Elizabeth Bishop, "Little Exercise at 4 A.M." *New Yorker,* 2 February 1946, p. 22.

50 Ruskin, *The Literary Criticism,* p. 67.

51 Bishop to Stevenson, "Letters from Elizabeth Bishop," p. 261 (also in Stevenson, *Elizabeth Bishop,* p. 66).

52 Wallace Stevens, "Of Modern Poetry," *Collected Poems,* p. 239.

«Infant Sight»
A COLD SPRING

1 Ashbery, *"The Complete Poems"* (review) *EBHA,* p. 203.

2 Bishop, "Gerard Manley Hopkins," p. 7.

3 W. B. Yeats, "The friends that have it I do wrong," *Variorum Edition of the*

Poems, ed. Peter Allt and Russell K. Alspach (New York: Macmillan, 1957), p. 778.

4   Gerard Manley Hopkins, "Pied Beauty" and "Spring," *Poems and Prose,* ed. W. H. Gardner (Baltimore: Penguin, 1953), pp. 28, 31.

5   Paz, *Children of the Mire,* p. 56.

6   *Baudelaire as a Literary Critic: Selected Essays,* trans. Lois Boe Hyslop and Francis E. Hyslop, Jr. (University Park: Pennsylvania State Univ. Press, 1964), p. 55.

7   George Herbert, "Man," *English Poems of George Herbert,* ed. C. A. Patrides (London: Dent, 1974), p. 106.

8   Irving Howe, *Decline of the New* (New York: Harcourt, Brace, 1970), pp. 19–20.

9   Paz, *Children of the Mire,* p. 55.

10 Richard Howard, lecture "On Translating Baudelaire" to an NEH Summer Seminar attended by the author, New York University, 13 June 1983.

11 Charles Feidelson, *Symbolism and American Literature* (Chicago: Phoenix, 1953), p. 45.

12 Paz, *Children of the Mire,* p. 119.

13 Bishop to Robert Lowell, 1 January 1948, Houghton Library.

14 Bishop, "A Brief Reminiscence and a Brief Tribute," p. 308.

15 Alan Williamson, "*A Cold Spring:* The Poet of Feeling," pp. 96–97.

16 Stevenson, *Elizabeth Bishop,* p. 12.

17 Ashbery, "*The Complete Poems*" (review), *EBHA,* pp. 203–4.

18 Brown, "Interview," p. 11.

19 Elizabeth Bishop, "It All Depends," p. 267; John Keats, *Selected Poems and Letters,* ed. Douglas Bush (Boston: Riverside Press, 1959), p. 261.

20 Anne Stevenson, "Letters from Elizabeth Bishop," p. 261.

21 Brown, "Interview," p. 11.

22 Nemerov, review of *Poems,* pp. 179–80.

23 Ashbery, "*The Complete Poems*" (review), EBHA, p. 204.

24 Stephen Stepanchev, *American Poetry since 1945,* pp. 69–70.

25 Stevenson, "Letters from Elizabeth Bishop," p. 261.

«*Driving to the Interior*»
QUESTIONS OF TRAVEL

1   Charles Tomlinson, "Elizabeth Bishop's New Book," p. 89.

2   Johnson, "Geography" (interview), p. 24.

3   Delmore Schwartz, "The Isolation of Modern Poetry," in *New Directions in Prose and Poetry: 1941,* ed. James Laughlin (Norfolk, Conn.: New Directions, 1941), p. 695.

4   Bishop to Robert Lowell, 21 March 1952, Houghton Library.

5   Bishop to Lowell, 28 June 1953, Houghton Library.

6   Robert Lowell, "Elizabeth Bishop 4" (poem), *History,* p. 198.

7   T. S. Eliot, "Ben Jonson," in Eliot, *Selected Essays,* new edition (New York: Harcourt, Brace & World, 1950), p. 128.

8   Mazzaro, "Elizabeth Bishop's Poems," p. 100.

9   Sir Kenneth Clark, *Landscape into Art* (1949; reprint ed., New York: Harper & Row, 1979), pp. 15–28.

10   Jan B. Gordon, "Days and Distances," p. 296. Cf. also Stepanchev, *American Poetry,* p. 70–79, and the preciosity that M. L. Rosenthal finds in *The Modern Poets,* pp. 253–54.

11   William Wordsworth to R. P. Gillies, 23 November 1814, quoted in Wordsworth, *Selected Poems and Prefaces,* ed. Jack Stillinger (Boston: Houghton Mifflin, 1965), p. 573.

12   Wallace Stevens, "Arrival at the Waldorf," *Collected Poems,* pp. 240–41.

13   Gordon, "Days and Distances," p. 301.

14   Bishop to Marianne Moore, 27 February 1956, Rosenbach Museum.

15   Tomlinson, "Elizabeth Bishop's New Book," p. 89.

16   Bishop to Lowell, 21 March 1952, Houghton Library.

17   Stevenson, "Letters from Elizabeth Bishop," p. 261.

18   Robert Lowell, "On 'Skunk Hour,'" in *The Contemporary Poet as Artist and Critic,* ed. Anthony Ostroff (Boston: Little, Brown, 1964), p. 108.

19   Robert Lowell, *Life Studies and For the Union Dead* (New York: Farrar, Straus and Giroux, 1964), p. 13.

20   Ian Hamilton, *Robert Lowell: A Biography* (New York: Random House, 1982), p. 232.

21   Robert Lowell to William Carlos Williams, 30 September 1957 (Beinecke Library, Yale University), quoted from Hamilton, *Robert Lowell,* p. 233. It is not my intent to understate the influence of Williams—Lowell concludes with the following postscript: "I see I forgot to say that I feel more and more technically indebted to you, growing young in my forties"—but to delineate a specific, and less well understood, debt to Bishop.

22   Robert Lowell to Bishop, 10 June 1957, Vassar College Library.

23   Lowell to Bishop, 3 December 1957, Vassar College Library.

24   Lowell to Bishop, 20 April 1958, Vassar College Library.

25   Lowell to Bishop, 11 September 1957, Vassar College Library.

26   Laurans, "'Old Correspondences': Prosodic Transformations in Elizabeth Bishop," p. 77; Lowell, "On 'Skunk Hour,'" p. 109; Robert Pinsky, *The Situation of Poetry,* p. 77.

27   Stanley Kunitz, "Talk with Robert Lowell," *New York Times Book Review,* 4 October 1964, pp. 34 +, quoted from *Profile of Robert Lowell,* ed. Jerome Mazzaro (Columbus, Ohio: Charles E. Merrill, 1971), p. 55.

28   Paz, "Elizabeth Bishop, or the Power of Reticence," p. 15 (also *EBHA,* p. 213).

29   Marie-Claire Blais, "Presentation of Elizabeth Bishop to the Jury," p. 7.

30   Charles Wagley, "Amazon Town: A Study of Man in the Tropics (New York: Macmillan, 1953), p. 227. See pp. 224–33 for a discussion of pagés and sacacas.

31   Ibid., p. 255.

32 Ibid., pp. 224–26.
33 Bishop, *The Ballad of the Burglar of Babylon,* unpaginated.
34 See Bishop, "A Brief Reminiscence and a Brief Tribute" (eulogy, W. H. Auden), p. 47 (also *EBHA,* p. 308).
35 Robert Lowell, dust jacket of Bishop's *Questions of Travel.*
36 Brown, "Interview," p. 10.
37 David Young, *Magical Realist Fiction* (New York: Longman, 1984), p. 419.
38 Tomlinson, "Elizabeth Bishop's New Book," pp. 88, 90–91.
39 Gordon, "Days and Distances," p. 300.
40 Bishop to Anne Stevenson, "Letters from Elizabeth Bishop," p. 261.

The Art of Losing
GEOGRAPHY III

1 Stevenson, "Letters from Elizabeth Bishop," p. 261.
2 Bloom, *"Geography III* by Elizabeth Bishop," pp. 29–30.
3 Lloyd Schwartz, "'One Art': The Poetry of Elizabeth Bishop, 1971–1976," pp. 48; Jarrell, *Poetry and the Age,* p. 235.
4 Stevenson, "Letters from Elizabeth Bishop," p. 262.
5 William Carlos Williams, "The Descent," *Pictures from Breughel and Other Poems* (New York: New Directions, 1962), p. 73.
6 Bloom, *"Geography III,"* p. 29.
7 Ibid., p. 30.
8 Lewis Thomas, *The Medusa and the Snail* (New York: Viking, 1979), p. 9.
9 Stevenson, "Letters from Elizabeth Bishop," p. 262.
10 Mazzacco, "A Poet of Landscape," p. 4.
11 Karl Malkoff, *Escape from the Self: A Study in Contemporary American Poetry and Poetics* (New York: Columbia Univ. Press, 1977), p. 3.
12 Stevenson, "Letters from Elizabeth Bishop," p. 261 (also Stevenson, *Elizabeth Bishop,* p. 66).
13 Ibid., p. 262.

Primary Sources
Books, Miscellaneous Prose,
Letters, and Interviews

BOOKS

North & South. Boston: Houghton Mifflin, 1946.
Poems: North & South—A Cold Spring. Boston: Houghton Mifflin, 1955.
The Diary of "Helena Morley," by Alice (Dayrell) Brant. Translated and edited by Elizabeth Bishop. New York, Farrar, Straus and Cudahy, 1957; reprint, New York: Ecco Press, 1977.
Brazil (with the editors of *Life* for the Life World Library). New York: Time-Life Books, 1962.
Questions of Travel. New York: Farrar, Straus and Giroux, 1966.
The Ballad of the Burglar of Babylon. New York: Farrar, Straus and Giroux, 1968.
The Complete Poems. New York: Farrar, Straus and Giroux, 1969.
An Anthology of Twentieth-Century Brazilian Poetry. Edited, with an Introduction, by Elizabeth Bishop and Emanuel Brasil. Middletown, Conn.: Wesleyan Univ. Press, 1972.
Geography III. New York: Farrar, Straus and Giroux, 1983.
The Complete Poems: 1927–1979. New York: Farrar, Straus and Giroux, 1983.
The Collected Prose. Edited, with an Introduction, by Robert Giroux. New York: Farrar, Straus and Giroux, 1984.

MISCELLANEOUS PROSE (A Selection)

"As We Like It." *Quarterly Review of Literature* 4 (1948): 135–39 (essay). [Excerpt in *EBHA*, pp. 278–79].
"A Brief Reminiscence and a Brief Tribute." *Harvard Advocate* (Auden issue) 108 (1975): 47–48 (eulogy). [Excerpt in *EBHA*, p. 308.]

"Dimensions for a Novel." *Vassar Journal of Undergraduate Studies* 8 (May 1934): 95–103 (essay).

Dust jacket of Robert Lowell's *Life Studies*. New York: Farrar, Straus and Cudahy, 1959. [*EBHA*, p. 285]

Flannery O'Connor: 1925–1964." *New York Review of Books* 3, no. 4 (1964): 21–22 (eulogy). [Excerpt in *EBHA*, p. 287.]

"Gerard Manley Hopkins: Notes on Timing in His Poetry." *Vassar Review* 23 (February 1934): 5–7 (essay). [Excerpt in *EBHA*, pp. 273–75.]

"An Inadequate Tribute" in *Randall Jarrell: 1914–1964*. Edited by Robert Lowell et al. New York: Farrar, Straus and Giroux, 20–21 (eulogy). [*EBHA*, p. 304.]

"It All Depends." In *Mid-Century American Poets*. Edited by John Ciardi. New York: Twayne, 1950, p. 267 (essay). [*EBHA*, p. 281.]

"The Manipulation of Mirrors." *New Republic*, 19 November 1956, pp. 23–24 (review). [Excerpt in *EBHA*, p. 283.]

"On Being Alone." *The Blue Pencil* 12 (June 1929): 18 (essay).

"A Sentimental Tribute." *Bryn Mawr Alumnae Bulletin* 43 (Spring 1962): 2–3 (eulogy).

"Then Came the Poor." *The Magazine: A Literary Journal* 1 (1934): 105–10 (story).

"Time's Andromedas." *Vassar Journal of Undergraduate Studies* 7 (May 1933): 102–22 (essay). [Excerpt in *EBHA*, pp. 271–72.]

LETTERS

Letters from Robert Lowell. Vassar College Library. Poughkeepsie, N.Y.

Letters to Robert Lowell. Houghton Library. Harvard University. Cambridge, Mass.

Letters to Marianne Moore. Marianne Moore Papers. Rosenbach Museum. Philadelphia, Pa.

Stevenson, Anne. "Letters from Elizabeth Bishop." *TLS*, 7 March 1980, pp. 261–62.

INTERVIEWS

Brown, Ashley. "An Interview with Elizabeth Bishop." *Shenandoah* 17, no. 2 (1966): 3–19.

Johnson, Alexandra. "Geography of the Imagination." *Christian Science Monitor*, 23 March 1978, pp. 24–25.

Spires, Elizabeth. "The Art of Poetry, XXVII: Elizabeth Bishop." *Paris Review*, no. 80 (Summer 1981): 56–83.

Starbuck, George. "'The Work!' A Conversation with Elizabeth Bishop." *Ploughshares* 3, nos. 3 and 4 (Spring 1977): 11–19.

Selected Critical and Bibliographic Sources

Alvarez, Anthony. "Imagism and Poetesses." *Kenyon Review* 19 (1957): 324–27.

Ashbery, John. "*The Complete Poems*" (review) *EBHA*, pp. 201–5. Originally appeared as "Throughout Is a Quality of Thingness." *New York Times Book Review,* 1 June 1969, pp. 8, 25.

———. "Second Presentation of Elizabeth Bishop." *World Literature Today* 51, no. 1 (1977): 10–11.

Bertin, Celia. "A Novelist's Poet." *World Literature Today* 51, no. 1 (1977): 16–17.

Bidart, Frank. "On Elizabeth Bishop." *World Literature Today* 51, no. 1 (1977): 19.

Blais, Marie-Claire. "Presentation of Elizabeth Bishop to the Jury." *World Literature Today* 51, no. 1 (1977): 7.

Bloom, Harold. "*Geography III* by Elizabeth Bishop." *New Republic,* 5 February 1977, pp. 29–30.

Bryan, Nancy Lee. "A Place for the Genuine: Elizabeth Bishop and The Factual Tradition in Modern American Poetry." Ph.D. diss. Claremont College, 1973.

Carter, Elliott. *A Mirror on Which to Dwell.* Speculum Musicae, Columbia, M35171, 1980 (phonograph record).

Ehrenpreis, Irvin. "Solitude and Isolation" (review of *Questions of Travel*). *Virginia Quarterly Review* 42 (Spring 1966): 332–33.

Emig, Janet A. "The Poet as Puzzle." *English Journal* 52, no. 3 (March 1963): 222–24.

Estess, Sybil P. "Elizabeth Bishop: The Delicate Art of Map Making." *Southern Review* 13 (1977), pp. 705–26.

———. "Toward the Interior: Epiphany in 'Cape Breton' as Representative Poem." *World Literature Today* 51, no. 1 (1977): 49–50.

Fowlie, Wallace. "Poetry of Silence." *Commonweal* 65, no. 19 (February 1957): 514–16.

Frankenberg, Lloyd. *Pleasure Dome.* Cambridge, Mass.: Riverside Press, 1949. Pp. 331–33.

Fraser, G. S. "Some Younger American Poets: Art and Reality." *Commentary* 23, no. 5 (May 1957): 461.

Garrigue, Jean. "Elizabeth Bishop's School" (review of *Questions of Travel*). *New Leader,* 6 December 1965, pp. 22–23.

Gordon, Jan B. "Days and Distances: The Cartographic Imagination of Elizabeth Bishop." *Salmagundi* 22–23 (1973): 294–305.

Gibbs, Barbara. Review of *North and South. Poetry* 69, no. 4 (January 1947): 228–31.

Honig, Edwin. "Poetry Chronicle." *Partisan Review* 23 (Winter 1956): 115–17.

Ivarsk, Anthony. "Elizabeth Bishop: 1976 Laureate of the *Books Abroad* / Neustadt International Prize for Literature." *Books Abroad* 50 (Spring 1976): 263–65.

Jarrell, Randall. *Poetry and the Age.* New York: Noonday, 1953.

Kalstone, David. "All Eye." *Partisan Review* 37 (1970): 310–15.

———. "Conjuring with Nature: Some Twentieth Century Readings of Pastoral." *Harvard English Studies II: Twentieth Century Literature in Retrospect.* Cambridge, Mass.: Harvard Univ. Press, 1971. Pp. 247–68.

———. *Five Temperaments.* New York: Oxford Univ. Press, 1977.

Keller, Lynn. "Words Worth a Thousand Postcards: The Bishop / Moore Correspondence." *American Literature* 55 (October 1983): 405–29.

Kirby-Smith, H. T., Jr. "Miss Bishop and Others," *Sewanee Review* 80 (Summer 1972): 483–96.

Laurans, Penelope. "'Old Correspondences': Prosodic Transformations in Elizabeth Bishop." In *EBHA*, pp. 75–99.

Lehman, David. "'In Prison': A Paradox Regained." In *EBHA*, pp. 61–74.

Lowell, Robert. Dust jacket of Elizabeth Bishop's *Questions of Travel.* New York: Farrar, Straus and Giroux, 1967.

———. *History.* New York: Farrar, Straus and Giroux, 1973.

———. "Thomas, Bishop, and Williams." *Sewanee Review* 55 (Summer 1947): 497–99.

MacMahon, Candace. *Elizabeth Bishop: A Bibliography.* Charlottesville, Va: Univ. Press of Virginia, 1980.

McNally, Nancy. "Elizabeth Bishop—The Discipline of Description." *Twentieth Century Literature* 11, no. 4 (January 1966): 189–201.

Mazzacco, Robert. "A Poet of Landscape." Review of *Questions of Travel. New York Review of Books,* 12 October 1967, pp. 4–6.

Mazzaro, Jerome. "Elizabeth Bishop's Poems." *Shenandoah* 20, no. 4 (Summer 1969): 98–100.

———. "Elizabeth Bishop and the Poetics of Impediment." *Salmagundi* 27 (1974): 118–44.

———. "Elizabeth Bishop's Particulars." *World Literature Today* 51, no. 1 (1977): 48–49.

Mills, Ralph J., Jr. *Contemporary American Poetry.* New York: Random House, 1965.

Moore, Marianne. "A Modest Expert: *North & South.*" *The Nation* 163 (1946): 354.

———. "Archaically New." In *Trial Balances,* edited by Ann Winslow. New York: Macmillan, 1935. Pp. 82–83.

Moore, Richard. "Elizabeth Bishop: 'The Fish.'" *Boston University Studies in English* 2, no. 4 (1956): 254–59.

Mortimer, Penelope. "Elizabeth Bishop's Prose." *World Literature Today* 51: no. 1 (1977): 17–18.

Moss, Howard. "The Canada-Brazil Connection." *World Literature Today,* 51, no. 1 (1977): 29–33.

Mullen, Richard. "Elizabeth Bishop's Surrealist Inheritance," *American Literature* 54 (March 1982): 63–80.

Nemerov, Howard. Review of *Poems. Poetry* 87 (December 1955): 179–80.

Paz, Octavio. "Elizabeth Bishop, or The Power of Reticence." *World Literature Today* 51, no. 1 (1977): 15–16. [Also in *EBHA*, pp. 211–13.]

Pinsky, Robert. *The Situation of Poetry.* Princeton: Princeton Univ. Press, 1976.

———. "The Idiom of a Self: Elizabeth Bishop and Wordsworth." In *EBHA*, pp. 49–60.

Rosenthal, M. L. *The Modern Poets.* New York: Oxford Univ. Press, 1960.

Schwartz, Lloyd. "'One Art': The Poetry of Elizabeth Bishop, 1971–1976." *Ploughshares* 3, nos. 3 and 4 (Spring 1977): 30–54.

Schwartz, Lloyd, and Sybil P. Estess, eds. *Elizabeth Bishop and Her Art* [*EBHA*]. Ann Arbor: Univ. of Michigan Press, 1983.

Sheehan, Donald. "The Silver Sensibility: Five Recent Books of American Poetry." *Contemporary Literature* 12, no. 1 (Winter 1971): 99–120.

Slater, Candace. "Brazil in the Poetry of Elizabeth Bishop." *World Literature Today* 51, no. 1 (1977): 34–35.

Southworth, James G. "The Poetry of Elizabeth Bishop." *College English* 20, no. 5 (February 1959): 213–16.

Spiegelman, Willard. "Landscape and Knowledge in the Poetry of Elizabeth Bishop." *Modern Poetry Studies* 6 (Winter 1975): 203–24.

Stepanchev, Stephen. *American Poetry since 1945.* New York: Harper and Row, 1965. Pp. 69–79.

Stevenson, Anne. *Elizabeth Bishop.* New Haven: Twayne Publishers, 1966.

Tomlinson, Charles. "Elizabeth Bishop's New Book." Review of *Questions of Travel. Shenandoah* 17 (Winter 1966): 88–91.

Vendler, Helen. "Domestication, Domesticity, and the Otherworldly." *World Literature Today* 51, no. 1 (1977), 23–28.

Unterecker, John. "Elizabeth Bishop." *American Writers: A Collection of Literary Biographies,* supp. 1, pt. 1 (New York: Scribners, 1979): pp. 72–97.

Wehr, Wesley. "Elizabeth Bishop: Conversations and Class Notes." *Antioch Review* 39 (Summer 1981): 319–28.

Williamson, Alan. "*A Cold Spring:* The Poet of Feeling." In *EBHA,* pp. 96–108.

Wyllie, Diana E. *Elizabeth Bishop and Howard Nemerov: A Reference Guide.* Boston: G. K. Hall, 1983.

Index